Breaking Bad and Dignity

Breaking Bad and Dignity

Unity and Fragmentation in the Serial Television Drama

Elliott Logan
University of Queensland, Australia

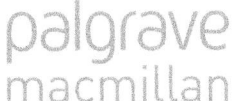

First published 2016 by
PALGRAVE MACMILLAN

Palgrave Macmillan in the UK is an imprint of Macmillan Publishers Limited, registered in England, company number 785998, of Houndmills, Basingstoke, Hampshire RG21 6XS.

Palgrave Macmillan in the US is a division of St Martin's Press LLC, 175 Fifth Avenue, New York, NY 10010.

Palgrave Macmillan is the global academic imprint of the above companies and has companies and representatives throughout the world.

Palgrave® and Macmillan® are registered trademarks in the United States, the United Kingdom, Europe and other countries.

ISBN 978–1–137–51372–4

This book is printed on paper suitable for recycling and made from fully managed and sustained forest sources. Logging, pulping and manufacturing processes are expected to conform to the environmental regulations of the country of origin.

A catalogue record for this book is available from the British Library.

Library of Congress Cataloging-in-Publication Data
Logan, Elliott, 1986–
Breaking bad and dignity: unity and fragmentation in the serial television drama / Elliott Logan, University of Queensland, Australia.
pages cm. — (Palgrave close readings in film and television)
Includes bibliographical references and index.
ISBN 978–1–137–51372–4
1. Breaking bad (Television program: 2008–2013)   I. Title.

PN1992.77.B74L64   2015
791.45'72—dc23   2015021859

Typeset by MPS Limited, Chennai, India.

For Ro

Contents

List of Figures   viii

Acknowledgements   ix

A Note on Episode Numbering   xi

Introduction   1

1   Humiliation and Shame in Season One   27

2   Pursuing Success in Season Two   56

3   Taking a Stand in Season Three   85

4   Inheritance and Legacy in Season Four   109

Conclusion: Facing Completion in Season Five   141

Notes   161

Bibliography   171

Index   176

List of Figures

I.1 'Breaking Bad': Walt looks past the camera
for acknowledgement of his stance   7

I.2 'And the Bag's in the River': Walt contemplates
Emilio's jawbone   22

1.1 'Breaking Bad': Walt dresses himself while ignoring
the needs of another   32

1.2 'Breaking Bad': Walt and Hank's different capacities
in social circles   44

2.1 'Breakage': Skyler mirrors Walt's projections of hardness   64

3.1 'Fly': Walt's inscrutable gaze   99

3.2 'Half Measures': Jesse confronts Gus   103

4.1 'Salud': Gus's oversight of his willed scene of carnage   130

4.2 'Face Off': Gus undone before Hector's gaze   138

C.1 'Felina': Jesse cradles his 'perfect' object   158

Acknowledgements

I am grateful for my experience of *Breaking Bad*, which fortuitously drew me back to criticism during a period of disconnection from it. It has been a privilege.

Thanks to Chris Penfold for believing in and supporting this project, and for allowing it the time needed. Thanks also to series editors John Gibbs and Douglas Pye for the same. This study began its life in the school of English, Media Studies, and Art History (now Communication and Arts) at the University of Queensland. That research was funded by an Australian Postgraduate Award, and I am grateful to both the University of Queensland and the Australian Government for that financial support.

Working at the University of Queensland provided the added benefit of the guidance, friendship, and support of many wonderful people there. Among many others, Alison Taylor, Huw Walmsley-Evans, Jess Hughes, Sam Lindop, Kate Warner, and Hano Pipic have across the years been crucial to the pleasure and good of working in the school. Early parts of the research were presented at seminars and conferences within the school, and I thank the organisers and audiences of those occasions for their stimulus and feedback. Aspects of the first chapter were presented in a paper at the School of Film, Media, and Journalism at Monash University. Thank you especially to Adrian Martin for his encouragements and suggestions on that paper, and for his continued support of the project since.

Lisa Bode and Jason Jacobs supervised me throughout the very long and difficult process of finding both my relationship to the series and my place within television studies, which at the outset of this work was to me almost entirely new scholarly terrain. I hope this book is suitable testament to their years of inspirational and friendly thought and teaching.

Along with Jason Jacobs, Steven Peacock provided early encouragement by giving me a venue in print for one of my first pieces of writing on *Breaking Bad*, and I have repeatedly benefited from his supportive remarks. I owe a great debt to the friendliness of Ted Nannicelli, who cheerfully read chapters of the book as they were produced. His incisive comments provided much-needed discipline and reassurance at crucial points. I was deeply fortunate for the privilege of having Sean

O'Sullivan and Trisha Dunleavy examine the thesis from which this study emerged. The generosity and enthusiasm of their response was a very moving reward after years of difficult work and doubt, and returning to their words throughout the preparation of this book has not only been a renewable source of encouragement, but has also brought home to me my own thoughts and ideas. Thank you.

My family have provided unstinting support, belief, and understanding. Thank you to my parents, Fran and Gil, and my siblings Shani, Calum, and Tim.

Ro has been alongside me every difficult and every good day; she has been unblinking in the face of what seemed like overwhelming crisis. These pages would not be here without her.

A Note on Episode Numbering

The first reference to an episode within each chapter notes the season to which it belongs and its position in that season. For example, 'Fly' is the tenth episode of season three, and so is noted this way: (3.10). The repetition of these details within each chapter is intended to help readers less familiar with the show maintain a sense of each episode's placement within the series.

Introduction

This book appreciates the artistry of *Breaking Bad* (AMC, 2008–2013). The series was prominent among a crop of expensive, 'high end' television serials from the US, the UK, and Europe that, from the 1990s onwards, drew frequent acclaim for extending and deepening television fiction's narrative and stylistic palette and its range of related achievements. A common touchstone for this discourse was the adjective 'cinematic'. As a term of both description and appreciative judgement, it was deployed with regularity in response to series such as, among others, *The Sopranos* (HBO, 1999–2007), *Six Feet Under* (HBO, 2001–2005), *Mad Men* (AMC, 2007–2015), *Forbrydelsen* (*The Killing*) (DR1, 2007–2012), *Game of Thrones* (HBO, 2010–), *Hannibal* (NBC, 2013–), and *Top of the Lake* (BBC Two, 2013). This suggested a view that the television dramas so described were aspiring to, and presumably in some cases realising, a 'height' of richness or sophistication of film style that had earlier been seen as the sole preserve of cinema. In Jason Jacobs's words, the validation of some television dramas in terms of their so-called 'cinematic' qualities can be understood as responding to the idea that television fiction had been 'textually anaemic when compared to film or literature'.[1] Readily available statements by key practitioners, among them some of *Breaking Bad*'s central creative personnel, do not discount intentions to work within certain cinematic traditions. As well, the following chapters demonstrate how, in the case of *Breaking Bad*, certain films may often provide appropriate registers of comparison with the period's television serials.

In spite of all this, the reading of *Breaking Bad* that I offer in this book presents a view of relationships between style and meaning in the series that resists being reduced to the discourse of the 'cinematic' in high-end television. Each chapter of the book instead elaborates how *Breaking*

Bad's expressiveness and meaning largely rest on its self-conscious handling of serial television form. In particular, across its length, the series is shown to make thematically significant the fact that serial television drama is produced in an unfolding series of discrete but nevertheless interrelated parts, namely episodes and seasons. What follows from this fact is that the textual composition of such works is characterised by what I will later argue is a peculiar tension between the unified and the fragmentary, between the discrete part and the greater whole, which are at once separate and connected.[2] The focus of the book's account is the way that relationships between various choices made in the series' design – choices of story, narrative, mise-en-scène, performance, and other aspects of film style such as editing – develop as patterned motifs arranged around this central tension. My interpretation of these relationships reveals how their significance first emerges and later continues to develop in relation to what I take to be the dramatic stakes of *dignity*, understood here as pivoting around the desire to act in such a way that one's inner self coheres with, and can be recognised by others through, one's outer presentation and deeds.

I begin by outlining how dignity – presented as a fragile state to be retrieved from humiliation – is dramatically salient in a scene from the pilot episode of *Breaking Bad* and how, in a range of ways, various dramatic stakes around dignity are expressed through tensions between the unified and the fragmentary. Moreover, I show how the handling of these tensions, especially in relation to our sense of Walt as a character, comes to invite an understanding of the scene's significance in ways that reveal the show's early self-reflection upon the kind of material that can generate and sustain interest in an ongoing serial drama. Roughly two-thirds of the way through the pilot ('Breaking Bad', 1.1), following his diagnosis of terminal lung cancer and his decision to embark on a criminal adventure, Walter White (Bryan Cranston) confronts the mockery of three teenaged boys as he and his pregnant wife Skyler (Anna Gunn) help their disabled son Walt Jr (R. J. Mitte) try on jeans in a clothing store. Importantly, the scene opens inside the curtained-off dressing room, within which Walt Jr, using crutches as a result of his cerebral palsy, struggles to pull up the jeans. We see him turn down his mother's off-screen offer of help, and instead reluctantly accept his father's assistance. Now examining the jeans in the mirror of the public shop floor, the family notice the taunting of a nearby football jock and his two friends. A grim-faced Walt tells Skyler not to interfere (*'Don't,'* he says, holding her back), and then disappears somewhere in the back of the store. In Walt's absence, Skyler goes to confront her son's tormentors, but is stopped in her tracks by Walt's dramatic re-appearance through the store's front door. As Skyler and Walt Jr look on, Walt kicks the main bully in the back of the knee, knocking him to the floor, where he stamps and grinds his foot into the young man's leg. Walt lets the bully up, and faces him off. In a hoarse whisper he says, 'What, are you waiting for your girlfriends? You better go – you better go. Take it – take your shot. *Take it!*' The three bullies leave through the front door, and Walt, with a wry smile, turns back to look past the camera in search of his family's acknowledgement as witnesses to this violence.

The scene in its outlines is immediately familiar from American films – of which there were many prominent examples in the 1990s – in which an ordinary, put-upon middle-aged man 'snaps' and outwardly projects his seething inner resentment in a display of righteously inflected violence, perhaps best typified by Michael Douglas's 'D-Fens' character in Joel Schumacher's 1993 film *Falling Down*. In her perceptive review of the film, Carol Clover claims that it distinguishes itself 'from the run-of-the-mill backlash fantasy' through the 'demographic precision with which it identifies its protagonist not as any white male, but as an Average White Male', 'surrounded by people who have claimed themselves his social victims and clamor for entitlement' – women, ethnic minorities, immigrants, elderly people.[3] *Breaking Bad* clearly lends itself to being understood in terms of late-twentieth century identity politics centring around white masculinity, as can be seen in quite a few of the essays gathered in David P. Pierson's edited collection on the series.[4] Yet in their generality such frameworks may actually somewhat inhibit more nuanced understandings of what is going on in *Breaking Bad* at the granular level of style through which the series' story is presented. They also have the added tendency – not unusual as a response to television fiction – to tether the show's significance to the time and place of its making and initial reception. Looking closely at the clothing store scene and thinking through its style brings into view choices not easily understood through any framework formed prior to, or away from, our encounter with the show itself, choices which may further be significant in relation to matters that go beyond the local bounds of the show's immediate social and political context. In taking this view of the scene and of the series more broadly, this book participates in the approach to film criticism advocated by Alex Clayton, among others, for whom an aspiration of good criticism is to discover and articulate the meaning of a work in 'its own terms', as those are found to be expressed in the fine details of its style.[5]

The clothing store scene begins by presenting a scenario in which a beleaguered young man is consumed in an activity traditionally associated with the domestic and the feminine, and this is presented in a way that marks out a strong division between public and private spaces. Around our awareness of this line pivots the central question of the sequence's opening moments: how is it appropriate for a man to be seen? We see that for Walt Jr the exposure of weakness to a woman is something to be avoided. However, the witnessing and helping presence of a man does not eliminate the need to avoid a sense of weakness exposed. The continued presence of this need is suggested in an eloquently modest way. Walt Jr buries his gaze in his father's shoulder, and Walt directs his own away from the mirror in which the spectacle of their interdependence is reflected. Important also is the fact we are in a space intended for the readying of the self for display and inspection before others, a private room for self-composure bracketed off from the public by a curtain. This gives the concern with private and public self-presentation a particularly theatrical inflection, and so raises the idea of re-creating and transforming the self through the act of stepping into or out of the public eye, or from a world that demands one kind of performance into that which demands another. So we are being told that we are to be concerned with the implications of everyday modes of presenting or performing the self, and of the discrepancies that arise between these performances in different contexts.

The bullies' blatant and cruel teasing of Walt Jr provides a framework that puts a sense of moral value at stake, and it is within such a framework that the scenario of a divided self can be made especially compelling as drama. We are asked to feel the injustice and humiliation of being subjected to the perverse wielding of self-proclaimed authority by the kind of shameless people who, if left to run rampant, would make a world unfit to live in. So our sympathy is not only for Walt Jr as the locus of these insults, but more so for Walt, who seems among his family the most agitated and stranded by his apparent lack of resources with which to appropriately confront or respond to their torment. A contrast is Skyler, who possesses a righteous self-confidence expressed in the fluency with which she moves to defend her son's honour, a quality highlighted by Walt's nervous vacillations, the two performances handled to contrast self-possession and discomposure. The moment invites our sympathetic recognition of the difficulty individuals in modern society confront when faced with situations that seem to demand some kind of swift, clear, and strongly demonstrative moral response.[6] This dimension of the scene is strongly brought into view if we consider the scenario's generic precedent in Hollywood Westerns, a common trope of which is those scenes showing the socially and morally disruptive force of malicious thugs seen off by the righteously applied violence of the hero gunslinger.[7] But in the lawful, peaceful bourgeois society that emerged from the period presented in those movies, there is no room left for violent, individual action.[8] So what we are shown instead is a confrontation with injustice that immediately spurs a desire for some kind of forceful, corrective moral act but that produces in Walt only a humiliating embodiment of impotence, one that betrays not only his helpless inability to stand in defence of his family, but also his pained preparedness to see injustice go unchallenged rather than suffer a further diminishment of his masculinity (his grimaced '*Don't*' to Skyler). We are asked to respond to an image of a man visibly divided against himself. The image is dramatically compelling because it suspends and intensifies our wish to see the character make a definitive choice. Such a choice would be one that could not only rescue him from his helpless impotence and self-division by striking back against those who would degrade his wife and son, but that could also bring into clarifying unity of focus his own status as a man able to stand for something.

Walt's entrance through the front door, and his ensuing violence, seemingly meets this wish. At the same time, though, it is handled in a way that troublingly complicates any sense of easy satisfaction, of simple 'wish fulfilment'. Crucial to this is the relationship between the moral stakes of Walt's assault and the fact that he is a teacher, and with the related choice that series creator Vince Gilligan makes: to have his schoolteacher character attack a youth of athletic build who appears to be about the age of a high school senior. These choices are significant within the generic context of the Western that I have already sketched out, and in relation to the scene's handling so that the public, theatrical nature of its setting is foregrounded for us. 'The reason the Western has the classic showdown between hero and villain take place on the main street of town,' writes Gilberto Perez, 'is that the matter at stake is not a merely personal but a public, a social matter.'[9] Such violence is therefore taken to have a socially instructive and transformative character, intended to, in Perez's words, 'foster [. . .] the burgeoning social good'.[10] Such an ambition connects with Walt's role as a schoolteacher, through which, in an earlier scene, we see him attempt to live out a desire to instruct and inspire young people with his committed speech about the fundamental wonder of chemistry as a basis for, and key to understanding, existence. It is telling that Walt resolutely fails to move them, and is there and later

humiliated by a clearly wealthy student's refusal to respect him or recognise his authority as a teacher.

These aspects of the dramatic scenario, setting, and character provide
the initial grounds for what I want to call, following George M. Wilson,
an 'oblique' view of the clothing store scene's details and of their
meaning.[11] From this view, the similarity between the young man Walt
attacks and the students before whom he was earlier humiliated now
inflects his ostensibly righteous defence of moral principle and family
honour with a tone of spiteful, personal revenge. Further to this is the
exacting way Walt carries out his attack by kicking the young man in
the leg and then stamping on his knee, as if to cripple him. Walt Jr's
use of crutches was the focus for the insults that incited Walt's rage,
and so his targeting the knee of his nemesis makes sense as Walt's desire
to force on the young bully the very condition he sees fit to mock. At
the same time, the bully's impression of Walt Jr's disability, and Walt's
impulse to direct his violent anger at those very body parts over which
his son is unable to assert full control, crafts a suggestive link not only
between the bully and Walt's students but also, even more disturbingly,
between the bully and Walt Jr. The link suggests that being taunted by
the teenaged kid he attacks is not the real source of Walt's humiliation –
in some 'deep down' way Walt's true humiliation is his own son, a son
who bears his own name and whose reflection in the mirror Walt felt
compelled to avoid.

That this aspect of Walt is unknown to him helps makes sense of the
very strange choice to have Walt disappear into the rear of the store
and then make his stand through an inexplicable, highly theatrical
re-appearance through the *front* door, its electronic 'ding' reinforcing
the slight sense of an orchestrated magic trick. The established theatrical quality of the scene gives this moment a touch of pantomime
stagecraft – the virtuous and the villainous played by one actor, making his backstage switch via the wings. And so, despite the ostensibly
ordinary, realistic situation, the moment suggests *Breaking Bad* as more
properly understood as a story of, and about, the theatrical desire for
superheroics. Inherent to such a desire is a personality fragmented along
the line separating one's ordinary life from its more extraordinary, fanciful projections.

Fittingly, Walt is somewhat incoherent in his violent heroics,
expressed in the way Cranston performs his verbal confrontation with
the bully: 'Take your shot – *take* it.' These are words that achieve their
contrast with Walt's earlier weakness by alluding, especially through
Cranston's hoarse whisper, to Clint Eastwood's particular mode of

masculine vocality. But rather than the calm collection and cruel self-discipline of Eastwood's Harry Callahan in Don Siegel's 1971 film *Dirty Harry*, Cranston performs Walt's violent stand as agitated and urgent, his breathing quickened and his movements jerky in their unfamiliarity to him. We are given a sense that this is a part of Walt's personality that he is unused to expressing or realising in action, and so it will take time for him to become more coherent in projecting his inner capacity for violence, to form it into a unified identity. The *Dirty Harry* resonance chimes with the evocation of superhero narratives to suggest that Walt might wish – again, in a 'deep down' and so not consciously meant or understood way – that his violence performed before the assembled audience might not only define a moral stance that could rescue him from his humiliation, but in doing so also transform his otherwise unremarkable life into a movie, one that could provide a more exciting narrative with ever stronger, more extreme opportunities for glory and dignified posturing. This is captured in the scene's final shot, of Walt cocking a wry grin that looks for approval just past the camera, towards his wife and son, almost directly towards us, as if in hope for some acknowledgement of his stance (Figure I.1). We are not given a reverse shot of their response as an answer. Instead we are challenged to judge for ourselves the moral valence of the stunningly transformative response to humiliation we have witnessed.

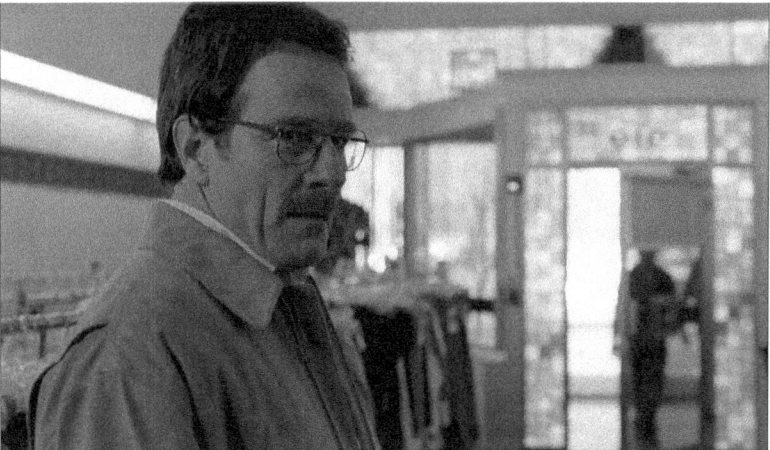

Figure I.1 'Breaking Bad': Walt looks past the camera for acknowledgement of his stance

These aspects of Walt's desperate grab to retrieve some sense of dignity present him as a good character for exploring through serial television storytelling: one whose personality and attributes are highly malleable and so available to ongoing modulation over time, rather than already sedimented into a fixed purity or essence of character, lacking the dynamism needed to generate continued drama and ongoing audience interest. At the outset of the book, this reading of one scene highlights the relevance and suitability of the title concepts to a study of relationships between serial television form, style, and meaning in *Breaking Bad*, and how they help to make clear an appreciative view of the series' artistry. The rest of the book is a detailed account of how that artistry can be seen to consist in the series' handling of a range of dramatic stakes around dignity. It is around those stakes, expressed through various tensions between the unified and the fragmentary, that *Breaking Bad*'s designs self-consciously address some of the most vital artistic challenges and opportunities of serial television drama as an ongoing form of seasonal storytelling, and in doing so achieve their precise grades of expressiveness and meaning.

Approach and organisation

The critical usefulness of this book's central concepts, and their role in its broader approach and organisation, should be viewed in light of the fact that serial television dramas like *Breaking Bad* and its peers noticeably amplify the already difficult problem of selection that critics confront in comparable art forms such as movie, novel, painting, and poem.

Art historian Michael Fried, outlining the approach he takes in his book *Menzel's Realism*, eloquently evokes such a problem as it is posed in Menzel's drawings and paintings:

> Much of the time I concentrate on individual paintings and drawings (and a few engravings), looking closely and trying to find words for what I see in an attempt to direct the reader's attention to features and aspects of those works that have either not been previously remarked or the significance of which has been – to my mind – misunderstood.[12]

Elsewhere, Fried values the achievement in certain sculptures and paintings of what he calls '*presentness*', or '*instantaneousness*', as if 'a single infinitely brief instant would be long enough to see everything, to experience the work in all its depth and fullness, to be forever convinced by it'.[13] Leaving aside the critical implications of 'instantaneousness' or 'presentness' as Fried conceives of them,[14] the point of juxtaposing the two quotes is simply to bring into relief how even an art form as wholly present as painting – in that any single work's entire form is present in any one moment – may yet persist in confronting the beholder with such richness and density of significant detail that its fuller understanding requires a sustained duration of effortful close attention, and that this density only deepens the necessity of *directing* one's focus. That is to say, heightens the need and difficulty of selecting those aspects of the work most worthy of appreciative attention, or most able to reward it, and to provide a basis from which to share that reward with others. ('But look at *this* part,' we might want to say, 'and see how it relates to these others.') The depth of this problem of selecting which details of a painting matter and, crucially, *how* they should be seen to matter, is well dramatised in writing by T. J. Clark's astonishing study *The Sight of Death*, in which the author journals his experiences repeatedly revisiting and reconsidering two Poussin landscapes at the Getty Museum in Los Angeles over a period of months.[15]

This is all to say that, in stark contrast to the sense of instantaneous conviction Fried values in response to certain sculptures and paintings, serial television dramas like *Breaking Bad* confront the critic with the extremity of their duration and what is surely the impossibility of immediately grasping, and the immense difficulty of eventually accounting for, their range and depth of achievement as a whole. To experience and closely study a television serial like *Breaking Bad* – or *The Sopranos*, or *Mad Men* – (whether for the first time or not) is more comparable to Clark's *ongoing* encounter with the Poussin landscapes, a persisting struggle with the enormity and depth of the world presented in the work.[16] Or, more accurately in regard to serial television, a persisting struggle with the enormity and depth of the world that *unfolds across* the work over a considerable span of time (months, years).

Perhaps what one most needs in order to make such an effort intelligible – not only to oneself but also, more importantly, to others – is that critical tool Christopher Ricks attributes to William Empson: '*the right handle to take hold of the bundle*. Or, rather, merely *a* right handle to take hold of the bundle'.[17] The wager of this book is that dignity – understood as a contingent mode of human expressiveness hinging on relative cohesion or division between a person's inner and outer – provides such a handle to take hold of *Breaking Bad* as an enormous bundle, a handle that has the strength and flexibility to allow aspects of the series to be turned over and around for examination in a number of illuminating and rewarding ways. It provides a conceptual basis from which, to quote Fried once more, I might 'find words for what I see in an attempt to direct the reader's attention to features and aspects of [the work] that have either not been previously remarked or the significance of which has been – to my mind – misunderstood'.[18]

This leads away from considerations of the particular approach this book takes to *Breaking Bad*, instead looking towards the broader tradition of critical writing on stylistic expression and meaning in which the book participates. Much writing about television fiction views its various works as, in Jacobs's words, 'a *relay* of cultural matter, say of national and local significance'.[19] This is a view of the form consistent with understandings of television as a medium of mass communication, which have underpinned much television studies work, and that have their roots in the idea that television finds its material basis in radio broadcasting rather than in other mediums or forms such as cinema, literature (prose or poetry), painting, or other graphic and sculptural arts.[20] An alternative way of approaching and writing about works of television fiction, one that this book takes up, is to understand them as '*expressive* artefacts, allowing us to calibrate the value of the artwork, and their creators' contributions to an ongoing tradition. The dominant comportment here is one of *submission* to the power and achievement of the work; critical activity is directed to illuminating both'.[21] This is related to the wider practice of expressive criticism, with a close model being expressive film criticism due to television fiction and movies finding a shared material basis in the elements of film style. Andrew Klevan describes expressive film criticism as a 'tradition of film scholarship which explores how the meanings, feelings, themes, ideas and happenings of a film are *achieved* by its organisation of style, while also highlighting how any achievement may reveal significant possibilities of the medium'.[22] For Clayton and Klevan, this involves 'bringing a realm of sounds, images, and actions to meet a realm of words and concepts'.[23]

Clayton and Klevan's statement joins hands with Fried's ambition – 'to find words for what I see in an attempt to direct the reader's attention'. And together, both articulations of approach point towards an understanding of description as being very much more than, in Stanley Cavell's words, 'preparations for saying something' ('something like items in a tabulation, with no suggestions about what is being counted or what the total might mean')[24]. Adrian Martin evokes this risk (of saying nothing) when he asks: 'why laboriously put into writing what is plainly evident for anyone to see on the screen in the first place – that Mitchum gets into a car and drives off?'[25] The question seems to suggest that a critical problem lies in V. F. Perkins's principle that the meanings of a film 'are not hidden in or behind the movie, and that my interpretation is not an attempt to clarify what the picture has obscured. I have written about things that I believe to be in the film for all to see, and to see the sense of'.[26] Yet saying this is not the same as saying that the movie in question makes available only one immediately and fully intelligible way of seeing it, and that to therefore describe in detail aspects of that movie would be a redundancy, that the movie itself could just as well stand in place of the criticism. As Klevan puts it:

> Description is not merely a necessary step on the way to the meat of analysis, it contains the analysis. Through careful choices about how to describe, discriminations are made subtly and implicitly. Description also reflects the impulse, true of much criticism on the arts, to articulate and share an experience. A film may be described differently, some things noticed, others not, and by reading the description we come to see a point of view. This may be *a* correct description, but not the only correct one: it is a *way of seeing* the film.[27]

This connects to Cavell's understanding of interpretation as, following Wittgenstein, 'seeing an aspect', which is to say, 'seeing something *as* something'.[28] In Perkins's words:

> No intra-textual interpretation ever is or ever could be a proof. Most often, it is a description of aspects of the film with suggested understandings of some ways they are patterned. Rhetoric is involved in developing the description so that it evokes a sense of how, seen this way, the film may affect us, or so that it invites participation in the pleasure of discovering this way in which various of the film's features hang together. But the ultimate appeal for conviction is to the reader's memory and renewed experience of the film.[29]

Through such an attitude, description comes to be far from inert indulgence. Rather, the effort to find words adequate to a detailed, discriminating account of individual artworks is instead *necessary* if we hope to arrive at any valid and shareable interpretation at all. Such work is relatively rare in television studies in comparison to other academic disciplines concerned with the meaning and value of artworks, for example film studies, literature, and art history.[30] As Jacobs has noted:

> I suppose a view of description as inert when compared to the energetic creation of new conceptualizations of the field might look askance at yet another account of the same text. But do we really want to forgo the richness of descriptive accuracy, the persuasive illumination of the appropriate construction of words which capture our experience (I am thinking of the writing on film by George Toles, Victor Perkins and William Rothman, among others)? I doubt whether we have even remotely enough of that in television studies.[31]

The authors whom Jacobs lists each exemplify, along with many others not listed, the best traditions of expressive film criticism. Klevan's account of that tradition, quoted above, reminds us of one aspect of what it puts at stake. This is in its aim of 'highlighting how any achievement may reveal significant possibilities of the medium'.[32] One risk of this ambition is to find oneself drifting towards Clement Greenberg's model of medium essentialism, which Jacobs and Peacock characterise as 'his insistence on the purity of medium-specific developments that were ring-fenced from contamination, borrowing or thievery from the other arts', an idea that remains 'a more or less explicit lining of thought in the scholarly study of film and television arts where phrases like "the possibilities of the medium" or "medium-specificity" are sounded with a thudding regularity'.[33] Further to this, there is the attendant inclination to settle on a fixed and pre-determined set of 'possibilities' defined by whatever is taken to be the materially limited ranges of expression possible through, or appropriate to, any given art form. In light of these pitfalls, this book proceeds carefully in regard to claims about serial television's specific 'possibilities' as an art form, while recognising that the title and general pitch of the study leans towards such considerations. Crucial to any claims this book makes about serial television drama in these terms is Cavell's idea of a medium. 'A medium,' Cavell writes, 'is something through which or by means of which something specific gets said or done in particular ways. It provides, one might say, particular ways to get through to someone, to make sense.'[34] It follows from Cavell that no medium can be defined or understood in advance of the artistic practice and criticism of individual works – a medium is rather *created through* those practices in an ongoing process of constitution.

This book's approach to serial television drama in these terms is reflected in the organisation of its four chapters, each of which considers an individual season. Respecting the show's organisation into seasons leads to an account that accentuates the series' gradual upbuilding over time through the development of what becomes its own internal expressive tradition. Rather than a strict division along thematic or stylistic lines alone, the chosen structure is further aimed to reflect, and afford reflection upon, the viewer's shifting involvement in the drama. That involvement is – like the form of the series itself – one that takes shape and moves through different senses of significance in time. The focus and progression of the chapters is further designed to home in on, while unfolding developing relationships between, specific thematic interests and their expression through particular elements of style at points of dramatic integration in narratively situated moments. Each chapter's focus on a certain theme is not intended to imply that theme's isolated treatment within the individual season alone. Rather, the arrangement reflects how particular facets of dignity as a dramatic subject are of special salience at certain points in the series' design, and are able to give precise significance to the aspects of serial television form that those designs address.

The book's structure further recognises the importance of the fact that *Breaking Bad*, like many of its US cable television contemporaries, consists of thirteen-episode seasons, with the exception of its fifth and final season, which was broken into two eight-episode parts.[35] For a long time it was standard practice in US television production for series to be initially ordered or commissioned in thirteen-episode batches, with the remainder of the seasonal order conditional on the performance of the initial thirteen-episode batch. But, as O'Sullivan points out:

> before *The Sopranos*, those first thirteen episodes had not been envisioned or consumed as a self-contained narrative cluster. The thirteen-episode uninterrupted complete season provided, for the first time in American television history, a distinct narrative form, one that was large enough to occupy significant time and space, but not so large as to turn into a vague sprawl.[36]

O'Sullivan's work explores the opportunities this form provides for the patterned design – and interruption – of *narrative* relationships between episodes. In particular, O'Sullivan finds in poetry an analogue for serial television like *The Sopranos* and *Breaking Bad*, as an art of segmented parts related through rhythmic structural patterns of unfolding repetition and variation.[37] The organisation of the book's chapters around seasons of *Breaking Bad* is intended to build on the identification of the thirteen-episode season as 'a new and significant unit of meaning' – or a new medium – to further explore the opportunities it affords for serialised *stylistic* and dramatic relationships.

O'Sullivan provocatively frames his contribution by reflecting on the fact that many recent studies of what he terms 'the new serials' 'have deployed the rhetoric of the new, rather than the discourse of the old – what is unprecedented within the realm of television or popular culture rather than what is adapted from poetic practice'.[38] Similarly, this book approaches *Breaking Bad* in terms of relationships between material choices of film style and achievements of expression and meaning that have a long-established basis in Hollywood filmmaking and related traditions of expressive mise-en-scène criticism. Within this tradition, cohesive choices of stylistic design closely inform our experience and sense of a film. As John Gibbs and Douglas Pye write:

> Every decision taken in making a film – where to place the camera, which lens to use, when to cut, how to place actors in space, how to clothe them – is taken in a specific context, informed by powerful conventions but unique to this moment in this film. Each decision – made in relation to the multiple patterns being built up across the film – develops the narrative and thematic web. Every shot is a view of something, every cut is from one specific view to another, every costume decision bears on considerations of character, situation, fashion context, colour design, and more. Much filmmaking seems to encourage us to view this complex tapestry of decision making as 'transparent', so that we are often unaware of the craft and artifice involved. But all this decision making is material and it has material effects on our experience of the film.[39]

The material here was written during a period of heightened interest in attending to style in serial television drama with the same pitch of attention that has been paid to style in cinema for some time. Within this scholarly context, one aim of the book is to show that it is enriching and indeed often *necessary* to consider how the fine-grained handling of stylistic detail in television serials like *Breaking Bad* is embedded within and patterned across such series, held together by the form's tension between the unified and the fragmentary.

Crucial to our sense of meaningful involvement in serial dramas is their capacity to have us live with and care about the deeds and experiences and fates of characters over long periods, into an indefinite future, and in the wake of a deep history of engagement with them. This fact about the attraction of serial drama to human viewing strongly guides my attention to *Breaking Bad*'s style. Harnessing the attention of each chapter is a focus on the experiences and stories of particular characters, in certain moments and across the series. My view of audience investment in character as a fulcrum of meaning reflects agreement with Raymond Durgnat's claim that:

> academic criticism often finds itself trying to attribute to stylistic features in themselves (cutting, camera-angles, etc.) artistic effects whose origin is simpler and more obvious. It is in the spectator's sharing of, and concern for, the experience of *these* characters in *these* predicaments. It is a simple empathy-sympathy – and no more uncritical than is our sympathy for friends and acquaintances in real life.
>
> Thus the spectator's response is largely to human experience. Undoubtedly, this experience is nuanced by, affected by, 'seen through', all the 'secondary characteristics' of style – cutting, camera-angle and movements, and so on. But in the dramatic films which are now the mainstream of the cinema, it is the function of these characteristics to relate themselves to, to build up, to add to, this 'resonance'.[40]

In this approach, the present book follows recent successful studies of individual films and television series that have been organised around character as a fulcrum of stylistic and dramatic achievement, namely Jacobs's study of *Deadwood* and Perkins's monograph on *La Règle du jeu* (*The Rules of the Game*) (Jean Renoir, 1937).[41]

As a work of appreciative criticism this book is further guided by T. S. Eliot's critical aim as summarised by Christopher Ricks. 'The idea,' writes Ricks, 'was not so much to show someone that a poem is good, as to go some way towards showing how it comes to be good, so very good.'[42] In much of what follows, this showing is led by *Breaking Bad*'s self-conscious exploration of its form as a serial television drama; call it the series' self-reflection on that form. This is not without risk, for the show and for my judgement of it. As Ricks warns, self-reflection as an artistic and critical principle, 'like all others, has always been tempted to escalate its claims, to make itself the one thing necessary, as if art's own nature were the only thing with which art were ever occupied. Then a proper self-attention becomes solipsism and self-regard, and poems are held to have no other subject than their own poemness'. Against such an attitude, Ricks has this to offer, and I will let his words ring here in the hope that their resonance finds harmony with what follows, both within *Breaking Bad* and my reading of it:

> Few things are more important in literary criticism than to protect the restored insights into the worth of disciplined self-reflection against its foes: those who have never had the imagination to see how much self-reflection could honorably effect, and those who have never had the imagination to see how it cannot honorably effect very much unless it be continually braced – as by the thrust of an opposing arch – against an equal respect for all the ways in which the reflection of something other than self (other than art itself) is indispensable.[43]

Serial television form and dignity

Fundamental to my reading of *Breaking Bad* is an understanding of the way in which serial television dramas like it are, in Sean O'Sullivan's words, 'broken on purpose'.[44] Sérgio Dias Branco describes television series as 'constructed piece by piece, segment by segment', each episode adding something in relation to the last, building with each new part the form of the series as a whole.[45] O'Sullivan claims that in this way, 'unlike the art of nonserialized fiction', serial television drama 'calls attention to itself as an array of parts; it is the art of fracture, of separation, and it is the art of the energy required to stitch together those pieces'.[46] The centrality of the part–whole relationship within serial television suggests an affinity with concerns important to cohesive filmmaking mise-en-scène and to related strands of film criticism that value achievements of balanced stylistic unity. In his history of mise-en-scène criticism in British film journals, John Gibbs points out how in the work of the *Movie* critics a 'major concern is the perception of links between different parts of the film', which sees an emphasis on the 'idea of a motif – the repeated visual element that acquires meaning through repetition'.[47]

As will become clear, the form of the motif and the accretion of 'meaning through repetition' are both central to my view of *Breaking Bad*'s achievement, and to what it reveals about serial television drama. Yet it is through the peculiarity of serial television's part–whole relationships that the artistic practice and criticism of serial television both differ from the filmmaking and film criticism to which Gibbs points. As Jacobs reminds us, it is important to consider how individual moments and episodes of a television serial 'have their own patterns and emphases but these are also intended to form part of a larger development even if that development is not yet filmed, written or planned'.[48] This means that a salient fact of serial television dramas is the way in which they are intentionally composed of, and understood as, episodes and seasons, each of which is a 'fragment' – 'something complete in itself and yet implying a larger whole'.[49] In Jacobs's words on *Deadwood* (HBO, 2004–2006), 'the friction and resolution, impasse and transcendence that the characters experience within scenes *ripple out* into the overall structure of each episode, so that scenes "speak" to scenes, and episodes are in conversation and negotiation with one another'.[50] *Rippling out*, conversation, and negotiation evoke an ongoing and not-yet settled jostling of internal relationships, the peculiar vitality of improvisation and openness to growth and other shaping impacts of human event and environmental pressure. Serial television dramas like *Breaking Bad* and its contemporary peers, then, participate in a tradition of filmmaking in which part–whole relationships are crucial to dramatic and stylistic achievement and appreciation. Yet as long-running works composed of fragments (episodes, seasons) that are only provisionally complete in relationship to the 'wider whole', television serials especially foreground and complicate *tensions* between part and whole.

All of this presents important issues for serial television criticism. For example, Jacobs and Peacock note how long-form television's seriality poses problems for criteria inherited from art forms in which the 'unity' of a given work is more clearly and definitively achieved:

> the fluid consistency of a TV drama with the ability to run on forever makes mischief with the criterion of coherence. How do we judge a television work's unity if it is open-ended, changing and building across episodes, still in flux? How can we make decisive discriminations of a particular moment if its relationship to the (incomplete) whole is as yet undeclared or undecided?[51]

Relevant to how exactly these issues matter to this project is the fact that I began the study while *Breaking Bad*'s third season was still unfolding in 2010. Yet, the second part of the show's fifth and final season concluded in 2013, more than a year before I finished writing. So, in contrast to the more 'live' unfolding Jacobs and Peacock evoke, this book responds to *Breaking Bad* as a work in which all part–whole relationships *have* been declared and decided insofar as they are no longer 'provisional', no longer open to revision and development.

Nonetheless, the narrative and stylistic form of the show is intended to inhere in the structures of serial television drama, and so the series remains shot through with the tensions between unity and fragmentation pointed to above. As O'Sullivan noted shortly after the broadcast of the series' penultimate episode ('Granite State', 5.15), and so in the shadow of the series' ultimate completion, *Breaking Bad* is 'a show fundamentally invested in the tension between movement and shape'.[52] That is to say, the show's narrative and stylistic designs are, throughout and across its vast array of episodes and seasons, intended to explore the ways in which apparently dislocated part and seemingly cohesive whole coalesce and collapse. It thus follows that any appreciation for the expressiveness and meaning of those designs cannot be divorced from considerations of the unified in tension with the fragmentary.

Two sequences on either side of the gap between season one and season five exemplify how *Breaking Bad* makes these aspects of serial television thematically significant in relation to dignity. Both sequences centre on the need to dispose of a body. In the pilot episode, Walt and Jesse (Aaron Paul) attempt to make a distribution deal with mid-level distributor 'Krazy-8' (Maximino Arciniega) and his cousin Emilio (John Koyama), who together force Walt to demonstrate his cooking method at gunpoint. Walt escapes by throwing a powder into hot water to produce a cloud of gas, and he traps both men in the RV to die. Episode two ('Cat's in the Bag . . .', 1.2) ends with Jesse disobeying Walt's instruction to buy a particular plastic tub in which to dissolve Emilio's body with hydrofluoric acid – he instead chooses to use an enamel bathtub. The consequence is the pulpy, putrefied mass that remains of Emilio crashing down through the corroded ceiling of Jesse's hallway from the bathroom above. Episode three ('And the Bag's in the River', 1.3) opens with a sequence showing the disgusting cleanup in detail.[53] Walt and Jesse, revolted, lump viscera into buckets, and scrub caustic soda and salt into the floorboards to erase the traces of Emilio's blood seeping into the wood. Intercut with this process is a flashback to Walt's earlier life as a researcher. He and a female colleague collate on a chalkboard all of the separate chemical elements that combine to constitute the human body, providing a distanced, scientific narration of chemical cohesion atop the images of bodily decomposition. As we hear Walt and his colleague express their astonishment at the low levels of calcium needed to make a human skeleton, we see Walt pick up and consider a fragment of jawbone, and toss it into a bucket. Iron is discussed next, and the image shows Walt find a slightly melted pistol, which is also thrown into the bucket, equalising the status of human bone and mechanical tool. The sequence ends with Walt's voice from the past saying, 'There's got to be more to a human being than that', while the image shows him in the present pouring Emilio's liquefied remains into a toilet, and flushing them.

Episode six of season five ('Buyout', 5.6) also opens with the cleanup of a murder committed at the end of the previous episode. In 'Dead Freight' (5.5), Walt and Jesse plan and execute a heist of chemicals from a train, and in the final moments of both the episode and the heist, their accomplice Todd (Jesse Plemons) shoots dead a young boy who accidentally comes across the crime scene while riding his trail bike. In the harrowing 'Buyout' sequence, the taking apart of the trail bike is shown in close-up detail that makes its destruction, in the dramatic context of a young boy's senseless murder, symbolic of the piece-by-piece dismantling of a human being. A jigsaw tearing a rubber tyre from its wheel evokes skin stripped from bone, and the collapse of the engine from its housing onto the floor has the expressive weight of a human heart or soul ripped from its bodily cage.

Crucial to the meaning of the sequences, and of their relationship to one another, is Vince Gilligan's choice of a scientist – effectively a chemical engineer – as his show's main character. Part of the reason for this choice is of course to provide a readily plausible avenue of dramaturgical connection between an otherwise ordinary character and the meth trade. But Walt's status as a scientist further provides a resource for the show to give concrete, dramatic shape to a pervasive technological mentality that has become characteristic of life in industrialised societies. Tzvetan Todorov provides a rich description of this mentality and its implications in his study of moral life in the Nazi and Soviet concentration camps.[54] His following remarks help make clear how this modern psychological condition is relevant to the present book:

> What made this immense evil possible, I believe, are two common, altogether ordinary attributes of our daily lives: the fragmentation of the world we live in and the depersonalization of our relations with others. These came about as a result of a progressive transformation, not exactly of people, but of their societies. Internal fragmentation is the consequence of an increasingly specialized working world and its inevitable compartmentalization; depersonalization comes from a transference of instrumental thought to the realm of human relations. [. . .]
>
> It is in this sense that we can hold our industrial and technological civilization responsible for the camps, not because any spectacular

industrial measures were required to carry out the mass murders and bring about suffering of boundless proportions (in Germany, these measures amounted to little more than gunpowder, poison, and fire; a Russia less rich in these simple things killed its people largely by cold, hunger, and disease) but because a technological mentality invaded the human world as well. This development is tragic because one cannot imagine its ever ending; the tendency towards increasing specialization and efficiency has made its indelible mark on our history, and its devastating effect on what is properly the human world cannot be denied.[55]

These last, haunting claims justify bringing a study of mid-twentieth century totalitarianism to bear upon an early twenty-first century television crime drama. Sociopolitical readings of *Breaking Bad* tend to locate the series' significance within its immediate historical context, for example in relation to the 2008 global financial crisis and ensuing recession, or neoliberalism and identity politics.[56] By bringing *Breaking Bad* into contact with Todorov's study, this book shows how the series taps into and explores the dramatic potential of a much deeper historical cultural context, that of modern industrialised society itself. The importance of recognising this connection to a deeper historical context is captured well in Jacobs's words on *Deadwood*: 'What matters about *Deadwood* as much as its relationship to the contexts or time and place of its making is how it is able, like any good art, to transcend that time and place and continue to speak to us now and in the future'.[57]

The deep historical context of industrialised society, with its attendant technological mentality, provides such a way of reading how *Breaking Bad* handles its plastic stylistic elements in relation to serial form and dignity within the two sequences described above. Across the sequences – separated by five seasons of television – sound, framing, texture, performance, and dramatic structure each craft links that through points of difference express significant development. The first moments of 'Buyout' reach back to 'Bag's in the River' through a musical echo, recalling the earlier scene's opening note while deepening its pitch to achieve a more grave resonance. The first images also share an approach to *visual* composition. Each opens with a frame covered or filled in such a way that our view of the fictional world is one that denies us any orienting sense of spatial or dramatic context. In 'Bag's in the River', an inky blackness smothers the screen, only broken through by spatters of bright red that in their fibrous, fungal structure suggest a microscopic view from the inside of a diseased human lung. That we are actually looking *up through* the viscera of Emilio's dissolved body is revealed as the black and red mess is scooped up and wiped away by Walt and Jesse, who we see peering down at us through the glass 'floor'. 'Buyout' opens looking down, the frame aligned on the horizontal plane with the expanse of concrete floor that stretches from one side of the image to the other, filling the shot in a refusal of any other details of setting. A large shadow starts to creep along the ground from the bottom of the frame towards the top, eventually followed by its source: a reversing dirt-filled dump truck that seems to *glide* 'up' the shot before slotting into place; the graceful, slight bounce of the brakes locking suggests a gentle fit as the vehicle reaches its stop.

These links of scenario, sound, and framing invite comparison between the sequences, and draw out significant expressive differences achieved in the patterned handling of texture.[58] The flashback scenes that interrupt the opening of 'Bag's in the River' have as their characteristic features dry chalkboard calculations and consultations with neatly folded stacks of computer paper. And so they bring into relief the grotesque contaminations of the cleanup, which focus on Walt and Jesse's experiences of having to touch, smell, and unavoidably taste liquefied human remains as they exhaustedly kneel amidst the mess, slowly sponging Walt's victim into spattered buckets. The sponge provides a figure for the scene's textural qualities, an emblem of porousness and availability to violation, an object that soaks up whatever it comes into contact with, in contrast to Walt and Jesse's cloaking in smeared rubber aprons and gloves, a desperate attempt at separation to avoid being stained by this encounter.

Five seasons later, in 'Buyout', the handling of texture suggests how the qualities of the scientific world in the 'Bag's in the River' flashbacks have come to more broadly characterise or dominate the series' world in the present. In place of the earlier sequence's opening immersion in organic material is a distanced, imperial view of concrete flooring; the lines of the moulding into which the cement was poured (prior to its hardening) cut the surface into clear compartments. The dismantling of the bike is presented as a methodically neat piece-by-piece process, each metal, plastic, or rubber part that is taken becoming whole unto itself – be it screw, cowling, or exhaust pipe. The cleanup that opens 'Bag's in the River' is handled in a way that the sponge becomes its central figure, one that connects to the visceral evocation of lung at the sequence's beginning. 'Buyout', on the other hand, has the dump truck and the sealed plastic barrel as mechanical or machined technologies of smoothed edge that contain mess (organic or otherwise) while at the same time being impervious to its absorption.

Textures of surface and object connect with qualities of performance in the 'Buyout' sequence, which are further related to the handling of performance in 'Bag's in the River'. There, sopping up Emilio's remains is presented as an unspeakably horrific and degrading experience, and both Bryan Cranston and Aaron Paul convey a kind of deep, automatic repulsion. However, it is one that refuses what would be for us the easy comfort of the characters' simply *moral* outrage at what has been done to Emilio, instead shading that moral sense with their more immediate, instinctive disgust at their own skin, nostrils, and stomach being contaminated by filth. It is telling how Walt's overwhelming disgust is momentarily overcome less by any sense of moral violation and more by the curiosity he displays towards Emilio's fragment of jawbone (Figure I.2). By the fifth season, Cranston's performance as Walt, and the performances of those immediately around him in the 'Buyout' opening, displays no suggestion of contamination and automatic, involuntary expressiveness. Walt, together with Todd and hitman and fixer Mike Ehrmantraut (Jonathan Banks), dismantles the bike. While each man at first conveys an inner sense of the gravity of what they are about to do, as they get on with the work they project little outward disturbance, meeting their task with grim pragmatism and efficiency as if working overtime in an auto shop. If they are at all moved, whatever

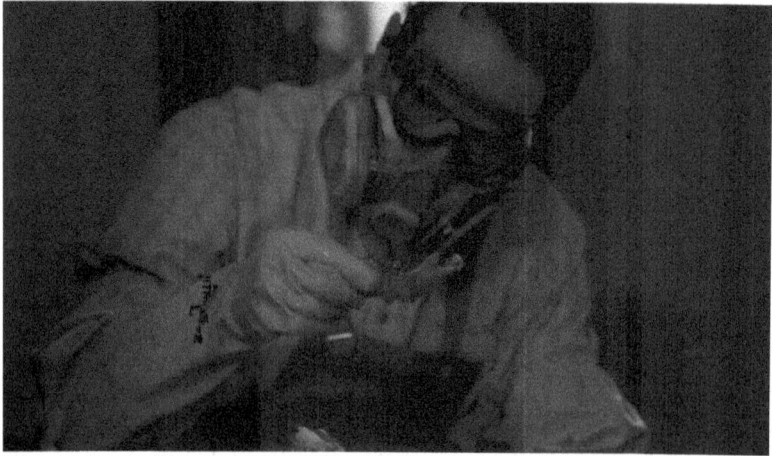

Figure I.2   'And the Bag's in the River': Walt contemplates Emilio's jawbone

feelings might move them are so successfully submerged as to exist only inside inner, private compartments, fully separate from others and so unable to touch – or be touched – by them. It is in this way that the 'Buyout' sequence represents the triumph and effect upon the world of Walt's mindset that in 'Bag's in the River' was frustrated by Jesse's refusal to buy a plastic tub. And so it is further telling that Jesse is the absent fig-ure from the 'Buyout' scene, refusing to participate in the dismantling – he instead smokes a cigarette outside. Jesse lacks the ability Walt displays in the immediate aftermath of gassing Emilio and Krazy-8 in the pilot episode ('Breaking Bad'). There, a shocked Jesse confronts Walt, saying, 'Hey – what'd you do to them?' Walt's answer comes as a patient, mono-tone lecture of chemical formula: 'Red phosphorous in the presence of moisture accelerated by heat yields phosphorous hydride – phosphine gas. One good whiff, and . . .' Jesse expresses the question as an issue of moral urgency, but Walt interprets and answers it as a technical problem, the solution to which is only a matter of scientific law and engineering. The consequences are elided by Walt's manner of trailing off, and giving a vague wave of his arm that avoids confronting and being moved by the human realm of death, and murder.

The rhyming of the opening sequences of 'Bag's in the River' and 'Buyout' captures how Walt's application of an instrumental mentality to human affairs turns individual people into parts of things, to be used to his ends and disposed of, the traces of their individuality effaced from the world by their dissolution into the chemical elements from which they were made. This interest is also manifest in methampheta-mine as a fully synthetic drug, engineered out of disparate chemical parts that, brought together, transform into a new molecule, the sale and use of which is shown in the series to corrode and break apart the bonds that join individuals in human community.

This reading of the sequences described above provides a basis for understanding them in relation to the handling of Walt's violence in the clothing store scene discussed earlier, and in such a way that involves the subject of dignity and its relevance to serial television form. In discussing the clothing store scene, I noted how it suggests a possible trajectory for Walt, one of increasing cohesion from a state of fragile self-division. The style of the 'Buyout' sequence expresses Walt's near-complete hardening, which, in comparison to his vacillat-ing indecision in the clothing store confrontation, imbues his stance with a perverse sense of dignity. This sense of Walt's manner relies on a particular understanding of dignity, one that is distinct from some more well-known formulations of the concept as an inherent, universal, and inviolable quality that all human beings possess by virtue of their being human, a status that puts them beyond worth or value. This universal conception of what is more properly termed *human* dignity is well articulated by George Kateb as working from the assumption 'that the dignity of every individual is equal to that of every other; which is to say that every human being has a *status* equal to that of all others'.[59] I have no desire to challenge this idea of human dignity in any way – as testament to its continued vitality, the scenes from 'Bag's in the River' and 'Buyout' draw their awful force from such a sense of human dignity being most grotesquely defiled.

Yet there is another way of understanding dignity as a much more contingent, fragile, and morally unfixed form of human *expressiveness*, one that is particularly resonant with the modern conditions of fragmentation pointed to earlier. Todorov arrives at such an understanding through the testimonies of concentration camp inmates about their attempts to attain or hold onto what they took to be a sense of their own dignity. Fighting back, singing on the way to the gas chambers, committing suicide, keeping clean (whether a prisoner washing himself, or a guard polishing his shoes), doing a job well (even if that job is to build a concentration camp's walls) – across the testimonies, actions as diverse and morally divergent as these are all found to be achievements of dignity.[60] (It is worth noting that as *achievements* of dignity these each leave implicit the corollary implication that a *state* of dignity is something that can be lost, or that can fail.) What Todorov arrives at is that common across these accounts of dignity is the wilful agreement between inner and outer, something like the visible restraint and mastery of expression seen in the 'Buyout' sequence described above. A quote from Todorov makes this clear:

> When one acts of one's own accord (for example by committing suicide) one demonstrates both that free will exists and that it is possible to establish an adequation between the internal and the external: purely internal decisions, as we have seen, do not lead to dignity. When I make a decision and act in accordance with that decision, that is dignity. [. . .] Dignity then becomes the capacity to satisfy, through one's actions, criteria that one has internalized. [61]

Todorov goes on to provide a rich illustration. 'One example of dignity so defined,' he writes, 'might be simply staying clean in circumstances where everything conspires to prevent it – where water is scarce, dirty, or frozen, the latrines far away, the climate severe.'[62] Dignity here is less a fixed, inviolable, *given* state, and more a contingent and provisional property of individuals in relation to others and to their environment, the attainment and loss of which is expressed and perceived through gesture, action, and manner over time (*'staying* clean').

This means that dignity is a mode of human expressiveness that can be tracked over periods, such as in moments, and the longer units of the weeks, seasons, and years of an individual's life, for example as a person grows old and their comportment may either give way or in some sense 'hold up' against the ravaging pressures of age. A further example suggests a less 'corporeal' link but one that is no less invested in the relationship between inner and outer, and that further links the theme or subject of dignity to the context of modern life. Robert Pippin summarises Henry James's treatment of morality in a modern historical context – one in which previously 'settled' assumptions and ways of life have collapsed and left in their wake great indeterminacy of identity, meaning, and value – in a way that strongly echoes *Breaking Bad*'s basic structure and dramatic issues:

> The novels are full of characters who begin their lives as quiet passengers on some busy train of life, and 'wake up' for one reason or another, insist on a turn at driving, and must then decide where to go (where it is worth going) and how to get there.[63]

What is at stake is something felt to be 'a free life', 'always shown to involve an "aware" or properly "felt" life', but what James's heroes and heroines encounter is 'a great, intensely felt, indisputably real limitation on such an exploration, something like the claims of others to be and to be treated as free, equally independent end-setting, end-seeking subjects'.[64] Here, too, a sense of dignified agreement between one's inner self and its outer realisation is at stake, and it is found to easily come into conflict with the moral claims of others.

It is the dramatic potential of the aspects of dignity outlined above that *Breaking Bad* taps and explores as a subject for serial television. A crucial hinge for the relationship *Breaking Bad* crafts between this subject and serial television drama is the form's peculiar facility for depicting the lives of fictional characters over very long periods of time. The expansiveness of narrative length is often seen by television scholars to be a central dimension of serial television's distinctiveness as a form.[65] For Jacobs and Peacock, it provides the opportunity for 'mutual inhabitancy' between viewer and show, based in 'the medium's ability to generate a shared history with us':

> the television 'houses' we get to return to again and again want us as long-term tenants [. . .] We live in to their familiarity and notice the adjustments in décor, light, the way a house reflects and shapes the lives of its inhabitants. Only television does this so regularly, with such insistent promotion of familiar spaces, people and objects.[66]

The quote points to serial television's tendency to closely track what are intimate and mutually shaping relationships between character and environment or context. This book argues that *Breaking Bad* discovers dignity as a major subject for this aspect of serial television by taking as its main dramatic material the issue of Walter White's fragmented personality and his gradual, willed transformation of self and world.

1
Humiliation and Shame in Season One

One notable aspect of *Breaking Bad*'s first season is the extent to which many of its most pivotal and engaging scenes revolve around characters facing situations in which they risk humiliating or shameful exposure. The pilot episode ('Breaking Bad', 1.1) introduces both Walt and Jesse through vulnerable moments of possible discovery and exposure by the police: first Walt in the opening sequence in the desert, later Jesse in the second act meth lab raid. Through cumulative instances of Walt's diminishment, the pilot's first act positions Walt within his dissatisfying inhabitation of ordinary life, from his breakfast with family through his day teaching high school and washing cars to his surprise birthday party, at which he is set against the more confident self-command of his DEA agent brother-in-law Hank (Dean Norris). A trajectory of decline is also traced by Jesse's shameful return to his family home in episode four ('Cancer Man', 1.4). Jesse's unexpected and somewhat unwelcome visit reveals, in his promising childhood drawings, a past of diligent application; he tries to recover this quality of character in episode five ('Gray Matter', 1.5) through his self-guided attempts to meet Walt's standard of cooking meth. In the same episode, the resentments of being surpassed and the humiliations of charity motivate Walt to reject free healthcare from a former colleague, and to affirm a sense of his dignified self-reliance by resuming his meth enterprise with Jesse.

The aim of this first chapter is to show how it is in the handling of humiliation and shame as dramatic material that *Breaking Bad* finds a solution to the problem that all first seasons of a television serial face: how to build, from a basis of character, space, and conflict, a dramatic structure that can attract viewers and also support ongoing growth and involvement.[1] What the first five episodes are seen to tap for the basis of a serialised drama is how the resentments and ambitions engendered by experiences of humiliation and shame can form deep reservoirs of potential psychological energy that can be drawn on as a renewable catalyst or propellant of human action. Such an aspect of psychology is important to practitioners of serial television as an ongoing form of drama, who must look for ways of sustaining viewer interest in the fiction against the threat of crucial narrative dynamics being exhausted or becoming stale. The first five episodes of *Breaking Bad* address this need by handling humiliation and shame, and their attendant resentments, so that they play a catalysing role in the series' drama that is not only suggested to be renewable, but that is also transformative of characters in terms of their identity and of their relationships to the world they inhabit.

Exposure and concealment

The opening sequence of the pilot episode provides a model for one of the central characteristics of *Breaking Bad*, plunging us into an extreme dramatic situation of mortal risk, handled so our involvement is above all keyed to the pressing threat of humiliating, shameful exposure, and the desperate need to be rescued from it. Walt, dressed only in underwear and a gasmask, flees along a desert road at the wheel of an RV, a man unconscious in the passenger seat beside him, and two other men sliding around in the back. (In a small but important detail, the passenger wears a gasmask, while the clearly more imperilled men in the back do not.) Walt crashes the vehicle off the road, and emerges to the sound of wailing sirens – surely the police closing in. Walt panics, but then controls himself enough to dress in a shirt and videotape a message to his family, after which he draws a pistol and strides out into the middle of the road. He aims his weapon and waits to suicidally confront the police. The scene ends, and we then witness for the first time the series' title sequence.

There are some aspects of the opening sequence's design that provide a crucial basis for our involvement in the drama and so are worth observing from the outset. *Breaking Bad* has been noted for its narrative complexity, sometimes highlighting its use of the 'cold open', which is inaugurated here.[2] Yet what actually happens is quite straightforward. Importantly, the events are extreme in such a way that, despite the cold open narrative technique withholding an orienting story context, there is a strong sense of *dramatic* clarity. This is partly achieved by integrating two generic forms – the crime drama and the Western – through which the scene quickly attunes us to a familiar set of dramatic stakes: fear of capture, and death, and in the face of these fears the wish to grapple for more than mere survival, for a final poise of dignity in the ultimate standoff. Of course, part of the reason for this approach to the opening is to rapidly earn the viewer's intense attachment to the show, an aim equally well met through the 'hook' of the cold open design. Throughout its five seasons, *Breaking Bad* will continue to experiment with the cold open sequence to different effects and with varying degrees of success. But in our first encounter with the technique here, in the form of a flashback structure, we are alerted to the series' participation in film noir tradition. This brings with it all the thematic concerns with agency that adhere to the handling of flashbacks in that genre.[3] Yet there is straightaway, at a more basic level, another implication of the cold open flashback pertinent to *Breaking Bad*'s status as a *serial* work, and that is the way in which it provides the viewer a 'sense of an ending' in a form predicated on the continued postponement or deferral of narrative conclusion. As one aspect of the cold open's purpose is to earn audience involvement by dislocating us from a stable, orienting narrative context, the signalling of an end point draws us in by slightly different means. The technique reassures us that we are 'going somewhere', that, in Jacobs's words on more closed narrative forms such as movies and plays, we know (or so we think) where we will be 'coming in to land',[4] providing a strong ratchet of anticipation by which the episode tightens our bind to the fiction.

In these aspects of the opening sequence we see Vince Gilligan (the episode's writer and director) declare and exercise his skills at television showmanship honed during his long spell as a writer and producer of *The X-Files* (Fox, 1993–2002), the network-based structure of which – a cold open and four acts – Gilligan would maintain in his work for AMC.[5] This is all to say that the arresting qualities of *Breaking Bad*'s immediate beginning are explicable as a showman's attempt to immediately secure viewer attention and commitment. Yet this fact does not represent the limit of the scene's achievement but rather the necessary grounds *for* its achievement. That achievement is to tighten our sympathetic involvement in Walt's fear of exposure so that we are somewhat blinded to or distant from more moral concerns that Walt's actions are at odds with, while making those alternative moral perspectives available all the while, so that we might retrospectively come to see how easily we slipped from alignment with the 'right and proper' position we would wish to take if we were less powerfully compelled by desires such as Walt's.

We are given a clear picture of Walt's vulnerability to exposure through the way in which the camera captures his stumbling exit from the RV. A high, wide shot places him beside the stranded vehicle as a puny figure alone against the surrounding landscape of imposing mesas and sky. It is an image of his isolation that at the same time allows him to be potentially caught in full view from any direction, putting him on the teetering precipice between insulating privacy and all-out discovery. The cut to a closer view lets us see this situation as one that imposes on Walt a sense of helplessness while also allowing that state's free expression in his temporary protection from being exposed to anyone but himself. Cranston at first plays Walt's response to his situation as one of impulsive anger. But with the first distant wailing of the sirens, he slides into unselfconscious despair and back again, and we cleave to the helpless sight of a man buffeted by conflicting waves of feeling whose clashes he cannot control or absorb. Turning his back to the camera, Cranston reaches up with his arms as if in resignation, but they are seized by rage as he pumps them down. Cranston then releases the tension of his limbs and fingers, as if Walt has already spent his energy – his limbs go loose as they come up again to rest with his hands clasped behind his head in a limp pose of surrender. Each exhalation becomes a deep and pained sigh as he aimlessly turns in circles on the spot, looking up and out into the middle distance, beyond his own resources for assistance. Now Walt seems to properly hear the sirens – he catches his breath and holds it, as if in reflex withdrawal against being unexpectedly stuck with everything out in the open. The intrusion of the outside world pulls him from his surrender to helplessness, and into panic at being seen in such a state. He releases his breath as a hyperventilating mantra – 'Oh my God, oh my God, oh my God' – and lets his hand flop loose at the wrists, flapping, an image of slightly effeminate distress that captures his weakness and indecision in the face of a crisis demanding firm resolve. These transitions of bodily expression position Walt as a man thoroughly out of his depth in unlikely and unfamiliar waters, and completely incapable of seeing his way through them. Ordinarily, of course, we would welcome such a situation being sorted out by the arrival of the police and their arrest of this man. (After all, from our knowledge of the series gleaned through advertising promotion and word of mouth, we know from the outset that Walt is a criminal, a drug dealer – possibly even a killer.) Yet, very soon after being snagged by Walt's moment of suspended breath, we are likely to find ourselves sharing his desire to manufacture some face-saving rescue against discovery and capture by the police, as Cranston begins to execute an extraordinary rebuilding of Walt's pitifully shattered self-command.

Our sympathy for Walt in this opening scene – as will come to be the case elsewhere in *Breaking Bad* – hinges on what George Toles finds to be crucial to our investment in Alfred Hitchcock's films. For Toles, many Hitchcock sequences work by somehow getting us to forget, for a moment or longer, our ordinary sense of moral direction and commitment, so that we might find ourselves wishing for good fortune to befall a character in his precarious attempt to kill his wife, as in Toles's reading of a sequence in *Dial M for Murder* (Alfred Hitchcock, 1954).[6] 'We venture into ethical territory as moviegoers,' writes Toles, 'not by locating the most responsible position for appraising others' wrongdoing, but by being drawn into a series of "wrong places" ourselves.'[7] The opening sequence draws us into such a series of 'wrong places' through our strongly felt desire that Walt rescue himself from his state of discomposure, in which he looked all about in vain hope of finding help from somewhere 'out there'. In comparison, what comes to impress us about Walt's more wilful response to the sirens is the way he abandons his blind hope of deliverance in favour of turning inward, where in only a few brief moments we witness him find and shape within himself something like a mental 'winch', a psychological mechanism with which to pull *himself* out of his mess.

Walt's first move towards controlling his appearance is to still his flapping hands by lightly pressing his fingers to his temples. This deliberate gesture gives a coherence of purpose to his previously disconnected parts of body and mind. Walt's placement of his hands by his eyes also blinkers his gaze from the world around him, which earlier intruded in the form of the sirens and set off his panic. Turning away from the world he is able to more strongly gather and focus his attention within himself. From this stable point Walt is able to act decisively, in contrast to his fumbling indecision a moment ago. He hurriedly grabs his shirt from its hanger attached to the RV's passenger-side rear-view mirror and begins to re-clothe himself. He covers up his nakedness while also attempting to retrieve, as a further sense of *psychological* cover, those aspects of his personality 'hung up' when he embarked on this criminal adventure. Toles reminds us that '[i]t is always enticing in movies to affiliate ourselves with the completion of a daunting task'.[8] And here Walt sets about the task of putting himself straight amidst a situation of seemingly irrecoverable collapse. So we might well feel an ambient relief at this point that *something* is being done about the situation, that shiftless panic has given way to purpose. We silently encourage Walt's actions, which, despite being hurried, speak to a much-needed measure of intent and control. Our view of Walt dressing himself is provided by

a shot taken from inside the RV – we eagerly look out through the passenger-side window, focussing our concern on Walt's fumbling efforts
to thread the buttons as quickly as he can, while in the foreground is
framed the passenger seat body lying still over the dashboard (Figure 1.1).
Despite the flashing beacon of the figure's bright red vest, my experience is that we are most likely to be projecting our greatest care towards
Walt's outside need to cover himself up.

The first time we watch the sequence we of course are given no
indication one way or another whether this person is dead or alive,
although his wearing a gasmask holds out some slither of hope for him.
Yet it is a fact of serial television like *Breaking Bad* that it is produced
so that it might last in the lives of its audience, to be revisited and
watched repeatedly, and for the meaning of events to be revised in light
of subsequent revelations. And so by the episode's end, as events come
full circle and we again witness Walt's desperate flight at the wheel of
the RV, we are in full possession of our knowledge that this young man
is Jesse and that Walt is most certain he is still alive.[9] So it becomes
salient to a retrospective appreciation of the opening sequence that, in
our immediately felt investment in Walt's need to cover himself up, we
have overlooked Jesse's unconscious body that is lying right in front of
us. As well, Gilligan and his editor Lynne Willingham (Kelley Dixon
and Skip McDonald would edit the remainder of the series) choose to

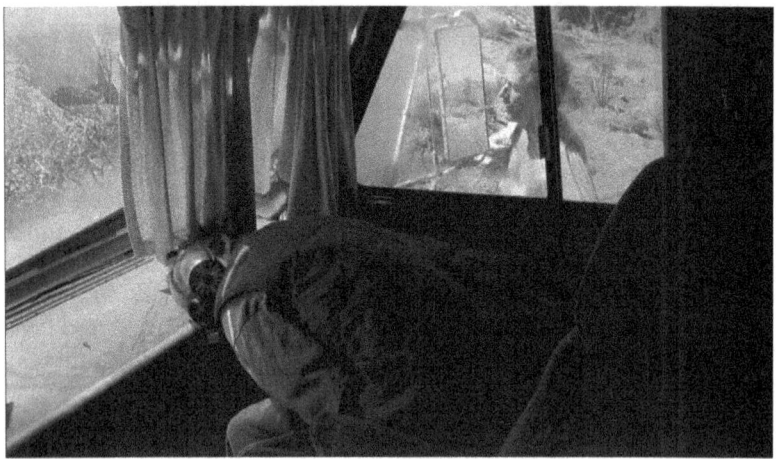

Figure 1.1   'Breaking Bad': Walt dresses himself while ignoring the needs of
another

present us with this view of Jesse's body twice in quick succession, so that a sense of his presence is suggested to be important to our view of Walt's actions. This is all to say that if we are to properly notice and care about the situation of this other character – of Jesse – we must to some extent 'step back' from our investment in Walt's sense of crisis that, more fully committed to, blinkers our view of what matters in such a way that what is at stake inside the RV fails to register against the 'more important' task outside.

In its quiet and still shots of the New Mexico landscape, the opening scene began by inviting us into a position of distanced contemplation, and then sharply shifted in focus and tone with the violent arrival of the careening RV, so that we let ourselves be plunged into close involvement in the drama as seen from Walt's perspective. Here those two viewing positions overlap – seeing the situation one way or another is not only a matter of the camera's selection of viewpoint but is also a matter of our own (retrospective) choice as to what we should care (or have cared) about.[10] The camera's positioning in this moment makes it available for us to discover (too late) how Walt's desire to restore his sense of self, which we have shared in, is pursued at the cost of caring about another person's grave need for help. In this way, Walt's patterns of splitting and cohesion between inner and outer are reflected in our own involvement in the drama, which sees us divided between competing ways of caring about what is happening from moment to moment. What is at stake in sharing Walt's 'blinkered' view is suggested when he returns inside the RV to retrieve a handgun from a dead man in the back and his wallet and video camera from the glove box in the front. Confronted with his partner's unconscious body slumped over the dashboard, Walt doesn't hesitate to plant his palm onto Jesse's face and push him to the side, removing this human impediment to the objects he feels he needs.

Yet by this stage we have likely also forgotten about our momentary concern for Jesse's situation. To plunge back into the RV, Walt – having thrown away his gasmask – must suck in and hold a deep breath. And so, watching a character with his breath held in a toxic atmosphere, we are keenly sensitive to mortal risk and we want him to hurry in his quest for the treasured objects: gun, wallet, camera. We don't register the pushing aside of Jesse as anything more than a desperate bid for safety and self-protection. Like Walt, we are focussed on completing the urgent task at hand, and we are now given another focus for that concern in his frantic grappling with the video camera, which he turns upon himself.

Walt videotapes something like a 'last testament', which, within the whole flashback structure of the episode, further connects the sequence to film noir, in particular to that paradigmatic example *Double Indemnity* (Billy Wilder, 1944). Wilder's movie begins with a different Walter, insurance salesman Walter Neff (Fred MacMurray), careening through the streets of Los Angeles in his car. (Also like his later namesake, Neff is concerned with covering himself up, using his coat to conceal a gunshot wound.) Neff sits down in his office and records into a Dictaphone his confession to murder, a confession addressed explicitly to his close associate and friend Barton Keyes (Edward G. Robinson). For Pippin, the confession aspect is only part of the point: 'Walter is also desperate for Keyes to hear his side of the story, which concentrates on his sympathy for the stepdaughter and the conscience he seems to grow the more time he spends with her'.[11]

The resonance between the two opening testaments is instructive mainly in terms of the substantial differences between them. In his confessional mode, Neff is resolute and coherent in ownership of his actions and the intentions that lay behind them. 'Yes, I killed him,' Neff says. 'I killed him for money, and a woman. I didn't get the money, and – I didn't get the woman.' By contrast, Walter White pointedly refuses to frame his video as a confession. 'To all law enforcement entities,' he begins, 'this is not an admission of guilt. I am speaking to my family now.' In contrast to Neff's voice recording, the videotape provides an opportunity for *Breaking Bad*'s opening to make visibly clear this 'split' mode of address that Walt desires. We see him engineer his image in this way when he begins to break down into tears, and so places his hand across the video camera lens to hide this display of 'weakness'. After sobbing for a few short moments, he removes his hand to reveal himself restored to a relative calm. This bears on the way that, like Neff before him, Walt is concerned to frame his misadventures in terms of love and good conscience:

> Skyler – you are the love of my life. I hope you know that. Walter Jr – you're my big man. There, there are going to be some . . . things, things that you'll come to learn about me in the next few days. I just want you to know that no matter how it may look, I only had you in my heart.

Any reading of Walt's speech must take account of the fact that it follows his hiding from view an unselfconscious revelation of overwhelming feeling. In light of this, Walt's devotions and 'deep down' cares of the heart are troublingly shaded by tones of doubt ('I hope you know that') and (self-) deceit. Walt's words capture how his dignified self-collection and containment depends on putting away some part of himself, while at the same time revealing a capacity for withholding. His wish to capture and contain a clear sense of self clouds his pledges of love, which are themselves held up as veils, a curtain to colour how things may look.

Walt's capacity to shed parts of himself is further plumbed moments after he leaves his videotape and ID in the sand. As he stands, Walt completes his clothing by remembering to button the last two holes of his shirt. He then draws himself taller and gently pulls his shoulders back, introducing a slightly military rigour to his posture and arms, which, now stiffened, he places and holds by his side. Upon hearing the sirens a moment ago, Walt used the connection between his fingertips and his temples to achieve a coherence of body and mind, which defied the panic-inducing threat of the police. His stiffened manner of standing now is even harder and less susceptible to being moved by the world around him. It is in this stance he is able to effect the most complete cleavage between his prior state of humiliating vulnerability and his emerging one of more dignified toughness. This transition seems to happen in a brief gesture akin to the moment in which an actor assumes character before alighting the stage. After sucking in several breaths as if preparing to submerge for some time, Walt shuts his eyes and shakes his head a little as he sharply exhales, and settles into a newly relaxed command of his body. This passage of breath seems to mark the passing and shaking off of the weaker aspects of Walt's self, because it is now that his eyes open to reveal a calm, narrow, predatory gaze that stares up from below the heavy eyelids that betray no trace of Walt's prior anguish.

As I will discuss in Chapter 2, *Breaking Bad* later develops and explores such moments of Cranston's performance as a crucial visual signature. In the first such instance here, Walt's capacity to concentrate himself in this way can be read as what Paul Schrader calls a 'decisive action' in response to an 'actual or potential disunity between man and his environment'.[12] Such action is transformative, as in *Taxi Driver* (Martin Scorsese, 1976), in which, according to George Kouvaros, the decisive action of Travis Bickle (Robert De Niro) at the film's bloody climax 'brings us face to face with the culmination of Travis's rage. From this point on in the film, we continue to see Travis, but we no longer hear from him in the same way'.[13] In Walt's decisive disclosure of toughness and self-mastery we are introduced to his extreme capacity for self-transformation, his ability to achieve an apparently complete divorce between different senses of himself, different sides of his being. Having adopted his mask of toughness, Walt strides up the small sandbank over which the RV has crashed, smoothly drawing the handgun from the back of his underwear. He takes his time to step deliberately into the middle of the road, choosing his spot and planting his feet, turning to face his as-yet unseen challengers, pivoting in a slight, yet graceful and fearless swing, as if his chosen stance provides him a linchpin.

My description cleaves to the qualities of honour and dignified virtue that adhere to our conventional notions of the Western gunslinger, in the image of which Walt rescues himself from simpering cowardice and panic. We are here seriously asked to consider and feel that Walt's stance is in some sense preferable to his earlier state of powerless collapse. This is in the way that the camera is now so close to Walt that the bottom edge of the frame is above the hem of his shirt, denying his partial nudity that was in the previous shot so obvious and unbalancing, emphatically framing the posture of extraordinary self-possession that in comparison to his earlier state is an undeniably more dignified position.

Yet at the same time, the way these final shots emphatically collude with Walt's self-image suggests that his actions to protect himself from exposure are indeed only partial concealments, self-deceptions rather than complete reconstitutions. The camera presents Walt's gunslinger stance as a cardboard cut-out of heroic individual responsibility that can perhaps elide, but not fully erase, what are to him the ordinary weaknesses and embarrassments that lie only temporarily out of sight. Those ordinary aspects of Walt's image he seeks to disguise are still caught out in the open. Here the opening sequence forecasts the psychological basis for Walt's extreme assertion of dignity, one that will be further established and explored through the flashback that constitutes most of the pilot episode: his failure to satisfyingly inhabit the ordinary.

Bases of diminishment

Across the first act, Cranston's performance is integrated with the handling of domestic spaces and the depiction of family routines in a way that we are to read as measuring Walt's perspective on the ordinary, and how it jostles with the competing views of others who share his situation. Following the opening sequence, these domestic scenes of humiliation and shame – which include Hank and Jesse – come to press upon and shape our sense of the postures through which the characters later express and realise aspirations for more dignified states of being.

After the title sequence, we are shown an exterior establishing shot of a modest suburban house just before first light. Unlike the RV in the desert, this house is grounded in a suburban environment associated with the peaceful upbuilding of family, rather than the violent individualism of the Western evoked by the cold open. Inside the house, having hauled himself from bed, Walt stands atop a small exercise contraption in the middle of his half-decorated nursery, plodding in place in a ritual gesture towards self-improvement. The deficit of spirit and heavy weight of habit expressed by his exercise makes it look more like half-hearted maintenance of his tolerated but seemingly unsatisfying condition. In comparison to the energy and immediacy the Western-inflected opening scenario elicited from Walt, in this space of domesticity he embodies spent or lost or surrendered vitality; it feels as if it is *his* lethargy, and not the weakness of the early sun, that suffuses his home with the claustrophobic shadows of a gloom-laden dawn. The choice of routine and its presentation here is suggestive: Walt's static exercise shows him exerting effort while staying in place. The scene then connects this image with a long arc of professional and personal stagnation when, after Walt's coughing brings his tired movements to a slow standstill, we are shown a plaque that hangs on the wall. Awarded by the Los Alamos Science Research Centre, it recognises Walt for his contribution to Nobel Prize-winning research; an extreme close-up focuses our attention on its date: 1985. Alongside, out of focus and so difficult to read, is an Award of Merit from the New Mexico Public School System. This weighting of focus places Walt's more remarkable, prestigious achievement as long past, as having passed, decades ago. It also suggests a weighting of value, in which a modest yet vital public contribution as an educator feels like wasted potential below the rarefied heights of Nobel recognition.

Of course, perhaps it's more common than not for bright, early possibilities cut so clear in youth to fade and be dulled by time's long, slow passage. But Walt's despondent response to the morning is set in a half-decorated nursery, a space in which energy, money, and time are being invested in preparation for the new life that will be raised here. Being shown these details we are reminded of the capacity of domestic interiors to give evidence of the construction or development of a family's life and world over time. *Breaking Bad* announces its interest here in using such spaces this way through its treatment of the nursery setting. We are shown the room in a way that places Walt's past, publicly recognised accomplishments of his late-twenties against he and his wife's present, more private achievement: creating a new human being, and building a hospitable place in which to care for it. The setting thus intersects Walt's extraordinary achievements that are now past with those more ordinary ones that are present and unfolding before him. Although he might justifiably take energising pride in both, Walt's careless exertions in this space suggest the risks and rewards of realising potential no longer lift his spirit, but stifle it under their burden. The scene's final image presents an undercurrent: Walt bends down and looks at the dial of his exercise machine; he looks to measure his progress.

The scene of Walt's birthday breakfast continues this concern with development through its brief, one-and-a-half minute sketch of the domestic everyday. Skyler tells Walt the strips arranged over his eggs in shape of the number '50' are 'veggie bacon', a caution against cholesterol intake, and then reminds him not to be home late from work, where she thinks he gets 'dicked around'. Walt Jr arrives at the table, complaining about the lack of hot water in the shower, nagging his parents to buy a whole new system. Walt coughs, and we find out he's been sick lately. Walt Jr sarcastically asks his dad: 'How does it feel to be old?' Walt replies: 'How does it feel to be a smart-ass?'

The modesty of the scene's handling invites being passed over quickly. *Breaking Bad*'s typical treatment of scenes such as this may seem to some eyes a conventional manifestation of American television's 'stylistic norms'. Adrian Martin describes the show's camera and editing style in this sense in his reading of a scene from season two:

> There are doubtless some conventional, predictable aspects to the televisual *mise-en-scène* and *découpage* [. . .] first, a high level of shot repetition [. . .] Second, a tendency to over-use the slightly shakey, hand-held effect (in almost every set up here) so beloved of TV drama – something that comes from the dual pressure of shooting quickly and wanting, at any cost, the ersatz realism of a 'you are there' aura. And third, a massive concentration of the all-inclusive, wide-scale master-shot [. . .][14]

Yet, as Martin goes on to note about the season two scene he discusses, it is in the series' find handling of details – often pivoting around performance – that such scenes find their interest and achieve significance. It is in this sense that, despite its apparently obvious stylistic simplicity or conventionality, the scene of Walt's birthday breakfast deserves attention. Its handling of the dramatic interaction between performers and characters gives an important picture of Walt's response to the state of his life at a point when more than half of it is over, and the trajectory of what remains seems fixed and given. The scene's first lines are about the danger of physical stagnation resulting from the past's accumulations, a lifetime of built-up fat clogging increasingly choked arteries that threaten to starve Walt of oxygen, or vitality. The next lines associate this strong image of gradual, invisible decay with our more clearly emerging sense of Walt's professional disappointments. Having asked what time he'll be home, Skyler scoldingly directs Walt to respect the confines of his employment: 'You get paid 'til five, you work 'til five – no later.' The psychological passions and rewards of exploring the unknown – Los Alamos – have been replaced with predictable exertions of minimal effort motivated only by a paycheque.

In our attachment to Walt we might, in sympathy, feel that working nine-to-five for what is only just a living would be a mean, dispiriting daily prospect. Yet a sense of Walt's life as leeched of spirit doesn't necessarily follow from his fairly ordinary work situation – suggested instead is that such an attitude, as well as our capacity to be sympathetic with it, stems from a tendency towards boredom and self-pitying humiliation. Klevan, discussing the basis for the development of Scottie's obsessive pursuits in *Vertigo* (Alfred Hitchcock, 1958), provides an account of boredom that usefully evokes its psychological location and what it puts at stake in terms of human connection to the world: 'One way of understanding the state of boredom is as an excess of imagination, and hence the failure to find sufficient stimulation in the ordinary aspects of life, those we also share with others'.[15] In its triangular dramatic structure of challenge and response between the parents and their son, the scene holds in tension such attitudes towards the ordinary. This is clear in the conversation around the hot water system. Establishing the family's mundane financial limitations (neither flush nor destitute, they are merely strained, or just restrained) the moment also works quiet contrasts of response to life's daily difficulties. Putting his crutches aside without expressing annoyance or expecting assistance, Walt Jr explains why he took so long to get to breakfast: 'There was no hot water – *again*.' Walt responds by turning from his son to painfully examine his unwanted veggie bacon, while Skyler, offscreen, rises to the provocation without hesitation: 'I have an easy fix for that,' she sharply but patiently offers, with a hint of playful drama as we study Walt's miserably irritated avoidance. 'You wake up early, and then you get to be the first person in the shower.' Carefully lowering himself to his chair, Walt Jr responds: 'I have an idea. How about: buy a new hot water heater, for the millionth, billionth time.' Skyler lets this slide past with a gently dismissive roll of her eye, seeming to flash the faint hint of a smile, which she tries to share with her grim husband.

In comparison to Walt, his son and wife find not having enough hot water for everybody's showers to be an occasion for a series of defiant but playful challenges. Their hardy involvement in the family's daily struggles – the temporary annoyance of a cold shower, the lifelong imposition of debilitating cerebral palsy – bring into relief Walt's withdrawal. Where Walt Jr and Skyler just get on with it and, by doing so, find a passing enjoyment in each other, Walt retreats into dissatisfaction with the ordinary situation they all share, which seems pale in comparison to those extraordinary, now unrealisable possibilities held in his past. Walt Jr and Skyler toss barbs between each other with a harmless ease that implies their ongoing regularity, yet they seem to painfully prick Walt. This pain marks the moment at the breakfast table as a quietly humiliating exposure of his felt inadequacy as a father and a man. It is an important early measure of Walt's character that his only, silent response is to shrink.

The scenes that follow sketch Walt's position in his working life, showing how he inhabits his roles as a science teacher and car wash cashier. The order in which they follow each other traces the downward trajectory of Walt's professional status over time, while also showing that he has now reached the bottom of his decline, and is stagnating in place. It is fitting that reductions in Walt's public visibility trace these diminishments. From his past recognition across an entire field of prestigious research, Walt is now reduced to weak attempts to assert authority over a classroom of students, and to avoid being seen as another faceless anybody serving customers behind a cash register; his inability to do so is highlighted by his reduction to just one of many workers who usually go unseen, crouched outside on wet concrete, scrubbing tyres. These sequences place Walt as a descendent of Ed Avery (James Mason) in Nicholas Ray's 1956 melodrama *Bigger Than Life*, which offers a compressed version of the diminishments we see Walt undergo. Ed is also a schoolteacher, who works a second, feminised job as a taxi dispatcher, which he keeps secret from his wife to avoid the humiliation of his financial inadequacy being exposed to her. Also like Walt, Ed is humiliated by his failure to provide his family an adequate hot water system. Diagnosed with a fatal inflammation of his arteries, Ed undergoes experimental cortisone treatments that unlock his repressed megalomania, allowing him to re-shape how others see him, until, at the end, doctors stabilise his medication and his desires submerge once again.[16] In *Breaking Bad*, the hiding-away of Walt's festering resentments does not dissipate but instead inflates his self-pitying sense of entitlement, which his cancer diagnosis then fully unleashes. It is suitable to *Breaking Bad*'s serial condition that the chosen disease is one that both presses on time (shortening life) and takes its time (months, years), and whose treatment does not promise a cure but only a temporary retreat. This will allow the series to closely track the ways that Walt's experience of mortality allows him to realise, over substantial lengths of time, dormant aspects of his personality, or to carve out new facets of it, transforming his image and being in relation to the shifting contexts of his treatment, work, and domestic life.

Through these early work scenes, integration of camera, performance, costume, object, and space express Walt's diminishments as – fittingly for these introductory parts of the series – spring-like *compressions* of his character, building-up a sense of dangerously harnessed potential energy that waits to be kinetically released. In this way, we are encouraged to find the basis for Walt's humiliations in his deep, unrealised desires for public recognition and esteem. I take this to be the issue of the conflict that ensues when Bogdan (Marius Stan), the car wash owner, orders Walt to step out from behind the register to wipe down cars. The moment reveals how Walt values the sliver of status his unstable position as a cashier allows when he firmly refuses to work below his station: 'Bogdan, *no* – we talked about this.' The impasse is broken in only a moment when Walt's resistance silently caves, setting up surrender as a habit. The way Cranston plays Walt's surrender in comparison to the previous gesture of resistance is telling. Walt's initial defiance is firm, but quiet and still. His manner pleads a little, as if making a veiled beg. By contrast, caving to Bogdan's demands, displaying his weakness again ('We talked about this'), Walt unleashes a small fury of energy: he slams down his biro (a flimsy impact) and – after stepping aside for Bogdan, who takes up the surrendered position – snags his arms by petulantly whipping off his jacket. Walt's desire to have his status recognised does not by itself excite his passions; the resentment of his perceived insult and the shame of his exposed weakness bring out a more vital, yet less graceful, display of spirit. That Walt's diminishment builds his resentful energy is shown when a student – who earlier made a public, classroom demonstration of Walt's powerlessness by dragging his chair across the ground to drown out Walt's voice – recognises Walt at the carwash as he scrubs the tyres of the young man's sports car. Walt tries to find reprieve from his exposure by retreating behind the vehicle, where he is reduced to working on his hands and knees. His scrubbing sublimates the repressed rage visible in his clenched jaw. This physical concealment does not relieve Walt's humiliation but amplifies its effects, heightening the gap between how he feels and how he acts. In what might suggest to us an early warning, Walt's flight from the pain of his humiliation only further distances him from a more dignified stance.

Different ways people can be visible to each other are used as mechanisms through which to introduce Hank in the following surprise party sequence. As Hank intuitively wields the force of his congenially bullish persona to make himself the focus of Walt's party, the scene sets this capacity to command respect against Walt's tendency to invite and pitifully absorb mockery. The men's contrasting capacities to be resistant to humiliation define them in opposition to each other, providing early points of comparison for tracing later developments. Our first sight of Hank is not of his face but a close-up of his pistol when, seated, he draws his Glock from his waist and points it ahead, a mock challenge to whoever confronts him. A tilt up reveals him to be a pit-bull of a barrel-chested man, who with his shaved head and imposing bulk might look at first like another iteration of the corrupt, racist, violent Vic Mackey (Michael Chiklis) of *The Shield* (FX, 2002–2008). There is a hint, though, that Mackey's more malevolent bravado is seemingly softened here just a bit by Hank's less aggressive charisma, his disarmingly fun way of being sociable, captured in Dean Norris's smile that, while slightly threatening in its crocodilian tooth line, spreads across and opens up his face, while the attendant laughter is delivered with full commitment of body, usually while leaning in towards the subject of his taunts, or giving them a friendly slap on the back.

By drawing on our awareness of the Vic Mackey type, however, the likeness inclines us to expect a similar character to emerge. Hank's first speech in the pilot meets these expectations, sketching him for the audience – both in the room, and watching the show – as a man of action who's quite casually been there and done that. Looking side-to-side as he speaks, canvassing the spread of the room as if everyone should be listening because they should all be interested, he draws the weapon and announces: 'Glock 22. That's my daily carry, 'kay? I mean, unless you're talkin' plus, b-plus loads, you can forget the nine mil', alright? Shit, I seen one of those, ah, bounce off a windshield one time.' Hank's speech echoes the similar words of Harry Callahan in the third of the Dirty Harry movies, *The Enforcer* (James Fargo, 1976), by associating masculine self-respect with violent, penetrative power.[17] Indeed, Hank shows his apparent invulnerability to penetration when he is unfazed by the attempt of his partner, Gomez (Steven Michael

Quezada) to pierce his self-inflation with the mocking line: 'Yeah, when you were shootin'!' However, there are moments in the first episode when this is given a less benignly boastful edge, tinged instead with a latent racism (he takes bets on whether a suspect is of the 'Latino persuasion', a 'beaner'), and we are invited to see as dangerously simplistic his tendency to cast his profession as a battle of good and evil, between the cops and the (usually Hispanic) 'bad guys'.

But before these later details emerge, Hank's speech also serves to highlight his and Walt's respective capacities to be apart from or cohere within a community. We see this when the choice is made to cut from Hank's close-up to a wide shot of the room. The cut releases us from Hank's orbit so we can see how everyone else is drawn in. If we look away from Hank's foregrounded moment in the middle of things we see Walt standing alone in the background behind Hank's circle, looking in, fidgeting with his cup of beer to seem occupied, just politely nodding to people who walk past him, cutting the figure of an awkward guest in his own home, uncomfortable playing the role of host, one that to be done well requires an intuitive sense of other people's complex and unpredictably fluctuating currents of feeling.

In this sense, the staging throughout the scene treats the living room of Walt's house as a theatrical space, a quality that is picked up on by both Walt and Hank, but in different ways. As Hank gathers an audience and projects (with the help of a prop) a dramatisation of a coherently possessed and secure self-identity, Walt seems paralysed by stage fright rather than at ease with domestic sociability, as if unaware of what his lines should be, and feeling badly outdone by a more natural performer. This suggests early on that Walt is a man who does not naturally inhabit the home, but feels it as a space that requires the conscious taking-on of a role, one that despite years of performance continues, or has come over time, to feel unfamiliar and uncomfortable – an ill-fitting costume. By treating the living room in this way, the wide shot of Hank's successful storytelling not only shows both Walt's marginalised position at his own party (we also glimpse him wander across the frame at the end of the previous scene) and Hank's centrality to it; it also asks us to measure their different capacities to get along with other people, to have others see them in a positive light, to draw people in and warm them by the energy they emit in social circles (Figure 1.2).

Walt's capacity to be humiliated or embarrassed by Hank in his own home and on his own birthday makes him an example of the melodramatic masculinity Deborah Thomas describes as a feature of many Hollywood movies, in which 'the theme of "becoming a man" [. . .]

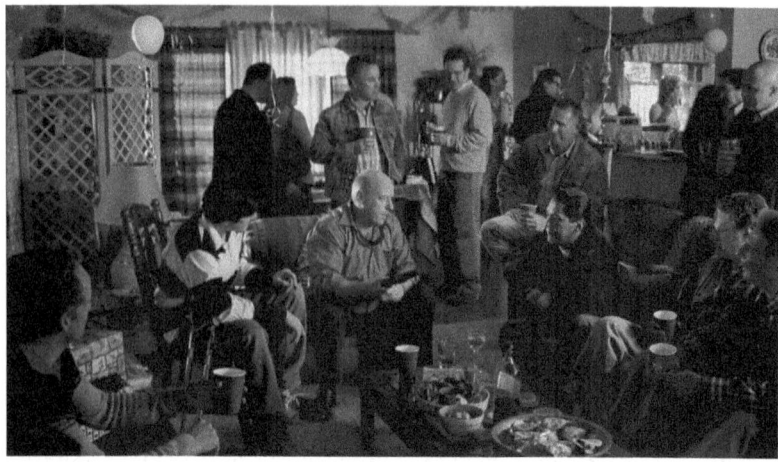

Figure 1.2   'Breaking Bad': Walt and Hank's different capacities in social circles

draws both on male-centred fantasies of augmentation and diminishment within the domestic space and on a flight into violence elsewhere'.[18] We see the attraction of such fantasies of 'a flight into violence elsewhere' after Walt's humiliation by Hank reaches its greatest height at the climax of Hank's supposed tribute to him. Whereas Walt can only hover around the room's edges, Hank widens his grip on the room with a boisterous call for attention, and proposes a toast to Walt. But as everyone else raises their own glasses, Hank takes Walt's beer from him as Walt moves to speak, leaving him silent and empty-handed but for the now-forgotten handgun that remains an emblem of his impotence. The next shot shows Walt at his most fully isolated, drinking alone while in the background his family together crowd around the televised glory of Hank's earlier meth lab raid. Walt returns to the group, intrigued by images of seized cash. If we think back to Walt's borrowing of the gunslinger pose in the opening sequence, this staging of his self-exile from and then return to the social gathering suggests that stories of strength and success received through media like television act as an avenue for Walt's imaginative escape from humiliation within the domestic.

Jesse also seeks to find a better sense of self through an identity borrowed from surrounding culture. Across episodes two ('Cat's in the Bag . . .', 1.2) and three ('And the Bag's in the River', 1.3), Jesse's interactions with Walt are handled so that they seem to paint a fairly coherent picture of Jesse as a small-time meth dealer barely able to see past the horizon of his next hit. Yet details in the brushwork of this characterisation suggest that the facets of Jesse made most prominent in these early episodes are not quite able to come together as a complete whole. There are small suggestions that there is something unlikely about the identity being framed for us. For instance, Jesse's introductory escape from the DEA suggests that his sensual inclinations distance him from the rationalist mentality of professional drug dealing. While heavily armed DEA agents ready their assault on the house, Emilio sits amidst the mess of the lab patiently scraping red phosphorous from match heads, a picture of diligent effort showing commitment to a moneymaking enterprise that has overtaken and rendered uninhabitable the home's interior. By contrast, we see Jesse hastily flee from a bedroom window down the street as the raid cuts short his sex with the woman who throws his clothes after him, revealing his capacity to see past material concerns, to glimpses of domestic pleasure and intimacy. Related to this is Jesse's need for the oblivion of getting high on meth, which he uses to become numb to the horrific reality of his attempt to dissolve Emilio's body. Here, Jesse's meth habit reveals his susceptibility to the world. It contrasts with the insulation Walt finds in his capacity for cold rationalisation, which he displays when he suggests Jesse cut off the arms and legs of Emilio's corpse as if he was casually eliminating from a chalkboard the remainder of a messy long division. So these first few episodes track Jesse's attempts to project an outward appearance as a dyed-in-the-wool member of the meth underworld, whose attitudes are embodied in Krazy-8 when, in the pilot episode, he unhesitatingly pulls a gun to kill Walt and Jesse. In contrast, Jesse's outward appearance conflicts with his inner sensitivity to companionship with others. This is shown in episode four ('Cancer Man'), when he keeps smoking meth so as not to be abandoned by his friends Skinny Pete (Charles Baker) and Combo (Rodney Rush), who exploit this need in order to get to his drugs.

In the same episode, after getting high with Skinny Pete and Combo, Jesse falls into a drug-induced psychosis and flees his house – which is now literally corroded by murder – and returns to his family home. This home is treated as a space that confronts Jesse with his childhood self as a monument to his unrealised potential, centrally in the form of memorabilia stored in a chest in his bedroom. Jesse's return home interrupts the dinner conversation of an upper-middle class family, a scene in which this couple (played by Tess Harper and Michael Bofshever) talk about their young son's apparent talent for woodwind instruments ('You really shine on that oboe, and I'm not just saying that.'). When we discover Jesse is their substantially older son, we can understand these later efforts of childrearing as perhaps somehow inspired by the shame of earlier failures (of both parents and offspring), and so see Jesse's life as an embodiment of lost possibility. Indeed, when he goes upstairs to sleep off his meth high over the course of the night and a day, we're shown emblems of Jesse's past potential: fairly skilful cartoons drawn by him as a child, and photographs of him smiling on the cusp of adolescence. These shots, and the later scene in Jesse's bedroom, treat the space as a shrine-like preservation of his unfulfilled promises, a memento of the past identity that no longer fits the young man Jesse has grown into. We see that the values Jesse's parents appear to be more successfully instilling in his brother, Jacob, once held their grip on their first son and his sense of the future, before that bright horizon fell dark.

Jesse reaches this vision of himself when he retrieves from his collection of memorabilia a test paper on which he has scrawled a crude and humiliating sketch of Walt sodomised by a test tube. Across the bottom of the test paper is Walt's caustic scrawl: 'Ridiculous! Apply yourself!' The already fading smile falls from Jesse's lips and his sparkling eyes go flat, pricked by this accusation that exposes his waste of potential. The scene, and Jesse's homecoming sequence, ends with a phone call from Combo, who enthusiastically offers to buy Jesse's remaining meth. The phone call arrives as if in response to Jesse's exposure to himself, his mobile phone opening up a line of escape to a different world that holds out an offer of respect and reward, an avenue to give slip those parts of himself that bear the shame of his past failures.

In the following scene, we see that it is through Jesse's pursuit of success, esteem, and companionship in the meth world that he seems most able to take command of himself. Jesse interrupts Walt at his home as the older man scrounges on his hands and knees to retrieve money accidentally sucked into the air conditioning. Walt hauls Jesse out back by the swimming pool. Despite Walt's humiliating assumption that he is wearing a wire, Jesse reveals why he came: 'Four grand,' he says, pulling a thick wad of fifty-dollar bills from his sweater, 'your share, from sellin' that batch. That's why I'm here.' Walt has no answer. 'Yeah, yeah, that's right,' continues Jesse, 'I didn't smoke it all.' Jesse throws into the air this money he could have so easily kept for himself and walks away as it flutters into the pool. He exits the scene head held high, having exposed the wrongness of Walt's estimations, leaving Walt as he began the scene, scrounging for money on hands and knees, as he pulls sodden notes from the pool with a leaf skimmer.

Walt's inhabitation of the domestic is presented in a way that not only evokes his past trajectory of personal decline and collapse, but also provides a measure for his anticipated future development of self-command, signalled in the cold open of the pilot episode. Those early scenes of Walt at work and at home give the impression of a man resigned (albeit resentfully) to who he has become. By comparison, Jesse is a young, relatively energetic man, and so it seems necessary for the series, in his homecoming sequence, to *confront* him with what he has failed to cultivate in himself. *Breaking Bad* negotiates this early confrontation around three instances in which Jesse fails to successfully find a place in four domestic spaces, four homes. The first two are the meth lab raided by Hank and the woman's bedroom from which he flees; the third is the house in which the ceiling collapses due to the corrosive effects of Jesse's involvement in Emilio's murder and complete dissolution; and the fourth is his parents' home, where the person he has become is no longer felt to belong, has split apart from who he was and who his parents are. So Jesse is being shown to us across these episodes as a young man whose shameful transgressions have led him into a criminal world, the depravity of which leaves him out of his depth. The episodes suggest that we might take his measure in the future by his capacity to respond to his history of shame by finding or constructing a domestic space he can inhabit as a home, or by coming into community with some people who are prepared to welcome him into a home despite the person he has become, or failed to become.

Development through aspiration

Breaking Bad's first four episodes show a repeated interest in staging scenes of potential or actual humiliation, handled in ways that suggest that the depicted events provide an impetus for Walt and Jesse's renewed cultivation of fallow capacities in response to past failures. This is important to the choice that Walt should start his meth cooking operation with a former student who his teaching was unable to reach. It allows Walt and Jesse's enterprise to become an avenue through which their aspirations to have other people recognise their personal quality and distinction – aspirations based in pasts of humiliating failure – may be channelled in ways that revive lagging beliefs in their abilities to educate, and to be educated. These stakes are given dramatic expression around the sense of dignity that may be achieved through work. 'Yet another form of dignity', writes Todorov, 'is the satisfaction derived from a job well done. Using one's skills or expertise to the best of one's ability can enable one to preserve [or restore] a measure of self-respect.'[19]

The first season conveys these developments around education and self-respect through sequences that will become another important visual signature of *Breaking Bad*: the meth cooking montages. These condense the cook into a couple of minutes in which its processes are orchestrated with an eclectic variety of music through striking uses of jump-cuts, dissolves, time-lapse, and other visual techniques of elision. Across the series they trace the development of Walt and Jesse's enterprise and relationship. In the second season montage we see the expansion of their productivity in a larger, more advanced lab, and the greater intimacy of their relationship as they take turns working, resting, and relaxing together ('4 Days Out', 2.9). Third season montages – in 'Sunset' (3.6) and 'Kafkaesque' (3.9) – trace the folding of their enterprise into corporate-owned, industrial-scale production.[20] The consequent dissolution of Walt and Jesse's partnership, and the instrumentalism of the meth world, is laid bare when in episode ten of season four ('Salud', 4.10) Jesse is 'sold' to a Mexican cartel after demonstrating his skill as a cook. A key montage in the fifth season shows the reunion of Walt and Jesse's partnership, and demonstrates their renewed capacity to be mobile while hiding in plain sight, by disguising their transplantable cooking operation within a domestic fumigation firm ('Hazard Pay', 5.3).

In this way, the cooking montages become a highly recognisable stylistic segment of the show. However, by eliciting instant recognition, the montages tend to arrest viewer attention in such a way that risks us sensing a self-conscious straining for novelty on the part of the show, and of a clear appearance of visual rhyming that might easily seem obvious. Yet the sequences, and the patterned relationships between them, are eloquently integrated with their dramatic contexts so that they serve the conventional function of marking some seemingly clear serial narrative development, while holding in tension the satisfactions of apparent progress with doubts as to the meaning or value of what has been progressed.

That there is a sense of value or principle at stake in the first cooking montage is suggested in the scene that immediately precedes it. Walt brings to Jesse's house the lab equipment stolen from the high school, and their conversation conveys their different attitudes towards the work. For Jesse, a successful meth cook in which one can take pride is a matter of self-guided feeling and intuition, a subjective matter of 'art'. This can partly be seen in his refusal to heed Walt's advice about the proper use of laboratory glassware. 'This is a volumetric flask,' Walt points out, 'you wouldn't cook in one of these.' Jesse is unwavering in his self-guided sense of what works: 'Ah, yeah,' he replies, 'I do.' In his 'signature' of an inert chilli powder additive, Jesse instead holds firm to a fully self-generated set of criteria, taking no regard of any objective measure or judgement by others. Walt also holds firm to a set of principles as to what constitutes good work, but rather than being a subjective matter they instead seem inherited from his training within a tradition of scientific application and craftsmanship. In his enthusiastic appreciation of the glassware and its properties, Walt cleaves to a normative sense of what one 'should' do with such objects, what their proper given function is, in contrast to Jesse's more cavalier attitude in which the way things are used and valued is a matter of personal whim or ease.

These differences are expressed in the cooking montage through contrasts in bodily movement and the characters' different relationships to the objects and happenings around them. The practical realisation of Walt's pride in craftsmanship is shown by the camera's attention to the well-practiced fluidity of his movements, guided by an alertness to and intimate knowledge of his process, which enables him to predict outcomes and be prepared to respond to them. For instance, when Walt adds methylated spirits to a beaker of ground pseudoephedrine tablets and produces a cloud of fume, he calmly, lightly holds his hand atop the beaker until the fuming subsides. By contrast, Jesse seeks constant distraction from his work. As they each grind tablets, Walt concentrates on the precision, effectiveness, and cleanliness of his task, whereas Jesse spins in circles on his chair, working without a sense of direction. To Walt's visible annoyance Jesse listens to music and constantly fidgets to its beat, so he's unprepared when the boiling flask he is supposed to be watching quickly erupts, spewing toxic waste that should have been cleanly removed by the pipe Walt has to desperately fix in place a moment too late. What the montage contrasts here is the sense of Walt's grace conveyed by the way his movements appear thoughtfully, intentionally integrated with surrounding objects and processes, against Jesse's bodily incoherence that suggests his failure to attend to the marriage of his body parts and to their relationship with the world around him. The style of montage employed in the cooking sequences seems well suited to exploring these contrasts, and how they can shift over time. In moments, the sequences are intensely fragmented by jump-cutting in a way that conveys a mood of jittery agitation, but they also display a striking sense of cohesion. This is found in their marriage between the respective rhythms of meticulous process, gesture, cutting, and music, and their use of time-lapse as a way of locating a sequence structured around elision within a seemingly uninterrupted observation of time's passage.

The second cooking montage, in episode five ('Gray Matter'), follows Jesse's return to the meth business with an old friend, Badger (Matt Jones), in the wake of his attempt to get a legitimate job in real estate. (Reflecting his lack of education and training, Jesse was not offered a sales job as expected, but instead a position waving a sign on the footpath while dressed as a one-dollar bill.) The cooking montage in 'Gray Matter' draws upon the pilot episode's montage through variations of rhythm, pace, fragmentation, and cohesion. Through its patterned handling of these elements, the sequence suggests how, in response to his earlier humiliations detailed above, and in answer to Walt's example, Jesse strives for a more perfect outcome in a way that is shown to heighten the requirements of his self-respect. This second cooking sequence conveys Jesse's development under Walt's tutelage by giving him an opportunity to model for Badger Walt's enthusiasms, knowledge, and values. Jesse's grinding of pills now surprisingly mirrors Walt's in its focus and intensity, suggesting the shame Jesse displayed when over-boiling the flask ignited his aspiration to be recognised as self-sufficiently competent. We see how a lack of shame is an obstacle to education when, taking on Walt's approach, Jesse tries to reprimand Badger, who does his work with slow, weak disinterest and finds distraction in snacking from a nearby bag of chips. As Badger clowns with empty malt liquor bottles, we see how Jesse's increasing interest in work for its own sake manifests in frustration at his partner's lack of investment in the job at hand. In the first cooking montage, instead of helping to grind pills, Jesse at first mucked around with the video camera. 'Just shut up and help me,' said Walt. Now, as Badger uses a gasmask to get in Jesse's face with a Darth Vader impression, Jesse says, 'Are you gonna help me or what?' Here, Jesse grows-in to the authority of his new sense of status. The slower, closing shots of the montage show Jesse alone, staring with intent curiosity at drops of liquid slowly dripping from the condenser into a beaker. As hours pass by through time-lapse, the careless Badger retires to sleep while, in contrast, Jesse continues to work, testing pH levels and standing by his task as the yellow liquid in an Erlenmeyer flask transforms through a dissolve into a clear solution. These are stably held images of Jesse arrested by his newly focussed interest in his work, in Walt's chemistry and how its processes can cohere and transform.

This new focus is shown to expand Jesse's imagination of his own capacities when, assessing his product in the wake of the cook, he finds it doesn't meet the standards modelled by Walt and tosses it out, to begin again. The earlier post-cook assessment of Walt's product in the pilot episode gives important context for this later moment. Picking over Walt's shards of perfectly clear crystal, Jesse expresses his new respect for Walt's skills. Turning to Walt, he exclaims in disbelief, 'This is pure glass. . . . You're a goddamn artist. This is *art*, Mr White.' What Jesse earlier considered his own, unteachable, art ('So don't be tellin' me') he now sees as more properly residing with Walt, the scientist. However, this enthusiasm sees Jesse move to surrender himself to the drug's power over him. Rubbing his hands together in agitated excitement he says, 'Man, I gotta – I gotta try this.' When Walt intervenes by saying, 'No, no – No, we only sell it; we don't use it,' Jesse refuses this criterion of self-respect, this moral index: 'Okay, since when? Listen, you've been watchin' way too much *Miami Vice. That ain't happenin'.*' This moment positions Jesse as an addict apparently in total thrall to the way Walt's product promises to lift him beyond his ordinary sense of self. So the criteria of Jesse's self-respect can be measured by his capacity to resist this form of self-denial, to instead inhabit the world in a way that is unmediated by the deforming lens of a meth high.

Jesse's addiction allows his failure to meet the standard set by Walt's formula and its product to be a moment of humiliation, or humbling, that gives him an aspiration beyond once again servicing his desire for the base, animal, temporary satisfaction that he finds in the stained bowl of his meth pipe: pure stimulation of the central nervous system. After Badger applauds Jesse's work ('You are a *genius*, bro. This cankenstein is *unreal*') Jesse is able to reject Badger's opinion because he can now see with his own eyes: 'It's not right.' He tries to explain to Badger – 'It's . . . cloudy. It's not supposed to be cloudy, okay, that last time it was glass' – but Badger replies by lowering the bar of expectation: 'So what? Cloudy, not cloudy – It looks good enough to me!' Jesse repeats Badger's words to himself – 'Good enough' – as if remembering a familiar excuse, but one that now appears strange to him under the light of Walt's standards in pursuit of perfection. Seized by his imagination of a more perfect outcome, Jesse takes the tray of meth – which last time he wanted to smoke for himself – outside, and dumps it onto the ground, equalising its uniqueness and worth with dirt, erasing Badger's claims of the product's distinction and denying its addictive grip on himself. After failing another time, Jesse once again goes to trash the product, but is stopped by Badger. The moment restages Jesse's collapse under the weight of Skinny Pete and Combo's peer pressure described above, the moment in which he smoked himself to the point of psychosis rather than allow himself to be exposed to the loneliness of an empty house. Now, he wrestles the tray free from Badger and tosses it out the door, and their friendship breaks under the tension of addiction and its refusal – the two men fight so violently they trash the lab.

Jesse denies the meth's addictive power over him by pursuing its production not as a means to getting high, but as a way of achieving an ideal. The value of the meth no longer rests only in its physiological effect on Jesse's body, but in the extent to which its excellence can be recognised by others. Throwing out the meth represents Jesse's developing awareness of a value beyond gratification of base impulse, an elevation of his self-respect that measures Walt's influence on him as a teacher. However, Walt's response to the way Jesse valorises his skill just after their first cook together shows that his example to Jesse is not necessarily a valuable one, and that he does not prize Jesse's respect. Hearing Jesse now admire him as 'a goddamn artist', Walt sits seemingly dispirited and spent, and acknowledges Jesse's recognition of him with this ironic, deflating reply: 'Well, actually, it's just basic chemistry, but thank you, Jesse, I'm glad it's acceptable.' The spirit of these words is later reversed when Jesse proudly takes them up to display his new knowledge by presenting the lab equipment to Badger ('It's just basic chemistry, yo.'). So the patterns and variations across the first season's cooking montages show Jesse discover, in Walt's approach to chemistry, an example that can anchor and cohere his attempts at self-development, which can provide an alternative, more constructive satisfaction of desire than his drug use.

But doubts are invited about the personal qualities being developed. In comparison to his earlier decline into drug addiction, we are likely to admire the self-discipline and idealism that allows Jesse to throw his meth into the dirt. However, what this gesture also expresses is Jesse's belief, learned from Walt, that there is value worth pursuing in a more purely formed methamphetamine crystal that, on this basis, can stand out from and be recognised against the adulterated rest. This shows Jesse as susceptible to Walt's sensibility that values the coherence and unity found in scientific achievement or chemical engineering partly for its own sake, but also partly as the means to personal recognition above and beyond all others. But the distinction Walt and Jesse pursue is immorally directed, toward the 'better' production of illegal, socially destructive drugs. So the personal development the cooking montages convey, and which gives meaningful shape to their fragmented form, is of a kind that casts doubt on the value of an aesthetic unity or personal coherence that is not morally calibrated. The first season's cooking montages, then, show that at stake in the developments of character that *Breaking Bad* tracks are forms of growth and self-actualisation that realise either moral enrichment or a kind of moral desiccation. In particular, the compelling unities that the montages' rhythms of process, gesture, cutting, and time-lapse achieve suggest that moral bankruptcy might be concealed from us by aesthetically pleasing unities of form, in both the series' designs and the compelling stances and gestures of its characters.

The moral ambiguity of Walt's self-respect is further exposed in the first act of 'Gray Matter' when, attending the birthday party of former colleague Elliott Schwartz (Adam Godley), he refuses Elliott's charitable offer to pay for his treatment. Walt's refusal of Elliott's offer needs to be understood in light of the way that he experiences Elliott's lavish birthday party as a series of humiliations and embarrassments, for example his anxiety around the public unwrapping of his modest, privately sentimental birthday gift (a packet of ramen noodles). The fact that Walt's gift is received as a triumph does little to undo our sense of his brittle susceptibility to status anxiety; by comparison, Skyler expresses embarrassment only for Elliott's oblivious, juvenile display. Walt is also humiliatingly exposed in a short scene in which he must explain why his career has diverged from Elliott's. After explaining that he moved towards 'education', Walt is left painfully speechless when asked: 'Oh! Which university?' Our sense of Walt confronting a disparity between who he could have been and who he has become is strongest when he takes it upon himself to look around Elliott and Gretchen's wood-panelled library, replete with a mezzanine, and antique books on display. It is in Walt's awe at the library that Elliott and Gretchen's house is most clearly used as a space opposed to Walt's home, one that represents his unrealised potential. This is crystallised in a framed magazine cover celebrating the Schwartz's recent achievement, an echo of the nostalgic Los Alamos citation on Walt's nursery wall.

So the sequence's design is intended to present the Schwartzes, and Elliott in particular, as reminders to Walt of what he has failed to achieve with his life: socially recognisable success. This makes it possible to understand Elliott's apparently unmotivated offer of a job for Walt – with, Elliott stresses, 'the best' health insurance – as bringing home to Walt a sense of his failure, the result of which is his reliance on others, more accomplished than he, for his family's wellbeing. Walt's refusal of Elliott's offer reveals he considers the rescue line to be a humiliation so great that it must be avoided even if doing so contributes to the insecurity of his family. When Skyler confronts the hostility with which Walt tries to justify his rejection of the apparently humiliating implications of Elliott's offer, Walt starkly separates what he takes to be his own concerns from his wife's, and puts distance between himself and his renewed bond to Elliott. He turns on Skyler with a raised finger and voice: '*I* don't like the way you talk about *my* private affairs, to people who are not – even in our *lives* anymore.'

At stake in Walt's continued separation of his life from Elliott's is his opportunity to have recognised the brilliance of his individual excellence, a light that is not a reflection of other sources, but that shines only from within. Working for Elliott would require that Walt be prepared to live with the knowledge that his position at the now prospering company he earlier walked away from has been given by others, rather than earned solely by him, making his reliance on the support of friends a reminder of his failure years ago to achieve such success on his own. By refusing this, Walt pursues a solution in the harshly individualist world of the illegal drug trade, where his brilliance as a chemist can be made starkly apparent, and where his skill can be recognised and celebrated even as it is used in a way that corrodes the society that reduced him to the supposedly lesser station of high school teacher, and the familial obligations that left him with a half-decorated nursery rather than an expensive, polished library. Walt's strikingly different responses to these two spaces show him weigh the trappings of success against what is felt to be a trap of mediocre struggle, and the life of the mind over the world of everyday sociability and familial upbringing. It is in the library that Walt's eyes come alive, and he raises his gaze to the ceiling; it is also a space of aspiration that brings out his sickness, in a brace of wheezing coughs that break his reverie and send him stern-faced back out to the party.

Later in the episode, Walt wakes in bed to find Skyler absent. He looks at the books on her nightstand about fighting cancer and raising babies, and luxuriates in the scent of her moisturiser, and her pillow. The moment is akin but inverse to Jesse's ruminations upon his trunk of youth memorabilia. Walt is not confronted with the waste of his past but with what he stands to lose if he forfeits any hope for his future. In the next scene he tells Skyler he will pursue treatment. Just before the episode's end, Elliott's wife Gretchen (Jessica Hecht) calls Walt and reiterates Elliott's offer. Walt lies about having adequate insurance coverage, and, after hanging up the phone, crosses the street into Jesse's driveway. 'Wanna cook?' he asks, and the episode cuts to black. So in 'Gray Matter' Walt is given two chances to meet his material needs, two chances to escape from a future of criminality while allowing him more time to continue making a life with his wife and son. However, from his position of humiliation and resentment he rejects them both.

In an interview for the Archive of American Television, Vince Gilligan describes how the choice to have Walt reject Elliott's *'deus ex machina'* offer is the moment of which he is 'proudest', because of the way it gave he and his writers a greater sense of creative freedom:

> otherwise it would have been some Rube Goldberg 'device-of-the-week': 'I really hate bein' a meth cook, but, ah, okay, I've got ninety thousand dollars now, that's good – Oh shit! I left it by an open window and the wind blew it away!' Y'know? It would have gotten more and more mechanical, instead of driving from an innate character trait.[21]

Walt's two choices that refuse Elliott and Gretchen's charity locate his motivation to cook meth not in material necessity, but in his response to a life he experiences as humiliating. This takes the form of a stance that seeks to affirm a higher sense of his dignity by projecting his individual brilliance over and above all others, and by undermining the social bonds to a human world of marriage and family that have tied down his potential for so long.

2

Pursuing Success in Season Two

Nearing the end of its first season, *Breaking Bad* promises a future expansion of its depiction of Albuquerque's meth trade. In the penultimate episode, 'Crazy Handful of Nothin'' (1.6), Walt, undergoing what we see to be the degrading effects of chemotherapy – his nausea keeps him from work, his hair falls out in clumps – seeks to accelerate the earnings of Jesse's piecemeal, hand-to-hand meth deals. Walt decides they should get a contract with a mid-level distributor who is new on the local scene, the fearsomely psychotic Tuco (Raymond Cruz), a Mexican whose pent-up supply of manic violence is nicely captured by the sharp fit of energy with which he snorts crushed meth off the blade of his Bowie knife. After Tuco bashes and hospitalises Jesse, Walt seizes back a sense of personal control from the ravages of chemotherapy by shaving his head bald, and – now having hardened his weak and pliant appearance – confronting Tuco. When Tuco asks for a name, Walt baptises himself 'Heisenberg'. This not only evokes the difficulties of perception and knowledge posed by the uncertainty principle, but also implies that Walt is living-out a perhaps long-imagined fantasy of scientific recognition and fame, one tinged by the infamy of Heisenberg's wartime nuclear research for Nazi Germany, an association heightened by Walt's former work at Los Alamos.[1] After threatening Tuco with explosives ingeniously disguised as meth, Walt extracts a favourable business contract, and the fragile promise of a new, ongoing partnership is made.

Season one's final episode, 'A No Rough-Stuff-Type-Deal' (1.7), features two meetings in a junkyard between Walt and Jesse, and Tuco and his two henchmen. The meetings track the early working-out of this new relationship, and Walt's process of settling-in to his Heisenberg alter-ego, now replete with his props of a black pork-pie hat and black sunglasses (the hat a nod to the transformation pursued by the cancer-ridden protagonist of Kurosawa's 1952 film *Ikiru*), an identity further tied to the trademark of his esteemed product: its unique blue crystals. The second meeting is the episode's final sequence. Near its ending, Tuco viciously bashes in the face of one of his men, 'No-Doze' (Cesar Garcia), and has the limp body dragged into his car as Walt and Jesse look on in shock. Tuco promises Walt, and through him the series' writers promise the audience, more to come in regular instalments: 'Okay, Heisenberg! Next week . . .' he says. As Tuco drives away, Walt clumsily removes his sunglasses and replaces them with his prescription lenses, and the camera cranes up to show Walt and Jesse small within the expanse of the junkyard as they stagger down the path before them. The song 'Who's Gonna Save My Soul Now?' hauntingly plays out the season.

'Crazy Handful' presents Walt's initial realisation of his Heisenberg persona as his retrieval, from the indignities of chemotherapy, of a posture that expresses dignified courage, composure, strength, and vitality. The style of the ending of 'No Rough-Stuff' shifts our sense of the quality of Walt's new identity in two ways. Both Tuco's line about 'next week' and the craning camera movement are significantly joined to the fact of the season's ending and the potential of another season beyond it. This meeting between points of style and a juncture of seasonal television narrative presents Walt's deepened involvement in the meth business, and in his Heisenberg identity, not as shoring up our sense of his strength and self-possession but as opening out a wide horizon of chaotic, unpredictable violence. Tied to this is the attention to the awkwardness with which Walt replaces one set of glasses for the other, which represents Walt's attempt to shed his criminal identity as Heisenberg in favour of those props that signify his 'better' self as Walter White, as if to remove himself from involvement in this violence. This gesture figures Walt's new, apparently ruthless Heisenberg identity not as a fully self-possessed unity, but as a shaky veneer, part of a tactic of self-compartmentalisation that forms a defensive response against Tuco's bloody breaking-apart of a man's face.

So the first season ends by figuring Walt's personal fragmentation, which results from his deepened involvement in the depravities that attend assertions of status and attainments of glory in the meth world. And, because it explicitly promises more to come, it forecasts such fragmentation as a subject for the second season to further elaborate and explore. The main way that season two does this is by organising its central storylines around Walt and Jesse's expansion of their enterprise, motivated by the need for both stability and growth, insulating them-selves from risk while heightening the stakes and rewards of their business by building a franchised retail network. This can be seen as a reflection of the show's own need at this point to reinforce its identity as a series, while also building on what it has laid down in order to discover new avenues through which to continue generating compel-ling drama from its characters' lives. As O'Sullivan puts it, '[t]he second season [of a television serial] inevitably operates as a sequel, speaking in direct dialogue with the first season'.[2] For O'Sullivan, the problem confronting the creators of a television serial at this point is that of dis-covering how, or whether, what was put in place in the first season can continue to provide rich veins of story to be mined.[3]

This chapter examines how season two of *Breaking Bad* discovers and explores such veins in a range of dramatic scenarios that pivot around the depiction of Walt, Hank, and Jesse's respective forms of psycho-logical fragmentation, which emerge as the characters respond to the changed contexts in which they find themselves as the events depicted in season one ramify in a number of ways. It is important to note that although the central season two storylines examined in this chapter appear to take the series in a number of new directions – most clearly in terms of Walt and Jesse's attempt to build a retail network, and the vari-ous moves into Mexico as a new dramatic space – my account of how those storylines are handled shows that their meanings are not achieved solely 'within' season two as a fully discrete unit of storytelling. This is in the way that interpreting particular stylistic arrangements across the season often requires that we precisely 'place' them in relation to the show's internal dramatic and stylistic history stretching back to the first episode of season one. In these aspects of its design, *Breaking Bad*'s sec-ond season involves us in a process of registering echoes of the past in present moments. The recognition of these stylistic patterns being built up across the series risks being viewed as an empty 'memory game', as just a formalist puzzle of broken-up pieces waiting to be put back together over time. Yet Gilligan and his team dramatically integrate these stylistic patterns – both across the first two seasons, and within season two itself – so that they can be understood as reflecting upon the characters' own experiences of confronting their personal histories, and in doing so attempting to reconcile what has happened to them, or what they have done, with who they want to think of themselves as being (or as being capable of becoming).

The rest of the chapter explores this through three central storylines pivoting around Walt, Jesse, and Hank's changing situations within the meth world. These unfold side-by-side following Tuco's kidnapping of Walt and Jesse at the season's beginning: in episode four, 'Down' (2.4), Walt tries to restore stability to his domestic situation while in an adjacent plot Jesse's collapses; and across the remainder of the season, Hank pursues a promotion to the front lines of the Mexican drug war, while Jesse runs a crew of dealers while trying to foster a romantic relationship.

Doubts about coherence in 'Down'

'Down' marks something of a turning point for season two, at which the writers and the characters try to put to rest, and move on from, the violent disturbances that Tuco's presence brought to the series' world. Crucial to this process on the part of the characters is Walt's attempt to submerge his alter ego as Heisenberg and to inhabit, in contrast, his identity as a loving and responsible husband and father who can sustain a domestic environment of intimacy, within which the spoils of his success as a criminal can be enjoyed or acknowledged. Walt's performance before his family is compelling to us as viewers because of our awareness of it *as performance*,[4] particularly one that perilously seeks to avoid shameful discovery by making what we know to be a fractured sense of self appear as a coherent identity.

Season two's first episode, 'Seven Thirty-Seven' (2.1), ends with Tuco kidnapping Walt and Jesse as witnesses to his murder of No-Doze, and the aftermath of this event is explored across the next two episodes, 'Grilled' (2.2) and 'Bit By a Dead Bee' (2.3). Hank helps Skyler and Walt Jr search for Walt, eventually tracking down Jesse's car at Tuco's desert hideout where he waits with his mute, wheelchair bound uncle (Hector 'Tio' Salamanca, played by Mark Margolis) to take Walt to Mexico. (Tuco makes Jesse's disposability clear, and we are stirred by Walt's capacity for courage and loyalty when, as Tuco holds a gun to Jesse's head, Walt righteously admits his desire to kill Tuco, and saves Jesse's life, eventually shooting Tuco in the belly.) Walt and Jesse hide from Hank's arrival, and then witness the violent firefight in which he shoots Tuco dead. In episode three, Walt and Jesse return to Albuquerque and engineer separate alibis. Walt claims to have suffered a fugue state, which sees him endure a lengthy and expensive hospital stay, and Jesse arranges to be arrested in a local motel room with a prostitute, Wendy (Julia Minesci), who supports his story of 'partying' at the motel at the time Tuco was killed. The episode ends with Walt returned home amidst evident tensions between he and Skyler, which climaxes in her asking him if he has a second mobile phone. He denies it, but the lie doesn't convince. Walt attempts to plant a goodnight kiss on his wife's cheek, as if this gesture of intimacy could overcome the cold distance that suspicion about surface appearances has opened up between husband and wife; Skyler turns away from Walt and switches off her bedside lamp.

'Down' builds on this moment to depict similar domestic routines, of waking and having breakfast, in order to test Walt's capacity to perform a species of cook different to the type he performs in the meth world. Walt's approach to cooking meth is associated across the show with isolation and sovereignty as means to control the manufacture of a drug whose effect on users is guaranteed by chemistry and biology. This is made clear in 'Crazy Handful of Nothin'' when Walt reforms his partnership with Jesse. Standing amidst the chaos of the RV meth lab trashed by Jesse's disastrous cook with Badger, Walt says, 'This – the chemistry – is *my* realm. *I* am in charge of the cooking.' Alongside these claims Walt performs a series of hand gestures that seek to encompass the materials of the lab within his grasp, and to draw them into his very self; he punctuates his words 'my realm' by repeatedly drawing and pointing an outstretched finger into his chest. This makes the claim of Walt's domain over the laws of chemistry consonant with his domain over himself. By contrast, 'Down' shows how, in the kitchen and at the family table, successfully synthesising ingredients into a whole hinges on more human variables, notably those turning on a complex web of interpersonal connections, histories, moods, and responses. These conditions of human, domestic life are shared by serial television drama. The comparison associates *Breaking Bad*'s art form with a domestic world subject to contingency, variation, and unknowability, as opposed to the conditions of certainty, autonomy, and control Walt finds in the unbending formulae of chemistry. So structuring the episode around a series of 'cooks' in this way presents Walt's series of breakfasts as his attempts to impose on the domestic those conditions of sovereignty and mastery he enjoys through the scientific, which is presented elsewhere in the show as being opposed to the human everyday.

In the first breakfast sequence, Walt's attempt to elicit a mood of familial unity unsettles the family's normal view of him, and obstructs their usual capacity to participate in everyday routine together. This becomes a regular dynamic across the seasons, in scenes that show Walt attempting to stage an ensemble performance of normal family life that, invariably, comes to rest on his exercise of brute force. In 'Over' (2.10), Walt commandeers the Sunday barbecue celebrating his remission, imposing his will as a father by pressuring Walt Jr to drink so much tequila that he vomits into the swimming pool. Such scenes show Walt as a director unable to elicit the desired performances from his human actors, who obstinately refuse to behave as the marionettes his attempts at control wish them to be. In 'Down', despite – or because of – Walt's enthusiastic encouragement to follow him in sitting down and eating the lavish breakfast he has laid out, Walt Jr and Skyler hesitate. Walt Jr refrains from reaching for the food spread across the table, as if a guest unsure of protocol, and Skyler resists even taking her seat, her usual place within her family now alien to her. The mood of estrangement is especially highlighted by those shots that linger on Walt Jr and Skyler's mute expressions of misrecognition.

The pair is struck here by their shared sense in Walt of what James Naremore calls moments of 'expressive incoherence', in which '[t]he flicker of an eyelid, the hint of a smile, the movement of a hand – any muscular tension or fluctuation of tone' disrupts the 'emotional unity of an everyday performance'.[5] Across 'Down', Walt's expressive coherence fractures, revealing the images of marital and familial care and love he crafts are instead self-serving disguises insulating from exposure aspects of himself he is unable to bear. In these moments, trust between Walt and Skyler splinters; the wider disintegration that follows reveals their belief in each other's performances of self to be the load-bearing structure of their marriage, and of their individual frameworks of self-understanding.

After the first breakfast, perhaps sensing that his performance of normality has not found coherent grip on his wife – or maybe sensing that it *has*, and thinking that now is his time to make his real move – Walt unfolds, with emphatic casualness, an elaborate explanation about the suspected cell phone. 'What you *heard*,' Walt helpfully dictates to Skyler, 'was my cell phone *alarm*, going off.' A man telling his wife what it is that she hears and sees is an echo of George Cukor's *Gaslight* (1944). For Stanley Cavell, in Cukor's movie 'not only individual men are destroying [Paula's] mind, but the world of men, in its contradictions with itself, is destroying for her the idea and possibility of reality as such'.[6] In light of Cavell's remarks, the relation with *Gaslight* suggests that at stake in Skyler's response to Walt's lie is at least partly her capacity to be in coherent relation to herself. As Harry Frankfurt writes, discovering that we have been convincingly lied to by a friend or intimate 'exposes something about ourselves more disturbing than that we have merely miscalculated or made an error of judgment. It reveals that *our own* nature (i.e., our second nature) is unreliable, leading us to count on people who cannot be trusted.' This means not only that the liar is morally defective – 'it also shows that the victim is defective too. The liar betrays him, but he is betrayed by his own feelings as well'.[7] So part of Skyler's injury upon discovering she has been so lied to is the revelation of her deep indignity in allowing another, trusted person to command the relationship between her self and the world. So it is with this condition at stake that, for the remainder of 'Down', Skyler refuses to let Walt see or talk to her, taking possession of her interiority and expressiveness through a mask of blankness that refuses to respond in any readable way to her husband's words and gestures.

In the silences and hesitations between Walt and Skyler an awful mood of oppressiveness and hostile estrangement befalls the home throughout 'Down'. In the episode's final act we are given a glimmer of hope that there might be a reprieve. Skyler wakes (Walt's side of the bed is fully made, not slept in) to find the kitchen stove cold, the benches spotless. Walt has been sleeping on the couch, and he sits slouched there still. The repetitive domestic performances seem halted, and so we think that perhaps he is prepared at last, in his pose of surrender and despair, to shed his act that shields him from the shame of acknowledging how he has failed his wife. Skyler hesitantly sits in the opposite corner of the couch, her hands warily folded across her pregnant belly. Their respective stances express the state of their marriage: resigned exhaustion in the face of suspicion and uncertainty. Walt's speech extends an apology that strives to give voice to wrongdoing and failure ('I haven't been a good partner to you, and for that, I'm *very* sorry'), and which, to our relief, appears to restore his wished-for 'contact' with Skyler when she reaches out and takes his hand. But the bitter argument that follows Skyler's continued demands for a full acknowledgement – not of how Walt feels but what, exactly, he has done and how he will bear its consequences – results in a screamed ultimatum: 'No more excuses. No more apologies. No more of these, these *obvious, desperate* breakfasts. You don't want to lose contact with me, Walt? Good. Then tell me. *Now.*'

Walt responds by unveiling – in this domestic space – a facial expression crucial to his transformations of identity and achievements of success in the ruthless, violent meth world. This aspect of Cranston's performance is one of *Breaking Bad*'s most striking and significant visual signatures, which I describe at the beginning of Chapter 1: those spectacular moments in which the actor makes an interior hardness overtake Walt's face to rescue him from the psychological pain or discomfort of his frequent moments of vulnerability. Prior to 'Down', this expression features in key moments of Walt's development towards his alter ego in the meth world: his retrieval of dignified self-mastery from helplessness in the pilot's opening sequence ('Breaking Bad', 1.1), and his first transformative declaration as Heisenberg in 'Crazy Handful of Nothin''. After Skyler makes her demand that Walt drop his pretences, a close-up of his face lets us see him slip behind this mask. Although Walt's eyes are irritated by tears testifying to his distress only moments ago, his face is unmoved, his eyelids sitting heavy. He is a chess player calculating his response to a particularly unsettling move. He silently cocks his head back and away from Skyler, as if testing in his mind another of her angles, and then delivers a line of cruel detachment: 'Tell you what?' On paper this is a question but Cranston coldly delivers it as a statement, of Walt's refusal to invite or entertain further conversation and inquiry. His voice expresses a deliberate and measured gesture of withdrawal, its intonation matching the granite surface of Cranston's deadened green eyes. Skyler staggers away in shock as if confronted by the revelation of an intruder, and leaves.

The expression is disturbingly repeated in a similar confrontation in episode five, 'Breakage' (2.5), but not by Walt. At the end of 'Down', Skyler escapes from the constriction of her collapsing marriage to Walt by smoking a cigarette in the parking lot of a petrol station. Skyler's act in defiance of the baby she carries relates her to Kay Corleone (Diane Keaton), wife of the criminal patriarch Michael (Al Pacino) in *The Godfather* movies, who in the second part of that film series acknowledges her husband's evil by aborting their son, what is for him an unforgivable betrayal for which he grants a divorce. Through this parallel I see Skyler's choice to smoke while pregnant as enacting a secret wish to divorce herself from even this relation to the husband she is no longer able to recognise and know. However, in 'Breakage', a moment of performance sees Skyler move closer to, rather than further away from, Walt's way of being in the world, as if it provides a more ready and potent mode of self-protection. Walt discovers Skyler's cigarettes in their clogged toilet, and later, frustrated by his impotent response to the robbery of one of Jesse's dealers, he produces the sodden pack for Skyler as she sits on the living room floor and eats lunch at the coffee table. '*Perhaps* you might know something, about *this*,' he pronounces, triumphantly plonking down his trump card. This plumbs Walt's capacity to avoid the more widely corrosive effects of his expanding meth enterprise by degrading the people closest to him as a means to protect his self-righteous sense of superiority. Skyler at first looks down to her pregnant belly, her face creased by shame at denying her relation to the baby. 'Perhaps,' she whispers. But when she looks back up to Walt, this expression of shame melts away to defiant blankness. 'But then again,' she says, 'perhaps I don't, Walt. Perhaps I smoked them in a "fugue state".' Skyler mirrors Walt's projections of hardness that guard against the indignity of shame or humiliation by refusing her exposure to another (Figure 2.1). The scene's end nicely captures the effects of such refusal. When Walt extends his hand to assist Skyler to her feet, a symbolic offer of care, Skyler violently bats away his arm, no longer able to even bear his touch.

It is worth noting that Walt and Skyler's marriage collapses into silence and distance not as a result of entirely ordinary betrayals, but within the context of Walt's involvement in a violent, moneymaking criminal enterprise. So Walt's resulting alienation from Skyler can be read in relation to the preoccupation of American cinema, and culture more generally, with, in Gallafent's words, 'the way in which an idea of "success", presented through the image of the American dream of becoming rich, is to be understood in the context of a world in which nothing suggests how these riches might be realised or enjoyed'.[8] For Walt, it seems family does not provide a space in which the profits of his drug enterprise can be put to use and their value realised. He instead can only turn the domestic into something like a (tragic) theatre in which the ordinary acts of care his drug money is supposed to support are perverted and undermined as a self-serving disguise.

From season three, this will come to form something of a contrast with the characters of Gus Fring (Giancarlo Esposito) and his chemist

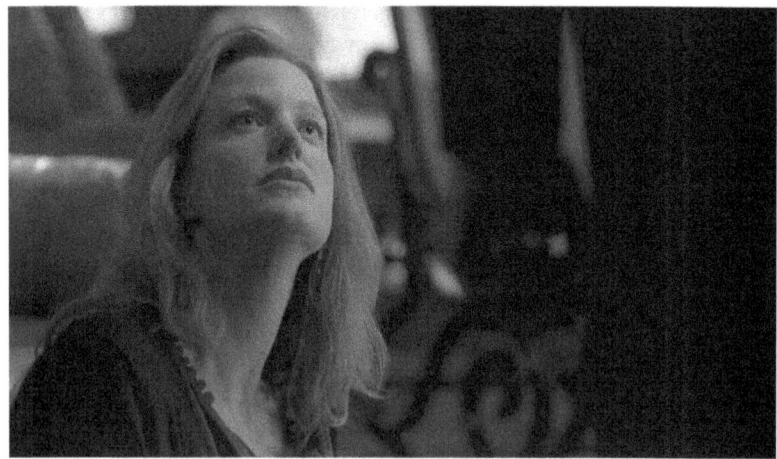

Figure 2.1   'Breakage': Skyler mirrors Walt's projections of hardness

Gale Boetticher (David Costabile), neither of whom is shown as needing to utilise a similarly doubled mode of theatrical performance in order to maintain stable and apparently pleasant domestic lives. Hank will track Gus's movements in episode nine of season four ('Bug', 4.9), and find they are an entirely habitual repetition of drives to and from his home and his legitimate places of work. So in Gus's case, it seems as though he is so entirely subsumed into his role as a respected local business figure leading a life of modest routine that there is no sense of a gap between his exterior and interior that might attract attention or suspicion from almost anyone else, presumably including his wife and children, who we never see. (The only signs of his children's existence are the toys on the floor of his house.)

We first see the interior of Gale's apartment when Gus visits him in the final episode of season three, 'Full Measure' (3.13). It is presented as a space entirely given over to the free expression of the self through the display of purposefully placed objects that evoke a desire to capture aspects of the world and their meanings. We see vintage photography equipment, books of political and economic theory, Aztec rugs, a collection of things with which the room seems to be at once chaotically overflowing and artfully arranged. The desire for publicity implied by artful display is tempered by the inherent privacy of Gale's domestic arrangement when Gus's visit is handled as an intrusion. When Gus takes a seat on the couch, Gale is left without a place to sit, and must quickly remove a pile of books from his computer chair. This is not a space intended to accommodate anyone but the individual who owns and has crafted it, and appreciates its qualities in private. That Gale is content in his own company is made apparent in the way that, prior to Gus's arrival, he is shown singing, with the perfect polish of frequent practice, both parts of a swing duet.[9] That the song is in Italian, and so is perhaps incomprehensible to Gale, strengthens the idea that he is able to appreciate not only the meaning of interpersonal communication (such as that conveyed through books, or his conversations with Walt), but also the different pleasure of *private* aesthetic experience, felt by and for him alone.

Neither the reassuring pleasures of Gus's obsessive routine, nor the hermitage of Gale's purely private pleasure in the self, strike me as desirable models of life. (This is despite the seductive mastery with which Esposito imbues Gus's rigour, and the endearingly childlike innocence with which Costabile conveys the joy Gale takes in the privately significant artefacts that constitute his life.) Gus's routine is shown as having calcified into empty habit, and Gale's privacy becomes emblematic of a morally bereft rejection of being in community with others. This is crystallised in the moral relativism and radical libertarianism by which, in episode six of season three ('Sunset', 6.3), Gale justifies his work in the socially corrosive meth trade. 'There's crime,' he says, 'and then there's *crime* . . . Consenting adults want what they want.' It is an isolation of the self from others that will leave Gale fatally vulnerable. But each aspect of the two characters points, in their own ways, to the quality that in 'Down' Walt is shown to lack: the capacity to be unembarrassed by one's life. Walt tries to compensate for this lack through his forceful attempts to direct his family life as a theatrical undertaking, betraying him as consumed with an idea of life as something like a melodrama of the self, through which his value as a man needs to be made manifest within a performative orchestration (or utilisation) of the people around him. The desire for the recognition of status and accomplishment on a public stage also animates Hank's season two storyline. We will see, however, that Hank provides an alternative view of how the melodramatic performance of the self may be modulated in relation to the shifting, provisional, ongoing nature of self-understanding.

Modulating performance on a bigger stage

I described in Chapter 1 how we are introduced to Hank during the sequence of Walt's birthday party in the pilot episode. That description showed how our earliest sense of Hank's character hinged on his confident command of personal performance in public space. Indeed, I noted how Hank's social gravity was so strong that he seemed to transform Walt's living room from a relatively private, intimate space into a theatre for the grand staging of his secure self-possession, invulnerable to the slights of others, such as when his partner Gomez mocks his skill with a weapon, or when both Gomez and Marie insult his weight. This sense of Hank's character is reaffirmed across the first season as we watch him confidently pursue a slowly developing case around the emergence of a new meth kingpin, who goes by the name 'Heisenberg'. Alongside this storyline, our view of Hank as a man of more or less harmless clumsiness in all affairs is reinforced by the ineptitude of his response to moments of challenging social intimacy. For example, Martin describes a moment from 'Breakage' in which Hank attempts to console Skyler's distress at Walt's disappearance: 'Hank is so ill at ease with displays of strong emotion from others (even his immediate family members) that he will do anything, or rather do something quite specific, to avoid contact with this emotion', in this case giving a brief, mechanical pat on the shoulder 'reluctantly, awkwardly, badly'.[10] Dean Norris's performance across these great many episodes builds up such a strong sense of unthinkingly secure self-assurance that we have no inclination to suspect anything of his character other than what we see on his big, brash surface.

Across the second season, however, a different, more interior dimension of Hank's character is revealed and gradually developed as he becomes more deeply involved in the meth world, as both a place of unpredictable violence and a stage for the assertion of identity and prestige.[11] Impressed by Hank's initiative, tenacity, and martial skill in tracking down and killing Tuco, in episode five ('Breakage') Hank's supervisor offers him a promotion to the El Paso office, across the border from the violence-ridden cartel stronghold of Juárez. Our view and sense of Hank's character develops as he responds to these changes to the context of his place in the meth world. This is tracked across multiple episodes through varied repetitions of his movements to and from public places – his supervisor's office, an open-plan workspace – and more private ones: empty corridors, elevators. Deborah Thomas's distinction between public and private spaces in Hollywood movies in terms of characters being either 'onstage' or 'offstage' shows how such spaces can be used to dramatise the fragmentation, or compartmentalisation, of a character's personality. Thomas's terms metaphorically refer 'to whether [the characters] are putting on a face and taking on a role for the benefit of others, or are revealing something like an "authentic" self that lies beneath the surface presentation'.[12]

We see the first fracture in our established view of Hank's character in episode five ('Breakage'), when, on his way to celebrate his promotion to El Paso, he finds himself in a rare moment of privacy after receiving the news of his promotion. Important context for this is given in the few scenes prior, in which Hank moves through a series of increasingly pressurised public places: Hank's supervisor puts Hank's identity at stake in the promotion, not only calling him a shark, but indeed a 'Great White'; Hank's own office becomes a hemmed-in space as his colleagues congregate to congratulate him, and as they leave he must wait behind in order to take more praise over the phone; the corridor then provides no respite, as passing officers stop to slap Hank on the back, forcing him to hold in place his face of good-willed cheer. The news of Hank's promotion has spread fast, and with it has widened the audience and the stage for the performance of excellence it demands. Hank's storyline is emerging at this point as one that expands the series' world; the phone call and the backslapping convey how such an expansion might be experienced as a pressure that closes in. The effect of such pressure on Hank is shown during his walk to the elevator on his way down to meet Gomez for lunch. Dean Norris allows a cluster of nervous tics to emerge from beneath the surface of Hank's normally unruffled manner. He has Hank anxiously swing his arms and slap his balled fist into his tensed palm, while letting out a series of sighs that try to give intentional direction to what seems to be a small spike of quickened breathing. Forced to wait for the lift, Hank jabs the elevator button, keen to get things moving again, as if a shark afraid of drowning. Inside the elevator these signs of latent nervousness, which cannot be concealed by gestures of absent-minded purpose, crest and break into a panic attack, a wave of breathless anxiety that obliterates Hank's self-composure. As Hank's loss of control peaks, the image cuts to an even, centred shot of the elevator doors opening to reveal Hank recovered; slight puzzlement and a couple of deep breaths are the only hints of his trauma. Any remaining vulnerability is hidden by the choice to have the camera watch from a distance as Hank joins his waiting colleagues, the three men silhouetted by sunlight coming through the glass doors of the lobby. From here, Hank forms a strong but featureless outline as he firmly clasps an arm around each man's shoulders. Lighting and staging express fragility solidly shrugged-off for a pose that strikes a picture of unity.

One way in which the scene comes to be important to *Breaking Bad*, and to my wider argument about the show's serial patterning of performances in space in relation to themes around personal cohesion or discomposure, is that it introduces the elevator in the DEA offices as a versatile dramatic space that can be used to repeatedly present different views of Hank's public and private modes of self-presentation. More immediately, the scene's function within the show's drama is to arrest the audience by sharply disrupting their likely settled view of Hank that has been affirmed by his largely unchanging characterisation across season one, and the first four episodes of season two. Part of the reason for this is of course to tap another vein of character potential that the series can mine.[13] One benefit of this would be to intensify the interest of viewers in Hank as a character of newly compelling and emerging depth, whose role is more than just that of a comically buffoonish bloodhound, entertainingly sniffing after Walt's/Heisenberg's trail.

Indeed, the compelling dismantling of Hank's established character becomes the focus of his storyline over episodes eight and nine, which follows his experiences working on a DEA operation to enlist the cartel turncoat 'Tortuga' (Danny Trejo) as an informant. Key to this are two scenes in which Hank faces the threat that he might be humiliatingly exposed as inadequate or weak. In each, he responds with an emphatic attempt to re-assert his usual control and authority.

In episode eight ('Negro y Azul', 2.8), on operation in Mexico, the limits of Hank's skill as a DEA agent – his ignorance of the political compromises of international work, his refusal to learn Spanish – are repeatedly exposed. These humiliating exposures peak when brokering a deal with Tortuga in a motel bedroom, in which Hank's masculine posturing is completely out of step with the domesticated nature of the negotiations: Tortuga in a dressing gown and slippers on the bed, bartering his allegiance for items in a homeware catalogue, the DEA agents each perched delicately around the room's edges. Mocked by Tortuga, Hank tries to assert himself through a hackneyed performance of 'bad cop': 'Hey! How about you stop jerkin' us off here! Where's the meet, and when's it goin' down?' The weakness of Hank's desperate aggression is plain in its failure to take hold against the room's mood of give-and-take between pragmatic, clear-eyed adversaries with no stock in role-play. Later in the same episode, Hank's professional standing is further diminished when he is confronted by the sight of Tortuga's disembodied head atop a crawling tortoise. The other agents riotously mock Hank's anxious queasiness, which he attempts to cover by grabbing an evidence bag from a truck. This saves Hank when a bomb concealed in Tortuga's head explodes, killing and horrifically maiming the other agents.

The consequence of this event is Hank's almost total surrender of his typically bombastic personality. In episode nine ('Better Call Saul', 2.9), following the bomb attack, Hank is shown lying in his bedroom with his eyes squeezed shut against the world. When Walt unexpectedly arrives, Hank tries to greet Walt with his customary energy, but anxiety and disbelief suffocate his vocal self-presentation. 'Hey buddy,' he breathlessly wheezes, and stutters through his usually boisterous 'What's up?', before losing faith in his performance and resuming an untypical silence, unable to convincingly re-assemble the dismantled parts of his persona.

Hank's move to El Paso and his involvement in the cross-border drug war provides a welcome expansion of *Breaking Bad*'s world, one that facilitates season two's wider project of exploring the broader context of the drug trade in which Walt and Jesse seek to increasingly establish themselves. There is no reason we couldn't have had an interesting development of Hank's character through his *successful* work in Mexico, seeing him develop his skills as a law enforcement officer, serving also as a conduit for a look into the workings of the transnational drug trade and war outside Albuquerque. But Gilligan and his writers choose to develop the character by staging a scenario in which Hank's grasp for higher success and glory leads him to confront a previously concealed or unknown aspect of himself, the exposure of which now threatens to unravel his identity, which has been built-up through his professional persona and accomplishments. So this puts at stake in the future development of his character whether or not he can retrieve from his humiliation what, in comparison, can be seen as a more dignified way of living in the world. How does it serve *Breaking Bad* for the makers of the show to deepen our involvement with Hank this way?

The reason is related to how the establishment of Hank across season one draws fairly stark, static lines of opposition between he and Walt. This is clearly illustrated in their respective ways of inhabiting social space during Walt's birthday party, described in Chapter 1. The way Hank's character is then revised across season two in the manner outlined above seems intended to complicate and blur that stark line of comparison, by developing both characters through their responses to humiliating exposures of inadequacy. The relationship becomes more like a fluctuating *interweaving* of the two characters' qualities, so that rather than merely being staged in direct opposition, aspects of one character can gradually be seen to in some ways intersect, overlap, or resonate with the other's. Toles's commentary on character doubles in Hitchcock's *Strangers on a Train* (1951) is useful here:

> For Bruno to function meaningfully as Guy's double, there must be core affinities between their characters. They need to be bound together inwardly to an even greater extent than they are bound by the machinations of the external plot. The double-spawning protagonist, whether in the spectral tales of German Romanticism, or the amnesia-saturated world of film noir, is not required to acknowledge, comprehend, or actively embrace the affinities he encounters in his secret sharer. But as the double's story proceeds, the topography on which his split figure moves acquires a volatile, dreamlike shiftiness. The man-with-a-double's capacity to hold fast to personal boundaries and oases of clear intention is treacherously impaired. What once seemed safely sequestered in a knowable and private inner life has somehow leaked outside, where it confronts us in the guise of an alien personage – formidable, slippery, menacing, opaque, yet peculiarly intimate as well.[14]

In a similar way, Hank and Walt can be seen to have 'spawned' each other – each man has helped bring out of the other some aspect of personality or character he didn't know he possessed. In both cases, in another parallel of Hitchcock's film, this occurs through a series of mere accidents by which Walt and Hank are, in turn, dragged from their settled, familiar worlds into contact with new, more extreme realms that reshape what there is for them to know about themselves. Walt's criminal adventure is only set in train because of Hank's offer of the ride-along on the meth lab raid, and it is only through his proximity to Walt's spiralling criminal vortex that Hank happens upon the confrontation with Tuco through which he earns his passport to the frontlines of Juárez. Yet at the same time these 'accidents' take place in ways that are in some sense 'wished for' or 'meant' by both men. In a way that seems largely unknown to Hank, they share a secret inner affinity, hence the capacity for their mutual (if unwitting) invitations and flirtations with one another to be so fully taken up to the point that each man's actions and pursuits warp the other.

It is such an affinity that Walt gestures towards when Hank rejects Walt's offer to be a confidant with whom Hank could share and examine his trauma. 'You and me,' Hank says, 'we don't have much of what you might call an "experiential overlap".' Walt differs – 'What if I told you that we do?' – and outlines to Hank how his cancer diagnosis relieved him of his pervasive fear of the world, and implores Hank to rediscover vitality through a generalised attitude of resentful aggression: 'Get up. Get out in the real world. And you *kick* that bastard as hard as you can right in the teeth.' That the two men are in some way psychologically connected or attuned is seen in the way that Walt's 'strength-through-violence' attitude to self-possession is enough to stir Hank to a more upright posture. This idea of their having in common an 'experiential overlap' is further figured, but also complicated, by the visual style of the scene. Alternating two-shots place the men in profile, facing the same direction while making it difficult to look at one another, a composition that highlights the physical similarity of Cranston and Norris, most prominent in their shaved scalps and the shared shape of their noses. The way the men are layered in the depth of the shot highlights this similarity. It is as if they are separate pieces, while unified because cut from the same shape. Yet the shallow focus separates them, marking some point of difference, while being unable to define its nature.

The significance of that difference emerges from the way we are shown Hank return to work at the DEA offices in Albuquerque. The sequence of Hank's return echoes his elevator-bound panic attack after being promoted in 'Breakage', and its designs are eloquent about the effort it takes Hank to try and return to his prior state of being. We once again see Hank bent over in the elevator, with his head against the wall, struggling to control his breathing. Ghostly yelping in the sound mix echoes the sonic expression of Hank's shell-shocked panic in the immediate wake of the bomb's explosion in Mexico. Hank composes a stoic face and then cautiously steps out from the elevator's protective enclosure into the open corridor. As he walks the hall, Hank takes determined possession of his posture; his gait is a taut concentration on and of himself. The sound of his boots' heavy fall on the floor gives a sense of trying to get a solid grip on things. Hank's inner energy is tied up, keeping from view his vulnerability to panic within. This image of Hank readying himself for the scrutiny of others is then juxtaposed with an exuberant public display when the next scene's soundtrack overlaps the image of this one. Hank's boisterous declaration of patriarchal presence bursts across the quiet intensity of his self-composure in the hallway: '*Honey*, I'm ho-*ome!*' Cut to Hank triumphantly making his way through the open-plan office, handing out high-fives as his workmates crowd around in an informal improvisation of celebratory welcome. The cut clashes private containments of anxious energy with a public release of confident projections. Where he tightly held on to himself in the private constraint of the corridor, in this more expansive public space he finds himself again able to exuberantly unfurl his usual banner of personality, and to welcome those around him into its fold. So the moment points up an aspect of inner personal fracture, yet we see how in Hank it allows separateness at a social level to be overcome. Hank breaks himself in two so as to keep his bent towards friendliness from falling apart.

After greeting the colleagues crowding around his boisterous return, Hank moves to wrap things up as the image cuts to a close-up. He starts to speak, saying 'Alright –', but the word snags in his throat; the closer view lets us see that his breath catches, a momentary paralysis that cuts off his self-projection. He just manages to squeeze out 'let's get back to work, for Christ's sake!' but reaches for a sharp emphasis on '*work*' to disguise his anxious pause that subtly disrupts the fluid ease of his otherwise self-possessed professional posture. Here, gestures we were previously likely to read as representing Hank's boorishly dominant self-confidence are transformed by their patterning across season two into acts of dignified self-composure, which represent Hank's successful struggle to overcome the crippling self-doubt and incoherence that obstructed him from inhabiting his public, social role as an officer of the law. Unlike the viciously individualist postures of self-mastery struck by Walt, Hank's recovery of a more dignified pose is presented as enabling him to again take genial command of his charisma in a way that gathers people around him, and corrals their collective energies *against* the likes of Walt. This points to *Breaking Bad* as a television fiction that, by its second season, starts to expand its depiction of the existential and moral malleability of its characters. It designs their pursuits of heightened success to catalyse a *range* of movements between states of indignity and dignity, a range that challenges us to measure their respective capacities to cohere or fragment the bonds between individuals and the world of interpersonal sociability. Another important dimension of this is the way that season two measures Jesse's involvement in the meth business alongside his attempts to foster romantic commitment.

Sustaining romantic commitment

Tuco's kidnapping of Walt and Jesse provided the catalyst for Hank's season two storyline, and also sets in motion Jesse's storyline over approximately the same episodes. But where it provided an opportunity for Hank to elevate his status (despite his traumas he is able to return a hero), it leads to a spiralling decline in Jesse's fortunes. After Walt and Jesse return to Albuquerque in episode three ('Bit by a Dead Bee'), the DEA seize Jesse's cash, and then in episode four ('Down') – alongside the disintegration of Walt's marriage described above – Jesse's parents evict him, leaving him without a place or resources of his own. Jesse's situation here is an echo of the pivotal moment of his development in episode four of season one ('Cancer Man'), when, suffering drug-induced psychosis, he fled his house corroded by the murder of Emilio and tried to return to his family home, which was itself found to be haunted by the history of mistrust and failure between Jesse and his parents.[15]

This echo allows us to read episode five of season two, 'Breakage', as representing a second chance for Jesse to build an untainted, uncorrupted home in which he can live, one that is his own and that allows an opportunity to surmount the humiliating and shameful failures of his past. Having borrowed some cash from Walt, he pays for the RV to be stored securely at the junkyard, and, under the naively assumed name 'Jesse Jackson', pays cash to rent one side of a duplex from Jane Margolis (Krysten Ritter), who manages the complex on behalf of her father. Krysten Ritter is a beautiful young woman, and she is presented here in a way that is likely to remind us of Mia Wallace, Uma Thurman's character in Quentin Tarantino's *Pulp Fiction* (1994), who is the wife of the central mobster and who accidentally overdoses on heroin at the end of a whirlwind night of hesitant romance with Vincent Vega (John Travolta), a hard drug-using but charismatic hitman. Like Mia,

Jane's jet-black hair is cut in 1950s pageboy style, and her red lipstick burns against pale skin and generally black costumes. The costuming and makeup of course also bring to mind the figure of the *femme fatale*, coding Jane as having a latent interest in outlaw behaviour. We see that criminality is a source of fascination rather than repulsion for Jane when, having refused Jesse's suspicious offer of cash ('My dad's not really a "make exceptions" kind of guy, trust me'), she relents and allows him to rent the property with his clearly suspect means. The gesture also hints that the characters have personal history in common, because Jane's choice seems moved by Jesse's self-pitying story about being estranged from his family. So these details introduce Jane as a possible partner for Jesse, marking her as having the potential to be a criminal's wife, and also as a young person, like him, looking to make-up for some past failure of the bond between parent and child. As well, for some viewers the resonance between Jane and Mia Wallace may raise a dark spectre in the possibility that Jane might well descend into the more degraded aspects of Jesse's world.

With Jesse's domestic situation re-established, the rest of his storyline in the episode is about work. Having stabilised the fallout from the kidnapping by Tuco, Walt is keen to get cooking again, to pay for what he calls 'the world's most expensive alibi'. Jesse needs to get business moving as well: 'I got bills, man,' he tells Walt. 'Rent, yo – *responsibilities!*' Jesse refuses to start dealing, though, because of his DEA profile. He proposes instead that he and Walt re-style their operation: '*We* got to be Tuco.' The plan is for Walt to cook, and for Jesse to oversee a team of independent dealers, expanding the territory of their small-time enterprise, and its volume of sales and profit. Walt and Jesse's new business model is floated in the same episode in which Hank is promoted to El Paso. Contriving this coincidence, Gilligan and his writers invite us to read the promise of Jesse's romantic involvement with Jane and the expansion of his business with Walt alongside the disintegration of Hank's sense of self over the same span of episodes.

'Breakage' shows Jesse's business and his status grow through its dealing montage, which is significantly varied from the one in 'Crazy Handful of Nothin'', an episode that was also about Walt and Jesse's attempts to move their business model away from direct retail. The earlier sequence shows an increasingly exhausted Jesse walking around various nightspots on his own, handing over tiny packets of meth in exchange for a few folded notes. The later montage shows Jesse over a longer period of nights and days, removed from the risk of hand-to-hand dealing, orchestrating by day over the phone the dealing and dynamism that drives the business's growth by night. In ramped-up shots, Jesse drives on freeways, talks on his mobile, drops hefty bundles of meth around the city and collects thick stacks of cash. Instead of deepening isolation and exhaustion, this later montage expresses surging energy and interconnection: Jesse's new capacity to tap into and organise quick, broad flows of resources (both products and people), and to accumulate growing piles of money.

The following episodes explore how expanding the business leads to cracks in its structure. In episode six ('Peekaboo', 2.6), Jesse retaliates against a gruesome couple of meth addicts, a man and a woman of scabby faces and hellish cackles, who in the previous episode stole money and drugs from Skinny Pete at knifepoint. After taking a hit of meth to muster the required performance of aggression, Jesse goes to confront the couple in their house. Its dilapidated outside conceals a nightmare of complete domestic disintegration within, at the heart of which is a mute, apparently malnourished little boy left alone to explore the piles of trash and filth accumulated by his addict parents. While waiting for them to turn up, Jesse feeds the boy and plays 'peekaboo' with him, and attempts throughout the episode to shield him from the violence and depravity of events, which climax in the boy's mother crushing his father's head with a stolen ATM. The house and its sad inhabitants represent the ruinous effect of Jesse's business upon the world of family and the promise of its healthy continuity, the child's muteness eloquent about meth's corrosion of human expression and interpersonal communication, which Jesse's peekaboo game seeks to rekindle. Yet it is the excessively destructive violence that is unleashed in the house that becomes key to the acceleration of Jesse's commercial success when, in episode seven ('Negro y Azul'), Walt encourages a rumour to spread that Jesse defends their business with baroque, murderous violence, and pins on this reputation the growth of their operation into new territories. So the development of Jesse's business is shown to pivot in part on a fragmentation between his more domesticated and peaceful private self, and the ruthless violence of his concocted, aggrandised public persona.

These sharply divided sides of Jesse rub up against each other in 'Negro y Azul' during an important meeting between Jesse and Jane on the steps of their duplex, when their mutual interest in drawing introduces the possibility that Jane could reconnect Jesse with his childhood artistic potential. Jane is sketching a design for a tattoo, and explains that she works part-time at a local parlour. Jesse offers that he 'used to be a draw-er' as well, but when Jane asks why he stopped doing so he has no answer. He instead asks why a tattoo artist doesn't have any tattoos herself. 'That's way too big of a commitment,' Jane replies. One function of the choice to give the characters a shared interest in different forms of pop culture drawing is to strengthen the ambient sense of their romantic potential. More pointedly, though, the way the characters each articulate this interest raises a tension between their latent desires to create or experience aesthetic unity, and their sense of being personally in flux, disconnected from or afraid of absolutely committing to parts of themselves ('used to be', 'that's way too big of a commitment'). The scene's ending attaches this problem or tension to the threat that Jesse's criminal commercial success poses to the duo's potential as a romantic couple. A man on a chopper-style motorbike rides past the duplex. He sees Jesse 'Jackson' and calls out, 'Hey man! You're Pinkman! You're the man. Everyone's been talkin' about you!' The moment drives a split between Jesse's private and public identities, his role as an up-and-coming drug dealer putting pressure on his attempts to cohere and commit to a romantic world two people can fully inhabit.

Key to the series' treatment of such intrusion is its use of Jesse's townhouse as a space able to track side-by-side over time the development of both Jesse's business and his romance. Crucial to this is the way that the changing décor of the space measures material success alongside romantic commitment, and how a motif of lighting and time of day unfolds around Jesse and Jane's capacity to join the world outside, together, in defiance of the intrusions of Jesse's work as a drug dealer. Adrian Martin points to the cinematic expressive potential of homes on film in his account of *How Green Was My Valley* (John Ford, 1941):

> A home-space defined not just by its drawable architecture or floor plan [. . .] but by the repeated vantage points, vistas, and configurations that Ford bestows upon it, shot by shot. Vantage points, vistas, and configurations that soak up emotion, repetition, ritual, become saturated with these things and then, in turn, imprint them upon living, evolving bodies – which fold in or strike out against this framing as the vicissitudes of history, story, and psychology enter the picture.[16]

The handling of Jesse's townhouse across the second half of season two exemplifies how serial television drama is able to extend such expressive opportunities of domestic spaces in film. It is worth revisiting a pertinent Jacobs and Peacock passage quoted in the introduction, which captures this quality of extension or expansion:

> the television "houses" we get to return to again and again want us as long-term tenants, as we become in the offices of Sterling, Cooper, Draper, Pryce. We live into their familiarity and notice the adjustments in décor, light, the way a house absorbs, reflects and shapes the lives of its inhabitants. Only television does this so regularly, with such insistent promotion of familiar spaces, people, and objects.[17]

Preparing the ground for such accretion, when Jesse shows his prospective drug dealing crew his home prior to outlining his business model in episode five ('Breakage'), its empty interior is a blank canvas on which to paint his life anew. Jesse's 'virtual tour' envisions the empty space's potential: a plasma TV on the wall, plush armchairs, and a candle-lit water feature as a romantic touch. Jesse's first piece of furniture is the TV, and at the end of episode seven ('Negro y Azul') it is a point around which Jesse and Jane come together. An earlier sequence showed Hank witness bodies blown apart by the drug war in Mexico; in Albuquerque, the drug economy's material spoils allow Jesse and Jane to form an intimate bond through each other's joined fingertips as they sit on folding chairs and wait for the TV's signal to connect. Jesse and Jane consummate their growing sexual interest in-between 'Negro y Azul' and the following 'Better Call Saul', which after its title sequence shows the couple in post-coital embrace on Jesse's bedroom floor. Jesse draws attention to the relationship as a motor to mature and solidify his life, and to his townhouse as a space in which to realise these changes: 'I really need to get some furniture,' he admits. Moments later, Jesse suggests they smoke pot and get high. The room's Venetian blinds cast strips of shadow, and of brown, dusk light, expressing private intimacy shuttering the outside. However, Jesse's offer of drugs promises a darker veil against contact with the world. Jane finds the resources to say no, confiding her history of addiction, and gently leaves without pushing away Jesse himself.

This marks the beginning of a motif in which light is related to staying in or leaving the house, the development of which dovetails with Jesse's ascendency in the meth world. Over the next few episodes, Walt and Jesse reach towards new heights of success. In episode nine ('4 Days Out', 4.9), Walt and Jesse embark on their four-day cooking marathon, producing enough meth to net $672,000 each. At the episode's end, Walt discovers he is in remission, and in the following episode ('Over', 2.10), having cooked enough to support his family, claims that once he and Jesse sell their supply he will retire from the business. In episode eleven ('Mandala', 2.11), Walt is set up with – but does not meet – a mysterious, large-scale supplier, with the ability to finance a massive deal. Over these episodes, changes to Jesse's furniture show how his romance develops alongside this growth in the business. At the end of 'Better Call Saul', Jesse's new bed arrives, and is hastily thrown onto the living room floor for spontaneous sex. In '4 Days Out', it has been moved to the bedroom and covered with yellow sheets, milk crate nightstands on both sides. In that episode, bright morning light illuminates and expands the space of the bedroom when Jane proposes they drive to Santa Fe to see the Georgia O'Keeffe museum. The clarity of the new day's light harmonises with the possibility of Jane showing Jesse bits of the world he didn't know existed. This goes unrealised when Walt calls and insists that he and Jesse embark on their marathon four-day cook in the desert. The division this business drives between Jesse and Jane is figured by the way the call interrupts the couple's breakfast together, with Jesse taking the phone from the kitchen into the bedroom, which now becomes a space of privacy and seclusion. In 'Over', the couple enjoy a more adult, cooked breakfast (in contrast to the children's cereal Jane eats in '4 Days Out'); here, warm, mid-morning sunlight is again associated with the promise of a day together free of Jesse's obligations to his business. In the same episode, the bedside milk crates are replaced with more purposeful and permanent wooden tables, and the room's uses expanded with a computer and drum kit in the corners; in place of the living room's folding seats are sturdier leather armchairs. The ostentatious expenditure of easy drug money becomes a deeper investment testifying to and supporting domestic commitment. Despite Jesse's attempts to fracture his identity and action along public and private lines, the development of his apartment's décor shows them intertwine around the increasing intimacy and solidity of his life with Jane.

The lighting of the scene in which Jesse offers Jane pot after they have sex casts their room as a shuttered place alternating between shadow and dying light. The lighting captures what their respective abilities to resist or surrender to addiction put at stake. Their relationship seems an edge that might cut their various ties, plunging them more deeply into a dark interior of self-obsession or mutual co-dependency that refuses the world, or instead severing that sense of insular need to rather foster their contact with an outside world of light and community. There is a failure to realise this brighter prospect in episode ten ('Over'), when

Jane refuses to introduce Jesse to her father, Donald (John de Lancie), instead treating Jesse with the polite distance of a landlord, introducing him as 'the new tenant'. Later, when Jesse angrily confronts a nonplussed Jane, she pointedly refuses to recognise any mutual commitment: 'Who's "us"?' Jesse absorbs the cruel blow of this rejection by smoking meth, alone, in the decaying brown light of the late afternoon, his face hidden in shadow. This aspect of drug use in the relationship is well characterised by Jacobs's description of socially destructive forms of sexual intimacy in *Deadwood*, as 'a kind of savage annihilation that cuts its participants off from the rest of the world, "a darkling plain", emphasised by the pitch blackness which surrounds both characters as they converse in an intimate post-coital moment'.[18]

The stakes of Jesse and Jane's relationship reach crisis point in episode eleven ('Mandala'). In the episode's cold open, we see a young boy shoot Combo dead as retaliation against Walt and Jesse's intrusion onto competition-held street corners. As in 'Peekaboo', Jesse's bid for success is again tainted by the perversion or destruction of young life. Jesse's response to this event buckles the walls he strived to impose between his life as a drug dealer and his life with Jane. The couple sit in front of the TV in the same decaying light that bathed Jesse's despairing drug use in 'Over'. Jesse admits to Jane he is a dealer, and takes responsibility for Combo's murder. 'I need you to leave,' he says. But what he says next drives in another direction as a tacit invitation: 'I'm going to smoke some crystal, and I just think you should go, being that you're in the program and all.' If Jesse's admission that he is a criminal who is responsible in some way for a murder puts distance between himself and Jane, the invitation here presents drug use as an activity that might in some way recover their earlier intimacy from its corruption by Jesse's criminal success. Jane tries to steer Jesse away from his addiction: 'We could get out of here,' she suggests. The line frames the domestic world, sullied by Jesse's actions in the meth world, as a place from which to escape, but Jane cannot articulate a particular space of alternative possibility. Perhaps it is this inability to conceptualise or imagine a feasibly alternative future, one that requires her to break off her connection to Jesse, that leads Jane to fail in her second attempt to reject what Jesse had to offer in 'Better Call Saul': an intimacy based in the intoxication of drugs, rather than a shared commitment to encounter together each other's multifaceted selves, shifting under the pressures of time. In Jane's pivotal moment of choice by the front door, light and darkness express this contrast between an enlivened, organic world outside and a static oblivion within. As Jane's hand hesitates on the doorknob, a profile shot is chosen so that we can glimpse warmer, brighter light on the other side of the blind hanging over the door. Jane's proximity to the outside allows in sounds of nature and growth in the form of fluttering birdcalls. Turning away from the door and its light in her moment of choice, Jane moves back into the room's darkness, its shadows submerging her face into depthless black. As she walks from the front door to Jesse's bedroom she now takes the fully unified form of the silhouette, emptied of the variety of details whose shifting interplay makes recognisable our individual, personal identities from the generic shape of the human body.

The final act of 'Mandala', and parts of the next, penultimate episode, 'Phoenix' (2.12), compress Jesse and Jane's descent into addiction. These are the same episodes in which Walt meets the mysterious big-time distributor, who turns out to be Gus Fring, the owner of a regional fried chicken franchise, Los Pollos Hermanos. As performed by Giancarlo Esposito, Gus is a powerfully compelling figure on the screen, projecting an enigmatic aura of deliberate self-composure and restraint, exemplified by the economic poise of his speech and the stiff-backed relaxation of his mannerisms, which seem at once eminently casual while being carefully selected and astutely deployed. 'Phoenix' opens with Walt successfully making his one million dollar deal with Gus, a last-minute transaction that causes him to miss the birth of his daughter, Holly. Across these episodes, the interior of Jesse's townhouse is again an index of growth, but now it shows more malign development. We see a sudden bloom of empty beer bottles, fast food junk, carelessly discarded cigarette butts, and other detritus of hard drug use. This moves their previously warm, flourishing domestic space towards the nightmarish warren of depravity that imprisoned the mute child of 'Peekaboo', a sign of a toxic quality to Jesse and Jane's potential to become parents, and representing the accelerated dissolution of whatever marriage they might have had.

The scene of Jesse's first heroin high can be read in light of the significance I have given to the earlier moment in which he and Jane share their interests in drawing. That meeting of the couple on the steps outside their duplex articulated their respective desires for the creation and experience of aesthetic unity in tension with their experiences of disconnection and fragmentation. Their drug use is presented as if it might overcome that tension and meet their desire. The manner in which Jane tutors Jesse in the process of shooting up is intimate; her whispered advice and cautions, and her guiding touch on his arm, express the couple's closeness. When Jesse asks Jane what the heroin will feel like, Jane voices a belief that it might bring them together: 'You'll see – I'll meet you there,' she says. As the drug flows into Jesse's veins his features coalesce into a singular picture of intoxicating satisfaction, and as he gently leans back to lie on the bed his movement is married to music expressive of the lightly swaying flight of a feather. As a song that croons of dreams and enchantment swells on the soundtrack, an overhead shot of Jesse cranes directly upward and lifts his body with it, carrying him up and away from the bed to a height that makes visible the tops of the set's fake walls.[19] Down below, Jane reclines onto the bed, consumed with her own high, separate and alone. The scene figures the aspect of addiction that psychologist Peter Adams calls 'fragmented intimacy', in which 'fragmentation leads to deteriorating relationships, splitting, and separations', but also 'leads in the other direction towards a binding but unloving closeness'.[20] So heroin is presented as an injectable aesthetic sensation that gives Jesse an overwhelming sense of personal unity and harmony with his surroundings, yet it is also conveyed as an artificial, confected experience that severs his connection to Jane and to the (now fake) world beyond his own sense of self. Jane's recapitulation to addiction can be viewed as a consequence of her deepened entwinement in Jesse's life through which she seeks to overcome the fracture of her own world that in 'Over' temporarily shattered the couple's romantic bond to each other. Similarly, Jesse's inability to successfully maintain a fragmented self makes him more vulnerable to the knowledge of his moral failures. His drug use is an escape from how his success and glory in the meth business has sowed such fractious and murderous effects upon the world, an escape that allows a sense of heightened unity between him, Jane, and the world around them, while veiling the breakdown of those connections.

This aspect of the couple's heroin use is reinforced in the penultimate episode ('Phoenix') when the storyline of their romance merges with the storyline of Jesse and Walt's massive deal with Gus. Walt refuses to pay Jesse his half of the cash for fear that in his addicted state the money would be a death sentence. Jesse, lolling in the first waves of a high, lets slip to Jane that Walt owes him $480,000. Jane's superficial resemblance to the *femme fatale* now becomes an aspect of her personality when she hatches and leads Jesse on a scheme to blackmail Walt. After Walt reluctantly hands over the cash that night, the pair plans what to do with the money, plotting a naïve future life in New Zealand, because, Jesse says, 'That's where they made *Lord of the Rings*'. Jesse suggests Jane can be an artist, painting 'the local castles and shit,' and he will be 'a bush pilot'. (Their childishness will amplify the pain of Walt's later failure to act as a parent to either of them.) They both pledge to get clean so they can realise this new life. But when Walt later returns to retrieve the money – after a chance conversation with Jane's father convinces him not to give up on Jesse – he finds the couple passed out in bed together, used needles and a burnt spoon on the bedside table. Trying to wake Jesse, Walt knocks Jane onto her back. She vomits, and starts choking. Walt instinctively moves to intervene, but stops himself. He stands still as she convulses, and after a few moments she chokes to death. Through his agitation and tears, Walt composes himself, and the episode ends. The impossibility of Jesse and Jane's aestheticised fantasy of life with money makes sense of this return to heroin. The pair is unable to turn the money, status, and glory Jesse earns in the meth business into a different life through which they can feel in coherent, meaningful relation to themselves, each other, and the world. This is a state of being they can only attain by the strict repetition and diminishing returns of getting high on heroin, an always-identical aesthetic experience of unity that for Jane results in death, a state of absolute fixity and autonomy from the world.

So it is fitting that images at once highlighting connection and showing the obliteration of unity climax Jesse and Jane's storyline and give coherence to what were initially scattered parts of the second season. The final episode, 'ABQ' (2.13), seems to reach a stunning climax when Skyler demands a separation, after biding her time while Walt recovers from surgery to remove the remains of his tumour. She drives away with their baby, and leaves Walt alone; he sits by the backyard swimming pool and, like us, contemplates this radical dismantling of the family that supposedly provided the very *raison d'être* of his life as a criminal. This is intercut with scenes of a clearly distracted and exhausted Donald Margolis, Jane's father, returning to his work as an air traffic controller following her death. As we are shown two planes move into each other's paths on Donald's screen, we cut back to Walt by the swimming pool. A few beats of silence are torn apart by a booming explosion in the sky. The camera gives spectacular views of the chaos, spiralling down through the air as if a falling piece of debris. This aerial perspective spreads out Albuquerque below as neat clutches of houses and lines of road that form both boundaries and seams, at once cutting up and stitching-together a patchwork visible only from above. And as it falls the camera turns upwards, showing what must be the shredded parts of people and their possessions scattered aflame to the winds, to land at random in the backyards and homes of strangers. A pink teddy bear, scorched and disfigured, lands in Walt's pool, and from below the water we watch it sink down towards us as Walt peers over the pool's edge, perplexed by what has happened. The image changes from colour to black and white, while leaving the teddy a vivid and violent pink. A fade to black and the season ends.

But as viewers we don't share Walt's perplexity because the bleaching of colour to black and white connects this image that concludes the season to the images that opened it. Season two is marked by a series of four enigmatic flashforwards that begin in the first episode and culminate in the last. Each pivots around the pink teddy bear, and provides a black and white glimpse of some inexplicable catastrophe that will unfold around Walt's house. The episodes chosen to give these glimpses contain in their titles pieces of a perfectly formed puzzle: 'Seven Thirty-Seven', 'Down', 'Over', 'ABQ'. Through these pieces of episodes, season two's sense of unity emerges in fragments. Similarly, a spectacle of fragments scattered over the city, which is presented as being a consequence of Jane's death, makes visible only to viewers the unity of her entwinement in a social fabric, this interconnection invisible on the ground within the fiction, where profound separateness is shown to haunt the characters. Perfect unity requires a certain fixity and completeness, autonomy from the deforming pressures of a world shifting across time. The relevance of this to the storyline of Jesse and Jane's romance, and of her death, is heightened by the visual allusion that the season's final image makes to the famous underwater shot that closes the flashback structure of *Sunset Boulevard* (Billy Wilder, 1950), that of a dead William Holden floating facedown in a swimming pool as police officers look down into the water from the edge. That movie can be taken as being about a fantasy of success that seeks to overcome, through the lasting fixity of the filmed image, terrible isolation and the irrevocable degradations of time. Gilligan uses Jesse's season two storyline to show us how fixity, completeness, and autonomy are qualities in conflict with the availability of television serials and their characters to continued development, and presents them as aesthetic values inimical to the varieties of growth and degradation over time that are a condition of ongoing human life. In Jesse and Jane's storyline across season two, fixed unity is associated with the denial of contact with the world of people beyond the self, and with the destruction of human community as a consequence of the glorified notions of self-identity Jesse and Walt pursue through their success in the meth world.

By contrast, it is in Hank that season two shows us a character able to grow into a more benign relationship to the variously marbled, flexible facets of his personality. Hank's storyline of personal crisis ends on an image of him re-joining with energy and vitality a meeting of his fellows on a public stage. In 'ABQ', Hank's storyline once again merges with Walt's when, following Walt's million-dollar sale to Gus, Hank notices Heisenberg's blue meth cropping up once more, but now all over the region, beyond the limits of Albuquerque and New Mexico. It is around the figure of Gus, and the machine of his corporate enterprise, that the third season will turn: they provide the series a new villain, and a central new dramatic space in the form of the superlab. In this underground factory *Breaking Bad* will find a space of perfect autonomy, repetition, and unity. It is a space that will pose a drastic threat to choice and consequence as tangible forces that make stances of glory, morality, and dignity compelling as grounds for the forming and tightening of human solidarity.

3
Taking a Stand in Season Three

The superlab appears for the first time in episode five of season three, 'Más' (3.5), in a scene in which Gus shows Walt the massive underground room and its equipment. The scene marks the height of Gus's pitch to employ Walt as his cook, which he first makes in the season's opening episode, 'No Más' (3.1). The offer is 'three million dollars, for three months of your time'. Yet Walt, after a barely concealed moment of enticement, turns it down, surely at least partly out of guilt over Jane's death and the ensuing plane crash, but more explicitly because earlier in the episode Skyler petitioned him for divorce. 'I have money', Walt tells Gus. 'I have more money than I know how to spend. What I don't have is my family.'

This is a modest, quiet, and pathetically tinged instance of what is a key dramatic staple of *Breaking Bad* – those moments in which characters stake their sense of dignity and honour or virtue by taking some kind of declarative, forceful stand, often appearing to embrace what seems the more difficult or sacrificial of the choices they confront. These scenarios as expressions of dignified self-command are especially prominent in the series' first season, from Walt's suicidal standoff with the 'police' at the start of the pilot episode, through his later refusal of chemotherapy, and then his identify-forging demand for compensation from Tuco in 'Crazy Handful of Nothin' (1.6). Seemingly in keeping with such demands for recognition are Walt, Jesse, and Hank's pursuits of success across season two, which, as I described in the previous chapter, hinge on their desires for heightened forms of visibility. Marbled throughout the treatment of those storylines, though, were inflections of the characters' needs or desires to *avoid* such exposure, to protect and shield the self from the scrutinising gaze of others through privacy or anonymity.

The beginning episodes of season three forecast the ambition of Gilligan and his writers to take up a renewed interest in such wishes for self-concealment. Following Walt's initial refusal of his offer, Gus puts in motion a scheme to entice Walt back into the business through the superlab's promise of security, a plot that unfolds alongside Walt's attempt to reclaim his role as a husband and father. (Adjacent to these events is the arrival in Albuquerque of twin, menacingly silent Mexican cartel assassins [Luis and Daniel Moncada], who it will emerge are seeking vengeance against Walt for the killing of Tuco, their cousin.) In episode three, 'I.F.T.' (3.3), Walt moves back in against Skyler's wishes; this resumption of an earlier state of affairs is mirrored in the episode's parallel plot in which Hank is again offered the dangerous promotion to El Paso that catalysed his season two storyline. Walt buttresses his forced reunion of the family with performative gestures of care (preparing grilled cheese sandwiches, feeding the baby bottled milk) that present a charade of fatherly love and responsibility, undermining Skyler's attempts to (rightly) paint him as a toxic influence. And in episode four, 'Green Light' (3.4), Hank's public self-inflation in response to his renewed promotion begins, in private, to collapse around him as he sinks once again into a pit of anxiety and fear that becomes manifest in temporarily crippling panic attacks. Indeed it is only Jesse who, after losing his last remaining contact with Jane in the form of her endlessly repeated voicemail message, seems fully prepared to resume his risky public career.

What might seem to be the tired repetition or rehashing of season two's familiar scenarios (such as Walt's vacillating attempt to 'go legit' from season two's 'Over' [2.10], and Hank's El Paso promotion) is instead a *deepening* of the earlier season's interests in insulating and concealing the self from a wider human world.[1] This is achieved through the season's central plotline about the meth business becoming corporate and industrial, the central symbol of which is the superlab. That space becomes emblematic of the kind of total compartmentalisation and resultant specialisation that Todorov sees as eroding moral conscience and responsibility.[2] As an illustration, Todorov describes the psychology of a man like Reinhardt Heydrich: 'his sleep is never disturbed by the millions of deaths that took place on his orders,' Todorov writes. 'He never sees a single suffering face; all he does is manipulate large and odourless numbers.'[3] 'He never sees a single suffering face' – the example is perfectly eloquent about the ultimate, untouchable refusal of a shared human world.

This chapter explores how season three handles such withdrawal from responsibility for a shared world in ways that can be seen to address a problem that serial television dramas come to face as they expand to such length. There emerges at this point a difficult-to-negotiate gap between the latest point in the series and the now faraway origins of its story in the first episode and season.[4] If these beginnings represent our initial points of attachment to a show, then as the series expands it risks losing touch with, or in some sense 'betraying', the initiating grounds of our involvement in the fiction. As O'Sullivan puts it,

> the first season – the beloved object – is now officially outnumbered, and will get increasingly outnumbered as the seasons increase; so the beloved object must be rescued from the increasing sprawl (by mourning the first season's diminishment), or the sprawl must be allowed to recontextualize the meanings [. . .] of the first season.[5]

Within the context outlined above, one of an extraordinarily diminished sense of exposure to and personal responsibility for the world, season three of *Breaking Bad* is able to make especially compelling and significant what I have claimed is the first season's central dramatic scenario: the retrieval of one's dignity by publicly taking a stand. The remainder of the chapter examines how season three's achievement is to at once heighten the stakes and intensity of such scenarios, while not only complicating, but also to some extent dismantling, their mystique as one of the show's most crucial dramatic tropes.

Facing one another in 'Más' and 'One Minute'

In season two, Hank's performance of lightly worn toughness was shown as allowing him to successfully avoid his vulnerability to anxiety and self-doubt in a way that gathered people around his projections of confident self-command and coherence. In episode five of season three, 'Más', aspects of that performance of self are repeated with significant variation in a domestic context, when Marie presses Hank to explain why he turned down the El Paso promotion the second time around. The scene is part of the storyline begun in 'Green Light', in which Hank turns down the El Paso promotion ostensibly to continue his threadbare pursuit of Heisenberg, which causes tension with his partner Gomez. Throughout this storyline the rightness of Hank's instinct is in conflict with his apparent need to use the weak Heisenberg case as a tactic to avoid his fears and his history of vulnerability to them; his pursuit of a deeply felt intuition is at the same time a continued retreat from what he knows to be true about himself. The pain of being torn in two ways like this must be especially brought home to Hank when Gomez quits the Heisenberg case, telling Hank he has accepted the El Paso promotion in Hank's place.

Hank continues his retreat from what threatens to humiliate or otherwise wound him when, in the next scene, he returns home at the same time as Marie is getting ready for work. Marie finds Hank undressing in the bathroom, removing his clothes as if exhausted by carrying a burden. She seeks to lift his obviously heavy mood with a cheerfully energetic question: 'Did you catch your bad guys?' Hank's 'No' in response attempts to shed the weight he seems to feel without shifting it on to his wife. Marie is trying to relieve Hank's burden in her own way, but the kindness of her question elevates her husband's life to a melodrama of heroic, victorious good guys, which must unfortunately sharpen his awareness of being unable to step up and play such a role. While Hank showers, Marie sits perched on the vanity and tries to keep up a conversation across the shower curtain separating them. Testing deeper waters with a noticeably hesitant voice (a shift from the earlier line delivery, which made a strident show of support), Marie raises the fact that Gomez accepted the status-boosting promotion to El Paso. After Hank gives only a curt 'Yeah' in response, Marie tries to edge in closer with her next line: 'I was just . . . wondering how you feel about that?' Hank puts his hands on his hips and juts his chest forward a bit. This echoes a much earlier gesture, from episode six of season one ('Crazy Handful of Nothin'), in which Hank puffs out his chest as a playful expression of masculine superiority while facing off against Walt during a game of poker. Here, Hank seems to absent-mindedly repeat a version of that gesture. Now it is crafted less as a confident boast than as a defensive stance, as Marie tries to get around his conventional posture of collected confidence, which denies any interior depth that could sustain penetrating exploration.

Staying on the surface, their exchange takes on an air of rote rehearsal. 'I turned it down, end of story,' offers Hank, rolling his head as if trying to find relief from a weight around his neck. 'Good! Good,' chirps Marie. 'Jesus, God knows I'm relieved.' But Marie's display of enthusiasm and relief is coloured by her uncertainty of its reception by Hank. As she offers 'Good!' she looks away from the shower, tilting her head as if struggling to sense her husband's response. On 'relieved' Marie keeps her lips taut across her mouth; the arch of her eyebrow and her wide, fixed stare are, like her hunched shoulders, caught up in the suspense. Unable to see each other through the curtain separating them, each partner offers firm sentiments whose meanings are cut through with signs the other cannot read. The curtain's placement makes visible the gap between how Hank projects himself and what Marie can understand of him. At stake in this division between the couple is whether Hank will seek to avoid a humiliating exposure at the cost of an unbridgeable space between he and Marie. It is at this point that Marie leans against the shower recess to reduce distance as an obstacle to conversation.[6] Having come in closer, she puts a question posing the clearest threat to Hank's sense of self: 'Did you not want to go?'

The delivery is central to our understanding of what is at stake in Hank's storyline. Betsy Brandt's tender vocality resists the easy availability and certainty of a fixed position that has been already taken up and which will be defiantly held onto. Instead of allowing easy judgement or accusation to creep into Marie's voice, Brandt understands the line as a sincere, searching question. The actress's quiet delicacy and sympathy of tone suggest Marie's awareness and acceptance of what her question's answer might mean for both herself and Hank: the dawn of a long, deeply submerged understanding gone unspoken that is just now coming to cast their marriage in a new light, its revelations carrying the potential to give a revitalising new start, or to result in a devastating loss of old securities. The question brings up an unexplored aspect of the past whose built-up weight pushes both characters to breaking point. As it weighs on Hank the camera presses in and scrutinises his face in tight close-up; he squeezes his shoulders and winces, being needled. Marie keeps asking for explanation: 'I mean after what happened last time, it would make perfect sense for you to not want to go back.' Being ever more directly made to face his past, Hank releases an increasingly violent torrent of defensive self-justification:

> I'm onto some important stuff, right here, right now, and Mexico doesn't have a *damn* thing to do with it, and anyone who thinks that – (Long beat) I might end up doing some actual *good* out here, and all I get are these *bullshit* accusations. Everyone thinks I'm jerkin' off on this thing? Fine!

Rather than presenting marital disharmony as the clash of one determined stance against another, the performances here – the fragile invitation made through Brandt's delivery of Marie's question, and the violent opposition with which it is met – are handled to invite contrasts between hesitant openness to flux and hardened resistance against it.

In light of this, it is interesting to note the dialogue's subtle repetition of a protest Hank makes in an earlier episode, in another moment that, like this one in 'Más', pivots on the public exposure of a personally wounding inadequacy. In episode seven of season two ('Negro y Azul', 2.7), trying to overcome what he obviously feels is the belittlement of the motel bedroom negotiation with Tortuga, Hank stands up and yells: 'How about you stop jerkin' us off here!' The repetition of these words could of course be explained away as simply a manifestation of the character's typical patterns of speech, a turn of phrase that Hank – like any real person – might habitually reach for in a given situation. But its existence in the show is also a product of the writers' intentions: it wasn't reached for by Hank in the moment, but *put* there for him to say and for us to potentially recognise and remember. Why?

In 'Negro y Azul', Hank tries to make a defiant stance against the concessions of negotiation that require humility, flexibility, and patience. In other words, the very 'openness to flux' I have argued is articulated by Betsy Brandt's performance opposite Dean Norris in 'Más'. The repetition of the words, as with the repetition of Hank's puffing up his chest mentioned above – which are both convincingly performed by Norris as being delivered utterly without deliberate intent by Hank – makes available the idea of Hank unconsciously drawing upon gestures through which he might retrieve a sense of self he possessed more strongly in the past, which now threatens to slip away altogether under the weight of his recent history of traumatic self-disintegration. Serial television drama is especially, perhaps even uniquely, well suited to depicting how the building-up of personal history places pressure upon the always-shifting constitution of a person's present identity as a foundation for their future. This is drawn-upon through Dean Norris's repetition of Hank's gestures, performed in similar ways in earlier episodes as a bulwark against various challenges to his status as a man and a DEA agent. In contrast to how Betsy Brandt articulates Marie's preparedness to confront a new understanding of Hank, Norris's repetitions of earlier aspects of his performance become a marker of Hank's refusal to acknowledge his susceptibility to time, instead seeking to assert with violent force a position of absolute, fixed coherence, unable to be shifted by the weight of his own past. The final image of Hank and Marie's separateness in 'Más' figures these alienating effects of his futile attempt to preserve a past self-image as if it could be invulnerable to time. The questions Hank defensively screams are answered only by the sound of water running unseen down the drain. Visual and sonic designs meet to associate Hank's attempt to grasp a fixed image of himself with things slipping and spiralling away from him, as Marie falls from his reach and is left, like Hank, isolated and alone outside the frame, pushed away from marriage. Protecting his self-image by avoiding his own past, Hank also avoids his relation to Marie, whose intimate entwinement in Hank's personal history threatens his exposure to it, and so to a part of himself he wants to forget.

Hank takes another stand, but with different effect, following the events of the next, sixth episode of the season, 'Sunset' (3.6), in which Hank's near-capture of the RV is foiled when Walt's hoax call sees him convinced that Marie has been in a serious car accident. 'Sunset' ends with Gus meeting the cartel assassins pursuing their vendetta against Walt, and offering them Hank's life in exchange. The next episode, 'One Minute' (3.7), opens with Hank taking his own misplaced revenge on Jesse, beating him so viciously he is hospitalised. Helpful to a reading of Hank's storyline is this remark of Stanley Cavell's in regard to the characters in Hollywood comedies of remarriage:

> it will be a virtue of our heroes to be willing to suffer a certain indignity, as if what stands in the way of change, psychologically speaking, is a false dignity; or, socially speaking, as if the dignity of one part of society is the cause of the opposite part's indignity, a sure sign of a disordered state of affairs.[7]

The virtue of Hank's dignified stance against a world that would see him otherwise diminished or humiliated is plainly put at risk by his bashing of Jesse at the beginning of 'One Minute'. Near the episode's end, Hank confesses his crime and accepts its consequences: that he will be stripped of his status as a DEA agent. The stakes of this acceptance are suggested in the way that choices of style in 'One Minute' work upon motifs developed across Hank's season two post-traumatic stress storyline. This is achieved across two scenes in particular: when Hank leaves his office after refusing to speak with investigators, and when, leaving the building, he meets Marie in the elevator.

Hank's refusal to testify to the investigators is followed by a tellingly handled piece of business – the investigators peel back the dressing on Hank's knuckles and photograph his now naked bruises. Hank's body exposes what he refuses to confront, and so it is fitting that each of the men in the room avoids the others' eyes. They silently mirror Hank's inability to face, reflected back at him, what he cannot stand to see about himself. The following scene in which Hank collects his things from the office associates Hank's refusal to be witness to himself with his diminished identity as a DEA agent. This works on our memory of Hank's earlier moments of post-traumatic stress described in Chapter 2, in which his identity hinged on his ability to use the public spaces of the DEA offices as stages on which to project clamouring calls for the recognition of his status by others. This is further developed when, after refusing to talk with his investigators, Hank stands in his office with the lights turned off. Through the open Venetian blinds we can see out to the light- and noise-filled bustle of the open-plan space through which Hank will have to pass in order to leave. Despite this visual and aural connection, the darkness of Hank's office separates him from the rest of his colleagues, concealing his face in deep shadow.

I see Hank's refusal of light here as refusing his colleagues' scrutiny of him, an avoidance of the shaming gaze of others at the diminishment of his honour as a DEA agent. In this darkness he weighs in his hand, then removes from around his neck the lanyard carrying his identification as DEA. Casting a glance out the windows as if feeling the pressure of judging eyes upon him, or wanting to be sure he is evading their watch, Hank puts the lanyard in his bag in readiness for his walk through the office, where he can no longer declare himself as he used to. Leaving in shame, whereas in season two he returned from El Paso in self-declared glory, Hank's passage through the office is now in reverse: his walk is away from his space of work and recognition, not toward it; rather than unfurling a declaration of himself he is hunched and timid, drawn into himself as he was in 'Better Call Saul' when shown in private preparing for his public performance. In Chapter 1, I described how Dean Norris's weighty bulk is used to good effect when the pilot episode introduces Hank as a bear-like man whose heft commands attention in space. 'One Minute' shows Norris exploiting serial television's opportunities for actors to build upon deeply established patterns of how their bodies are available to the camera. Instead of easy and nimble command over the gravity of social attention, Norris shifts the weight of his bulk here to convey the resignation and collapse of that performance of self.

In 'Más', Hank's attempt to preserve his past persona took an aggressive form that drove Marie away from him, as if their very intimacy required him to confront those shameful parts of his self-knowledge he would rather avoid. But in 'One Minute', when Hank goes to take the elevator downstairs after his first meeting with the investigators, his being able to acknowledge his changed public identity is associated with his capacity to sustain a condition of marriage with Marie. In the second season, the elevator inside DEA headquarters is used as a private space in which Hank can reveal to himself (and the show can reveal to us) those aspects of his psychology in conflict with his public identity. In 'One Minute', Hank must share this space of private revelation with his wife when the elevator opens to reveal Marie waiting inside. The scene shows a test of whether intimacy with Marie presents a threat to Hank's identity to be met with a continued posture of refusal. From outside the elevator we watch the doors close. Cut to Hank nestling his face in Marie's shoulder, pushing himself into her embrace as he collapses and she holds him up, the couple joined by this revelation of these tears for each other. The elevator doors open, and Hank and Marie stand inside, apart, re-composed in postures of polite restraint.

This echoes Hank's recovery of his self-image from his moment of anxiety upon returning to work in 'Better Call Saul'. The surrender here is also momentary, passing. Its temporary quality enables Hank and Marie to restore a prior state of things but with a changed understanding of each other, a state of mutual poise in which they can confront the outside world together. Crucial to the significance of this gesture is Hank's hushed line as they walk towards the building's exit: 'I hope it goes without saying that we're not talking about this to anyone, okay?' As these words seek to close a circle around the marriage, they also raise, rather than deny, the experience in the elevator. What Hank and Marie know of his past is no longer out of bounds but up for intimate discussion, an aspect of *each other's* world, rather than of Hank's alone. No longer refusing Marie's intimacy as threatening exposure, Hank's hushed words of cautious self-protection are words to his wife that quietly promise a more hospitable ground for the couple's conversation, and so for the state of their marriage.

The scene marks Hank's transition from fixation on the control of his self-image towards its partial surrender, an acknowledgement of the limits of his capacity to fix and hold his identity in the face of a contingent world. This is made most explicit later in the episode when he and Marie sit together on the edge of their bed prior to his deposition. Hank listens as Marie invents evasions intended to diminish his responsibility: 'Years of training, and your body acted faster than your brain; you had no choice but to hit him, you had to fight back.' There is pathos to Marie's kind attempt to shield Hank's sense of himself from the consequences of his crime, sealing-off his criminal body from his well-meaning mind. Driving against the good intent of Marie's words is the way they undermine Hank's freedom of will that is the basis of the dignity he seeks to retrieve from this crisis of identity and moral stature. As Marie kindly seeks to avoid what they both know about his actions, Hank foregoes excuses in favour of revealing his recent history of psychological 'unravelling' since shooting Tuco. Further driving against what we thought Hank was capable of, Dean Norris – in contrast to his more typically brash presence in the series – locates and brings to the surface a tremulous voice pitched so that it carries Hank's fear at finding himself disarmed while conveying a measure of the strength his wounded openness allows him to invite and receive from Marie. 'It changed me,' he says. 'I swear to God, Marie, I think the universe is trying to tell me something. And I'm finally ready to listen. I'm just not the man I thought I was.' The revelation frees Hank to later provide a full and honest account of his crime against Jesse. After he hands across his badge and weapon as emblems of his now-surrendered status as a DEA agent, the camera tilts back up Hank's body to show that his ID badge is flipped-over, projecting nothing but a blank face. After a moment's hesitation, Hank gives a nod that secures the rightness of his choice, expressing a now proper fit between his knowledge of himself and his image in the world, one upon which his marriage to Marie might be sustained.

In comparison to our view of Walt, this associates Hank's capacity to suffer the indignity of his diminished status with a strongly possessed sense of moral clarity and virtue. Fittingly for a show about its protagonist's discovery of his unimagined capacities, the events of 'One Minute' suggest that of all *Breaking Bad*'s characters it is Hank – who first appears to us as a self-absorbed, racist buffoon – who holds within him the promise of good and the psychological capacity to realise it, prepared to face himself in other people and by doing so not vainly fight to hold the world in a condition of stasis, but to re-build the world every day, with each humanly shared gesture. In a brutal measure of the exposure to vulnerability this involves, the twin cartel assassins ambush Hank in an outdoor parking lot while he is on his way back home to Marie. Stripped of his weapon, he is left defenceless, but through sheer ingenuity and determination he mortally wounds one attacker with his car, and then, having himself been shot in the abdomen numerous times, shoots the other assassin dead while he is readying Hank's ritual execution by axe blade. The sequence ends on a wide, high shot of the carpark. The neat rows of cars and the sterility of the asphalt setting now abandoned of busy life are at odds with the scattered figures of the dead and wounded combatants and their blood spilling onto the ground, as at this halfway mark of the season a car alarm sounds a repeating note of distress.

Enclosed in repetition and anonymity

The shocking end of 'One Minute' conveys a sense that at the midpoint of season three *Breaking Bad*'s world is falling apart, spiralling out of control as it is punctured by the violent eruption of vengeful passions.

This seems in contrast to the way that, from episode five ('Más'), the superlab takes up a new position as the stabilising, secure centre of the series' meth world. The revelation of the superlab to Walt and to us comes amidst a concurrence of storylines concerned with self-concealment. Adjacent to Hank's refusal to face his past in El Paso is the plot of Gus's attempt to overcome Walt's refusal of his employment, which rests upon Walt's avoidance of who he must surely (by this point) know himself to be: 'I am not a criminal,' he tells Gus.

It is at this point that Gus takes Walt to the superlab, built beneath an industrial laundry. The room is a large underground bunker of solid concrete walls, overseen by a mezzanine catwalk. Its dominant colour is red, from the lighting to the painted catwalk and floor. The scene of the superlab's unveiling provides, for us as well as for Walt, a beguiling tour of a novel place, fitting treatment for a new centrepiece around which much of the season will move. Gus's enigmatic power is captured by the arresting draw of his seemingly unblinking eyes that demonstrate an almost inhuman mastery of instinct and reflex. Being led down into the ground by this figure, there is a sense, strengthened by the initial dimness and the red lighting, of being shown hell as an attraction by the agent of dark power who willed its unlikely construction. Walt appears gradually seduced by the space, and we are guided to be as well. As we look upon the lab from the mezzanine for the first time, the scene's music score imparts a mood of fairy tale nostalgia, tinged by trepidation in the faint and fragile choral humming, and coloured by the strange lure of lightly struck glockenspiel, evoking the sinister image of a music box wound by some invisible hand. As Walt moves down to the lab floor and unwraps with the joy of Christmas morning the equipment he is being offered to use at his will, the music confidently glides into a waltz, as if to mark the new forming of a close partnership, between Walt and the lab, between Walt and Gus. Gus tells Walt he will need two hundred pounds per week 'to make this economically viable', and that Walt will have 'excellent help'. But Walt refuses the employment, citing again his need to be with family. Yet by the end of the episode, he seems to have accepted the impossibility of retrieving that life as it was – he moves out of Skyler's house and accepts the job with Gus.

However, the show's writers conspire the events around Jesse's bashing in 'One Minute' so that they may have Gale replaced by Jesse, as if recognising that Gale is an unsuitable character around which to sustain a serial television story: too perfectly formed within himself and in relation to others, unable to continue generating the jagged irritations of interpersonal fracture that are the source of arresting drama. As Jesse and Walt fall into the routine of working in the superlab together, the spirited harmony expressed by the cooking montage in 'Sunset' gives way to tediousness and alienating anonymity, which is shown in the opening sequence of episode nine, 'Kafkaesque' (3.9). The sequence uses a television advertisement for Gus's fast food chain as an ironic metaphor for Walt and Jesse's dissatisfying transition from entrepreneurship to corporate employment. A dissolve from a slow-motion shot of fried chicken tumbling through the air into an entrancing cascade of Walt's (now Gus's) blue crystal meth moves the sequence from a commercialised fantasy of authentic, family-owned, artisanal craftsmanship to Walt and Jesse's reality of employment in corporate, industrial production.[8] Jump-cut repetitions of Walt and Jesse weighing and packing meth into plastic crates are scored by a highly repetitive tune whose jaunty tenor clashes with Walt and Jesse's weary labours. These rhythmic repetitions of identical actions let one batch stand for multiple batches: just as actions across any one cycle of the process are indistinguishable, no batch is different from another. So the editing conveys Walt and Jesse's experience of cooking in the superlab as the tedious repetition of an always-identical process. It is pictured as a Sisyphean horror. 'The hell of Sisyphus,' Toles writes, 'is one where repetition has put an end to singularity as an attribute of experience. Memory has no function there.'[9] The professionalisation and industrialisation of Walt and Jesse's work puts an end to a sense of serial progression and the memories and histories of meaningful development it can build. Chapter 1 described how, in the first season, being driven to achieve quality was a catalyst for personal development and transformation. Here, the darker possibility of an obsession with quality is realised: the risk of settling-in to 'fixation and rigidity'.[10]

The rest of the opening sequence of 'Kafkaesque', which traces the meth's new mode of distribution, suggests how, apart from the perfect routines and formulas necessary to industrial-scale production and profits, Gus's corporation submerges Walt and Jesse's public identities, enveloping them in anonymity. The camera tracks crates of meth wheeled from the lab, weighed and packaged by a line of Hispanic workers rendered faceless by surgical masks, to then be immersed in barrels of fry batter bearing the Los Pollos Hermanos logo, and finally trucked away from the rural distribution centre to be trafficked regionally under the banner of Gus's legitimate food empire. The effect is Walt's work absorbed into the wider output of Gus's corporate entity, so that like Gus and Walt himself, his achievements 'hide in plain sight', appreciable only in private as a personal secret. The sequence fittingly closes by capturing Gus as a master of sight and enigmatic surface. He presents a depthless silhouette standing watch over the trucks rolling out his expanding empire – the only visible detail is the lens of his eyeglasses, catching and reflecting back the light of the world.

The following episode, 'Fly' (3.10), expresses the crisis of spirit or character to which Walt and Jesse's specialised industrial routine, and the material security for which they surrendered glory for anonymity, gives rise. The episode focuses upon Walt and Jesse's efforts to kill a fly inside their sterile superlab. As Walt's obsession becomes increasingly manic, Jesse puts sedatives in his coffee. Walt drifts into slurred, drugged-up ruminations about how he has 'lived too long', and the episode climaxes around the moment that the truth about Jane's death threatens to come out, with Jesse perched dangerously atop a stepladder in his pursuit of the insect . . .

Gilligan explains that the financial and scheduling contingencies of the season motivated the episode's design: 'it was a bottle episode, and the reason for doing a bottle episode is to help keep your schedule and stay on budget'.[11] Responding to these production contingencies, Gilligan and his team shaped an episode that excludes the series' world outside the superlab. This pragmatic choice gives the strongest expression yet of the anomie of Walt and Jesse's work there. The episode's concentration in and on this environment removes Walt and Jesse, and the viewer, from the pressures of time and social commitment being in the outside world involves. The superlab's indistinguishable cycles of strict repetition interrupt linear progressions that give evidence of the ongoing transformation of human lives and the world. Towards the end of season two, Walt was distressed to learn his cancer had gone into massive remission ('4 Days Out', 2.9). 'Fly' crystallises the reason for this distress, by diminishing the pressures of mortality that had previously given purpose and vitality to the remains of Walt's life.

In this context, the fly's intrusion injects novelty that allows spontaneity and improvisation to be discovered in an otherwise entirely predictable environment. This is expressed by the mobility of camera movements representing the fly's point-of-view, which contrast with the stillness and slowness of camera movements associated with Walt, such as insistently static, drawn-out shots of him waking up, turning off his alarm, and getting out of bed. That the fly provokes Walt to creative improvisation is seen in how his pursuit of it becomes increasingly elaborate. From bashing the fly with a clipboard he moves to throwing his shoe – which smashes a light and showers him with glass – and building a swatter, with which he tries to beat the fly while balanced on the mezzanine railing. Walt slips. A wide shot makes the danger clear, letting us see his slack, out of control body clang hard against the enormous settling tank before falling to the floor in a crumpled heap. Walt's increasingly dangerous attempts to kill the fly enact what has been lost in the transition to the superlab, compressing the dynamic of *Breaking Bad*'s early episodes and seasons. Enabling Walt to play out a desire to 'prove himself' through dangerous endeavour in a risky environment, they allow for the extension of his capacities in response to unpredictable stimuli, rather than their reduction to a series of repetitive actions. They also give Walt a renewed vitality of purpose. Walt's fall from the mezzanine is key to this. By introducing mortal risk to his endeavour, it re-establishes his connection with an ideal worth more than material security and safety. His decision to risk fatal injury in the pursuit of the fly is an implicit rejoinder to the question Jesse yells at Walt in 'Kafkaesque', which heralds the beginning of their mutual crisis of spirit in the superlab: 'What's more important than money?' Jesse also joins Walt in his preparedness to risk his life in pursuit of the fly when, in an attempt to swat it, he clambers to the top of a ladder precariously perched on a wheeled table, in a dangerous poise that echoes *Breaking Bad*'s need at this point for elevated risk as a locus of continued audience investment in its drama.

However, the ending of 'Fly' exposes the hollowness of the pair's efforts through a resumption of earlier cycles that renew their crisis of purpose and meaning. Walt's enthusiasm for the hunt eventually fades under the influence of the sedatives slipped in his coffee by Jesse. The point of going on seems lost to him without a worthwhile end in sight or mind. He gives explicit voice to this in his drug-induced lament – 'I've lived too long' – and his regret that the cancer's remission has allowed the passage of time to lay waste to the shape and value of his past. Reflecting on the moments before he left for Jesse's house the night of Jane's death, when he was listening through the baby monitor to Skyler singing Holly a lullaby, Walt says: 'If I had just lived right up to that moment, and not one second more . . . that would have been perfect'. However, even this realisation cannot shake Walt to surrender completely his moral standing in the world. As he tries to hold still Jesse's fragile perch with his slack grip, Walt says, 'I'm sorry about Jane . . .' But that is all he can say. Unable to reconcile his sense of guilt with his felt need to maintain his moral standing before Jesse, Walt's putative confession becomes only a pat, albeit heartfelt, commiseration, to which Jesse, in his touching but tragic innocence of Walt's evil, says only, 'Me too.' So when Walt finally cedes that 'It's all contaminated' and lets

Jesse get on with the cook without him, it is a perverse image of their intimacy when we see Jesse tenderly put Walt to sleep on a couch, even being sure to delicately place his mentor's shoes in considerate alignment, a friendly gesture sadly at odds with our knowledge of Walt's irrevocable fracture of their companionship.

As Jesse gathers a bag of chemicals in the background, a quick lap dissolve suggests the resumption of repetitive cycles interfering with a sense of time's linear progression. At the day's end, Walt, now composed, having slipped the intoxicating grip of the sedatives that temporarily saw him drop the mask from his face, coldly implies Jesse has been stealing excess meth, and states that he 'won't be able' to defend him against Gus's violence; their resumption of industry dissolves their brief bond of intimacy into mistrust and distance. The cut to black as they part feels like an ending. But then there are some final, strange images, which echo the first shots after the title sequence. Walt sleeps alone in his display apartment bedroom. He stirs from his sleep, and we hear the buzzing of a fly. Walt turns and looks up, and a point of view shot brings into focus the blinking red light of the smoke alarm. Cut to an extreme close-up of the light blinking, its second blink casting the fly into silhouette. The light cuts out and the fly disappears from sight. A reverse shot silently cranes down into a close-up of Walt's fixed stare, at the light, down the camera (Figure 3.1). A jarring cut to black and the episode ends.

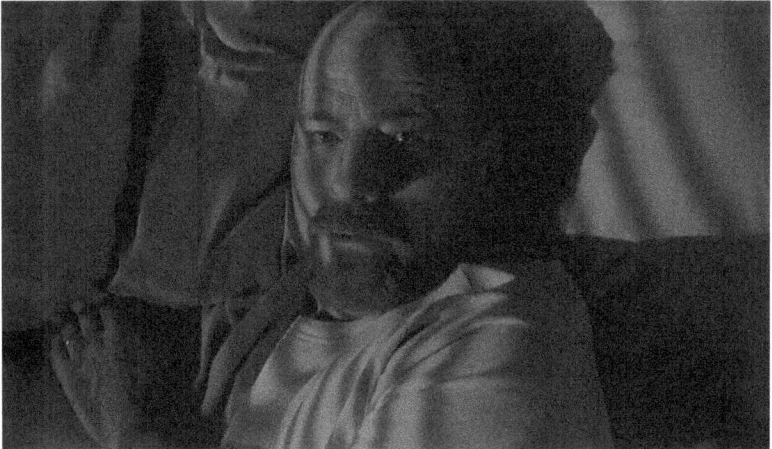

Figure 3.1   'Fly': Walt's inscrutable gaze

These final moments evoke a strange horror, related I think to the context of the episode's ruminations on the death of Jane and the deformation of Walt, and to the difficulty of reading Walt's expression in response to his apprehension of the light and fly above him. The moments' meaning is partly to do with how the red light, as a compelling attraction for Walt's gaze and for the camera, evokes HAL 9000 from Stanley Kubrick's *2001: A Space Odyssey* (1968). By silhouetting the mobile, agitated (and agitating) fly against the light that seems, like HAL, to cast a constant, unmoving, and merciless gaze, the scene draws on the connection with Kubrick's creation to juxtapose animal and machine agency. The moment does not clearly locate Walt in relation to these distinctions, but evokes their tensions within him. The fly, as a catalyst for Walt's waking, acts as a metaphorical haunting of his contamination of moral life, a weight that presses on him, especially when he is alone with his thoughts, even in the unconsciousness of sleep. Here the episode's dramatic links to the season two episode 'Phoenix' (2.12) form rich stylistic connections. The seemingly inexplicable close-ups of the insect in the cold open of 'Fly', which were accompanied only by the strange background whispering of a lullaby, now take sensible shape in relation to the much earlier season two scene of Walt listening to Skyler sing for Holly, his wife's disembodied voice carried to him through the baby monitoring machine, the blinking red light of which registered his daughter's vitality, which was in that moment unseen but nevertheless still felt. Walt is given here the human itch of conscience, unable – yet – to fully cohere with his morally upright sense of self the evil he has committed; his sleeplessness shows him tormented by a remnant of good gone to waste, which we might imagine pains him like a phantom limb. So he is not a machine, but a person, fractured within himself and haunted by his misdeeds and crimes, which have permanently torn the world's fabric, leaving his relationship to Jesse riven with hidden wounds that fester and infect, invisibly.

But neither does HAL sleep. And in that final shot we do not see an expression of inner torment, but something that looks more like deliberate and cold challenge, or scrutiny. Does the merciless gaze of one machine here meet that of another?

Returning to public spirit

This question, as a matter about the moral implications of Gus's corporate machine as a fully compartmentalised body, its parts autonomous and unified unto themselves, is explored through patterns of performance in a pivotal scene of the season's twelfth, penultimate episode, 'Half Measures' (3.12). If the superlab in 'Fly' represents the removal of Walt and Jesse from their entwinement in a social fabric, Jesse's attempt to sell the blue meth stolen from Gus through the poor souls he meets in rehab provides an avenue for renewed contact with moral commitment. It is through this plan that in episode eleven, 'Abiquiú' (3.11), Jesse meets a young woman, Andrea Cantillo (Emily Rios), and seduces her with the aim of getting her hooked back on the drug from which she is trying to escape. But when Jesse discovers Andrea has a six year-old son, Brock (Ian Posada), he instinctively abandons his attempt to become a pusher, and instead settles into a romantic relationship with Andrea, which comes already with a family in place and so represents something like a development on his earlier romance with Jane. It emerges that Andrea's little brother Tomás (Angelo Martinez) murdered Combo as a gang initiation, which we witnessed in episode eleven of season two ('Mandala', 2.11). 'Abiquiú' ends with Jesse buying some meth from the two dealers working the corner where Combo was murdered. As he takes the meth from Tomás, Jesse sees that it is blue.

'Half Measures' centres on Jesse's desire to avenge Combo's murder. This presents a crisis for Walt's allegiance to Gus's compartmentalised corporate machine, the sealed structure of which insulates him from the moral consequences of his place within it. His role as the underground engineer of the blue meth is divorced entirely from the destruction wrought by its sale on the surface, represented by a mute child abandoned to a disintegrating home in 'Peekaboo' (2.6), or a young boy whose childhood is cancelled by his transformation into a murderer. To protect this secure and insulated position Walt refuses to assist Jesse in his plan to poison Gus's dealers with ricin. News of Jesse's plot against his dealers gets to Gus by way of the hardened private eye, fixer, and hitman Mike. Mike and his silently menacing offsider Victor (Jeremiah Bitsui) kidnap Jesse off the street and take him to Gus's chicken farm, where Gus, Walt, and the two dealers wait.

The scene is staged by Gus in the form of a conventional, dispassionate business meeting, the various actors made to sit opposite each other around a table over which conflicting desires can be hammered into the same shape through rational negotiation to meet mutual self-interests. ('I understand that you have a problem with two of my employees,' Gus says to Jesse, as if a manager responding to a customer complaint.) What Gus seeks to do on this stage is subdue Jesse's strongly emerging desire for vengeance, or what can be called his thymotic passion to defend not only his own status but also that of others. This is a part of human solidarity not dominated by material desire or prudent reason, and which defies the limitation of human agency to the pursuit of material self-interest.[12] The concept of thymos has its origins in Plato's *Republic*, where he identifies the need in the City for people who are 'willing to sacrifice their material desires and wants'. In this sense, thymotic passion provides 'the basis on which private man is drawn out from the selfish life of desire and made to look toward the common good'.[13]

Jesse's thymotic passion is opposed to Gus's rationalist-technical mentality through contrasting qualities of deliberate fixity and instinctive urgency in the performances of Giancarlo Esposito and Aaron Paul. Throughout the scene, Esposito's talent is to present something like a 'negative image' of Gus's typical mode of carefully dialled poise that in public society puts across precise measures of distant politeness. Here Gus's capacity to seem distant from people is re-calibrated, so that his polite veneer is stripped of its warm projections of smile and chirp to disclose a menacingly cold abyss beneath, in which lies nothing but a machine-like purity of will to dominate and control those before him. This is seen in the moments after Gus delivers his command to Jesse: 'My men will come back inside,' he instructs, standing over the young man, 'and you will shake their hands and you will make peace.' 'No,' says Jesse. Mike shifts forward in his chair, and Walt issues an urgent intervention against Jesse's moral stand – '*Jesse!*' – but Gus swiftly extends a raised hand, and Walt immediately obeys his master's order to remain unmoved. Gus's eyebrows are arched in indignant surprise, but his expression remains tightly controlled, detached from fluid feeling (Figure 3.2). Jesse firms up his moral position by standing in defiance of Gus's looming presence, and, now on his own feet, he gives contemptuous voice to the two dealers' exploitation of Tomás as an instrument of murder, what Gus earlier elided as 'a problem with two of my employees'. 'These assholes of yours,' Jesse says, 'they got an eleven year-old *kid* doin' their killing for them.' Aaron Paul delivers these words in a low but intense whisper, in a way not dissimilar to Walt's Eastwood-like taunting of the bullies in the clothing store confrontation of the pilot episode. But unlike Walt's attempt to conjure an ironic cool, these words are righteously impassioned. By contrast, Esposito keeps Gus's expression unchanged, fixed in the rigour of his affront at the initial challenge to his authority. In comparison to our sense of Jesse's courage as the only one in the room prepared to move and stand in outrage before evil done to others, Gus appears calloused against moral degradation, a machine calibrated to be moved only by threats to its own dominance.

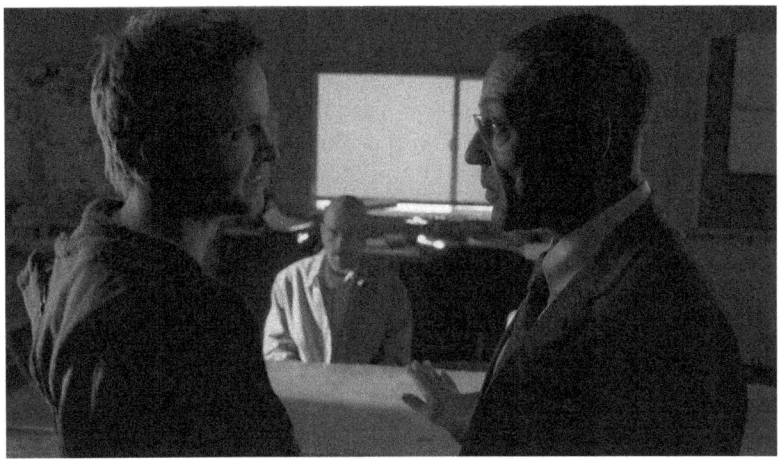

Figure 3.2   'Half Measures': Jesse confronts Gus

A different kind of moral impotence is shown when Jesse petitions Walt's outrage: 'You okay with this? You got anything to say here?' Walt can only look away, his hands and voice kept to himself, his eyes without direction that would move his other parts with coherent purpose. Maintaining his mute stillness in withdrawal from Jesse's moral commitment, Walt keeps to his private self. He is shown elsewhere to be a man capable of seemingly endless talk in the service of self-rationalisation, but when provoked to speak on another person's behalf possesses only the capacity for grim-faced silence. But while it is true that Walt's ambivalence looks undignified next to the unity of Gus's machined absoluteness, his indecisive position leaves room for the possibility of a moral shift.

A fragile peace settles when Jesse performs a weak, contemptuous and resentful handshake with his enemies. That night, Jesse lies in bed next to Andrea in pensive silence, his attention distracted from her, his gaze directed away, seemingly lost in his own thoughts, until the quiet separateness that has settled between the couple is disrupted by news that Andrea's brother has been found murdered. The sense we get here is of the community outside of these bedroom walls beset by Gus's marauding criminals, and of Jesse's growing sense of commitment to confronting their power, a melodramatic clash of good under siege by evil that is further pointed up by the choice to open the scene on a close-up of cheap plastic cowboy and Indian figurines on the nightstand. (This detail, perhaps only in retrospect of the episode's ending, suggests an ironic lining to the drama of villainy and heroism that promises to emerge.)[14]

Meanwhile, we see Walt sitting alongside Walt Jr in the lounge of his family home, watching TV with apparent distraction and agitation while Skyler prepares dinner at the table in the background. These scenes of disturbed absorption parallel Jesse and Walt, picturing the two men as now somehow estranged from their involvement in domestic family life. The meaning of the comparison is to show Walt moved by Jesse's example, the younger man's moral courage and clarity of benefit to Walt's soul, which is troubled and stirred from its earlier insulation against the suffering of others. This sense is heightened when Walt goes to turn off the TV news before dinner and overhears a broadcast about Tomás's murder. He is framed in the foreground, stopped by the horror of the report, his family in the background rendered as a distant concern by the deep staging and shallow focus, echoing the earlier shot that placed Jesse's courageous moral stand against Gus in sharp focus and clarity, and left Walt's inert and cowardly position out of focus in the background. And so despite the juvenile, plastic form in which a world of righteous violent action has been brought to mind in the 'cowboy and Indian' figurines, we feel stirred by Walt's growing sense of disquieted involvement in the world of violence outside the family home, and we perhaps anticipate or look forward to seeing his cowardice abandoned in favour of a renewed moral bond with his courageous young partner.

And so it is an astonishing and powerful moment when Walt breaks his stasis as he sits at the dinner table. He begins frozen in stilled silence while Skyler announces to Walt Jr that she and Walt might invest in a car wash, a money-laundering front intended to protect Walt from arrest and the family from ruin. Moments earlier Skyler demanded the news be turned off, keen to drive death from their home, while here she cheerily deepens her involvement in the very enterprise that robbed the young boy on the news of his life. As Skyler talks, the camera zooms in on Walt, sitting inert as he did alongside Gus. The droning score builds in volume and pitch to mute the conversation of his wife and son, the pressure upon Walt expressed by camera and sound building as his breathing quickens. Unlike Jesse, who seems to be capable of instinctively communicating moral concern through facial expression in immediate, clear response to the actions and plights of others, Walt is here again shown, as he was in the series' opening scene, to require an extreme scenario that allows for the communication of a moral stance through heightened effects of mise-en-scène and performative gesturing. This reaches its peak here when the building pressure of the drone turns to a sheer shriek of white noise that suddenly drops out to the sound of a door opening. Cut to Walt standing by the open front door, looking back behind the camera to his offscreen family: 'I'm sorry, I – I have to go.' He shuts the door, disappearing into the night. In contrast to his refusal to stand and leave Gus's side, Walt's empty seat at the family table stands as a symbol of his rediscovered capacity to pursue moral action in defiance of material, familial comforts, while also evoking an undercurrent of loss and cost, of absence, and of the unintelligibility of Walt's act to those supposedly closest to him.

The episode then ends with a heroic standoff and a shooting, a scenario repeated at the season's close in 'Full Measure'. In 'Half Measures', Jesse faces off against the dealers who killed Tomás. But as they draw their pistols, Walt drives over the dealers in his car. 'Full Measure' ends with Walt held at gunpoint by Mike and Victor. He is to be killed, and then replaced by Gale, in order to remove his threat to the security of Gus's operation and authority. Having anticipated this plot, Walt earlier discovered Gale's address, and so he phones Jesse and tells him to shoot Gale, leaving Mike and Victor unable to kill Walt who might now be Gus's only chemist. (The internal relationship of the episodes' titles – 'Half Measures' and 'Full Measure' – now suggests another, external point of relation, to Shakespeare's *Measure for Measure*, in their sharing with that play the drama of what a person is not only prepared to do themselves, but also have others do, to save their own life.) The style of both endings allows us to appreciate Jesse's and Walt's heroic stands in the face of death as dignified retrievals of the moral standing lost through their allegiance to the securities of Gus's superlab. Jesse's in particular does so through the way it is presented in the style of the Western standoff, thereby working within the frame earlier introduced by the crude cowboy and Indian figurines. Such stands embody what Todorov finds in moral values, which 'tell [him] there is something more precious than life itself, that staying human is more important than staying alive'.[15] It is important that this is historically figured in Westerns through violent public showdowns, this publicity necessary to working-out a political matter – which is to say a social or public issue – rather than a merely personal one (for example, say, of revenging romantic betrayal).[16] In keeping with this, Jesse confronts the two dealers at the site of Combo's killing: an open square. However, it is a space abandoned to post-industrial decline. Empty shells of buildings are hostile to a sense of community; the nighttime setting further limits public scrutiny. So the setting asks us to take the showdown not only as a matter of personal vengeance but also as a stance in defence of public, moral value, but then forecasts doubt as to whether this remains a possibility at all.

The showdown in 'Half Measures' is strongly reminiscent of the concentration upon gestures and objects in preparation for violence that marks the famous opening of *Once Upon a Time in the West* (Sergio Leone, 1968), which was screened for all prospective directors of *Breaking Bad*.[17] As Jesse walks towards the dealers in slow motion, our involvement is almost exclusively with him and the threat he faces. Extreme close-ups focus only on Jesse's gradual steps towards possible death, and on his grimly desperate stare. Long shots render his opponents as out-of-focus shapes taking up hostile positions, brought into close-up focus merely to let us see them cock their pistols. The design encourages us to be concerned for Jesse's mortal danger alone. So as Jesse approaches Gus's dealers to kill them and be killed, we see his murderous and suicidal standoff as not only justified, but also dignified as a gesture that demonstrates commitment to a value higher than life itself.

Similarly, the ending of 'Full Measure' elicits appreciation of Walt as courageously heroic by staging his self-willed salvation of his situation, from humiliating helplessness to a dignified self-mastery in the face of death. Victor intercepts Walt on his way to kill Gale and, inventing a story about a chemical leak, takes him to the superlab. Walt's long walk through the laundry with Victor at his back echoes Jesse's suspenseful, suicidal walk towards Gus's dealers and so similarly encourages our hope for Walt's moral, if not physical, triumph. A standoff is staged when Walt turns a corner and confronts Mike, who waits by the lab's entrance. Mike tells Walt to investigate the leak, but Walt hesitates. As Walt stares at the red glow of the lab's lights, which echoes the introduction of the space in 'Más' to forecast a descent to hell, Mike says: 'Walter, the sooner you figure out what this is, the sooner we all go home.' Mike's maintenance of his obviously false cover story is not an insult to Walt's perceptiveness but an offer for Walt to accept with honour this fatal consequence of his stance against Gus and beside Jesse, and so in effect to will Mike's murder of him – to abandon his humiliating avoidance of what he has sown, and 'figure out' his own death as a glorious sacrifice and penance, to imbue it with a sense of the dignity of individual responsibility for choice that Walt strikes in his gunslinger pose in the series' opening sequence.

However, Walt rediscovers his capacity to defend his vital interests first. He turns and begs: 'Please don't do this. Mike. You don't have to do this.' Here begins Walt's slide into the humiliation of trading away his values for his safety. His voice becoming agitated, he first gives up his skills and time: 'I'll cook. I'll cook for free, and there won't be any more trouble, I promise.' He then cashes in his murderous intervention that saved Jesse's life and further, by avenging the killings of Combo and Tomás, opposed Gus's ideology that validates their deaths as instrumentally worthwhile. 'I'll give you Jesse Pinkman,' Walt breathes with delicate hope, his eyebrows jumping at the prospect of saving his own life through his young partner's death. 'I'll take you right to him.' A wide shot shows Walt holding out each hand at his side, palms up, weighing Jesse's life against his own interests and his utility to Gus. Mike relents, but Walt uses his phone call that was supposed to betray Jesse to instead order him to kill Gale.

In this moment we are drastically upended. Did we earlier witness a heightened return to the aspects of Walt's character that in 'Half Measures' greeted the news of Tomás's exploitation with indifference, and with which, at the end of 'Fly', he relieved himself of his moral responsibility to defend Jesse against Gus's violence at the cost of his own security? Or were we instead, like Walt's audience in the scene, fooled by a skilled manipulation of his instinctive helplessness and fear, emotions no longer simply felt by Walt but also self-consciously *used* by him as a theatrical hide or trap, their appearance shaped here to gain mastery over Mike, the hardened, murderous criminal?

That it was indeed a performance is suggested by the fluent ease with which Walt recovers from his apparently consuming desperation through a drastic turnaround in his projection of self that contains no hint of surprise at the reversal. Without a weapon in hand he stares down Mike and Victor's pistols, and, his voice now deep and steady, coldly warns both men: 'You might wanna hold off,' he says, 'because your boss is gonna need me.' When Walt recites Gale's address, his deliberate enunciation of each syllable delights in unveiling the power his knowledge has now wrested from his armed opponents. We are relieved to see Walt step back from his undignified capitulation to the desire for his own life at the expense of Jesse's, just as we are glad that Walt's phone call interrupted Jesse as he was about to get high and so be unable to help Walt, and we may revel also as Walt glories in the power of this victory by triumphantly pulling his jacket onto his shoulders and relaxing into self-possession, now achieving the graceful compo-sure that he couldn't reach when flailing against the jacket's arms after being humiliated at the car wash in the pilot episode. But Walt's recita-tion of Gale's address verbally signs a death warrant. Walt's pleasure and

Mike's shock at the address's revelation are each tied to the fact that it means Gale's imminent murder at Jesse's hands. 'Full Measure' thus predicates our appreciation of Walt's heroism on Gale's killing, as 'Half Measures' locates Jesse's heroism in not only his suicidal intent towards himself, but also his murderous aims towards Gus's dealers.

The achievement of the endings lies in how they craft a tension between our appreciation of Walt and Jesse's stances as gloriously heroic and another available sense: that Jesse and Walt's dignified heroism, which we ratify by cleaving to its dramatically compelling image of might and will and justice, may actually be a hollow and morally repulsive assault that breaks up and destroys other people. We are thus drawn into two competing positions as viewers. We have thought that, in standing behind Jesse, we were placing ourselves against the inhuman and degrading instrumentalism of Gus's murderous corporate enterprise. Yet the self-deception of this view emerges in the season's final repetition at the end of 'Full Measure'. Here, Jesse points his pistol at Gale, who, whimpering as he vainly tries to shield himself, echoes Walt's earlier plea for Mike and Victor to recognise his humanity (and realise their own) by sparing his life: 'Please,' he begs, 'you don't have to do this.' The camera gently tracks in a slight arc that brings the lens and Jesse's gun barrel in line, the pistol now aimed directly at us. Tears roll down Jesse's face and his finger firms around the trigger, and we find ourselves hoping he will not pull it. (It is a sharp switch from our earlier hope that Walt's death-bringing phone call will reach Jesse in time.)

Figuring the idea of different viewing positions, the choice to bring us face-to-face with Jesse's pistol effects something like a 'reverse shot' of the earlier position we took up 'behind' Jesse at the end of 'Half Measures'. And it also echoes the final shot of 'Fly', in which Walt's cold gaze stares directly at us, and, much earlier, the shot that climaxes Walt's heroic stand in the clothing store scene of the pilot episode, in which he looks at the camera, and past it, to his family for their acknowledgement of the stand he has taken. When Gale opens the door to Jesse, Gilligan and his team take away all the dramatic, suspense-building tricks that they have so skilfully put on display up until that point – the 'race against time' ringing of the unheard mobile phone rattling against the CDs, the boiling of the kettle, the music Gale is listening to. They leave only silence, meekly filled by Gale's whimpers. Absent the comforts of melodrama, we are made to coldly confront the scene of death we have wished for. In it we might see the logical conclusion of the demand for dignity that Walt earlier stamps when, in the pilot episode, he viciously grinds a young man underfoot.

4

Inheritance and Legacy in Season Four

The force of season three's ending stems from tensions in serial television drama between the conclusive and the ongoing. The meeting of the fatal gunshot with the season's terminal cut to black marks Jesse's sudden murder of Gale as a terrible act of completion. At the same time, no small weight is carried in our felt awareness of how this must deform whatever remains of Jesse's life yet to be lived. The ending thus achieves its poise between a sense of events being irrevocably sealed and of their persisting force into a future they promise to always shape and limit. There are of course many celebrated films that similarly end by evoking the past's sometimes inescapable restriction of what may be possible in the future. The pathos of the final moments of Nicholas Ray's *In a Lonely Place* (1950), for example, depends upon, in James Harvey's words, the characters' shared recognition of 'too lateness', seen in their capacity to 'accept what cannot be unsaid or undone'.[1] Another case is Jacques Tourneur's *Out of the Past* (1947), in which the characters' histories leave them very little, but crucially some, just enough, room to act and so to retrieve a degree of their capacity to give intentional and therefore meaningful shape to their lives.[2]

Breaking Bad is distinct from those cinematic examples in the way that, as an ongoing television serial, it allows or obliges us (those of us prepared to continue with it) to not just imagine but to actually see how its characters go on to live with their pasts. As Jacobs writes of the tragic death of William Bullock in *Deadwood*: 'Television series allow us to experience the "after" of such terrible events, and witness the upbuilding of life as it continues'.[3] Whatever hope we have in what comes 'after', though, may also be tensioned against a sense that the past has accrued such oppressive force that it is felt to constrict or suffocate future options for action or change.

This chapter explores the significance of how *Breaking Bad*'s fourth season handles just such a sense of constriction and suffocation. My interpretation is informed in part by the fact that season four was produced amidst slow-moving behind-the-scenes negotiations concerning the show's future with AMC. For Gilligan and his team, these negotiations cast doubts upon the series' continuation, doubts that led to the final episode of season four, 'Face Off' (4.13), being provisionally intended to stand as the ultimate ending.[4] Yet by the time 'Face Off' screened in July 2011, AMC had agreed to a fifth and final season to be produced and broadcast across the following two years in two parts, each consisting of eight episodes.[5] My reading of season four explores how its unfolding design can be understood as a response to the situation (shared in different ways by both the show's writers and its characters) of being 'painted into a corner' by past events while at the same time sensing the shadow of an impending end. Crucial to the season's designs in this respect is its range of concerns with legacy, understood here as a matter of what can be left behind once something is finished. These two issues – the restrictions felt in the continued presence of the past, and the forward-looking desire for the achievement of a legacy – come to be played out, and are examined in the chapter's two sections below, in a number of storylines that emerge as the season proceeds.

The early episodes of the season revolve around the variety of immobilising situations in which the central characters find themselves in the aftermath of season three's events. Despite their rebellion against Gus, Walt and Jesse must confront the fact that he is more forcefully in control of them than ever before, while at the same time Jesse remains haunted by his murder of Gale. Hank is literally paralysed by his wounds received in the cartel ambush; his condition is one in which Marie also seems trapped. And Skyler attempts to re-shape the publicly presented story of her recent past so that it lines up with the path down which Walt has taken them both. The choice to concentrate the main characters in these variously 'stuck' conditions manifests a kind of storytelling inertia, and so also represents the creators risking a potentially diminished audience investment in the series by deflating our sense of its dramatic stakes.

However, it is in just such a risk that Gilligan and his team find the thematic material upon which the season will work. The basis for this discovery is how the storylines that are sketched above are presented in ways that self-consciously reflect the storytelling difficulties that the writers of the series confront at this point in its existence. And this self-consciousness is handled so that it in turn reflects upon what it must be like to live in a world that no longer seems to make available whatever is needed to stir, and to sustain and direct, the kind of desires and commitments through which one might conceive of and strive for a different future worth living in. And so what is put at stake early in the season is the question of whether, and how, such desire and commitment could be rediscovered and kept alive in the world that has been left in the wake of the events of season three. The foundation of such an enlivened or re-enlivened desire is not suggested to be some 'escape' from the past, as if its continued presence was necessarily an immobilising trap from which to be freed, but is instead shown to be found in the past itself, specifically in giving a special, future-oriented significance to certain objects that the characters receive from it.

That the most narratively important of these objects – a Los Pollos Hermanos napkin found in Gale's apartment, and a paper cup refilled for Hank by Gus Fring – come in the form of remains or likely future ruins is understood to suggest both the persistence and the fragility of meaningful links between past and present. The chapter's second half explores the meaning of a number of ways in which qualities of persistence and fragility, and the play of tensions between them, can be seen as crucial to a variety of designs across the season's later episodes and around its ending. Central to my reading of these parts of the season is the shift of narrational attention and dramatic intensity towards Gus Fring. Of particular focus is the handling of what emerges to be Gus's quest for vengeance against Don Eladio and Hector Salamanca. My interpretation of the climactic assassination sequence in episode ten, 'Salud' (4.10), views the unfolding of Gus's vendetta as a drama of paternal surrogacy, the fragile bonds of which put at stake the perpetuation or erasure of legacy, which within the fiction consists in the continued integrity, even beyond death, of a person's achievements and name.

How this is all relevant to the relationship between dignity and serial television form so far described in this book is crystallised in a scene between Walt and his son in 'Salud'. The previous episode ('Bug', 4.9) ends with the violent disintegration of Walt's relationship with Jesse, leaving Walt's face battered and bloodied. It is in this state that Walt Jr finds his father in 'Salud'. Partly under the influence of painkillers, but surely also torn by his failure of Jesse, Walt collapses into desperate, helpless sobbing, and must be comforted and placed in bed by his teenage son. The next morning, Walt tries to explain that he doesn't want 'last night' to be the memory Walt Jr carries of him, and tells Walt Jr about his only 'real' memory of his own father: formed as a five year-old, seeing his father lying in hospital near death, irretrievably cruelled by Huntington's disease, 'like there was nothing in him'. Then he force-fully says to Walt Jr: 'I don't want you to think of me the way I was last night. I don't want *that* to be the memory you have of me when I'm gone.' This sounds an echo that brings up Walt's speech to his family in season one's 'Gray Matter' (1.5), in which he refuses the infirmities sure to follow from chemotherapy, because 'that's how you would remember me – that's the worst part'.

These moments point to the way in which the concerns around humiliation and shame that animate *Breaking Bad*'s first season are also closely woven with the desire to leave behind an inheritance and legacy, which is of course one of *Breaking Bad*'s fundamental narrative catalysts from its very first episodes. While recognising this, I want to explore how, in season four, the series' interests in inheritance come together with its theme of dignity in ways that exploit the season's relationship to the show's increasingly deep internal history and what seems to be its nearing conclusion. It is in this way that season four's design embodies a certain sense of inheritance: as an aspect of human life and of art that offers a promise of lasting cohesion over time, while also being subject to ineluctable fragmentation and decay.

Paralysis and mobility

In a forecast of what will become its central concerns, season four opens in the past, specifically with the return of a face we thought we would never see alive again. Indeed, the season's first images are handled as a sort of exhumation. Following the enigmatic opening shot of a box cutter being used to slice through the plastic strap holding closed a crate (the hastily swung blade leaves its mark on the wood), our situation in the dark is opened up for us by the crate's lid being lifted to reveal Gale, bright-eyed in wonder, looking down at us in our wooden box. The cold open of 'Box Cutter' (4.1) goes on to show Gale – under the supervision of Victor and Gus – joyously receiving the great deliveries of laboratory equipment that when brought together will form the superlab. When Gus politely asks Gale how long he expects the assembly to take, Gale offers one month as a reasonable timetable. Victor, pen and clipboard in hand, takes his place at Gus's side, and offers a competing answer to Gus, delivered as a command for Gale: 'Two weeks.' The deliber-ate 'clunk' of pen on clipboard provides the full stop punctuation to Victor's immovable vocal tone – a bolt locking-in future plans. So the season begins with a scene of past unpacking in which a sense of jour-ney and discovery is mingled with tones of entrapment and fatedness.

After the title sequence, season four picks up immediately where season three left off. We are once again faced with Jesse holding out his pistol, and the gunshot that closed 'Full Measure' (3.13) continues to ring. It will not be easy to move past this momentary event; it will have ongoing resonance, an idea further suggested in the way that, in the immediate aftermath of the killing, as we hear onlookers call the police, the camera lingers on the multitude of fascinating objects left behind in Gale's apartment. The episode's final shot will return to the mystery of these objects in a camera move that snakes amongst the police investigators to settle on Gale's lab notes, the significance of which within the fiction lies – like Charles Foster Kane's 'Rosebud' – overlooked and unseen. Yet unlike the ultimate climax of *Citizen Kane* (Orson Welles, 1941), at which 'Rosebud is gone for ever and a significant moment has passed without notice',[6] the importance of things in *Breaking Bad*'s world stands a greater chance of persisting, of being passed on or recovered.

Yet across a great many of season four's early episodes, *Breaking Bad*'s past haunts the series in ways that can be seen as variously immobilising, in which the future pursuit of anything important or transformative is shown to be a weak hope at best. Throughout its seasons, *Breaking Bad* displays an interest in the persistence of the past by using the duration afforded by serial narrative to depict the lingering aftermath of extreme events, for example in season one dedicating two episodes – 'Cat's in the Bag . . .' (1.2), 'And the Bag's in the River' (1.3) – to Walt and Jesse's struggles to dispose of Emilio's body and decide what to do with the captive Krazy-8. Similarly, 'Box Cutter' immerses us in the difficult task the characters face of tying-off the many loose ends dangling at season three's bloody conclusion, and also in the similar problem faced by the series' writers: how to stabilise the fictional world so that the chaos wrought earlier doesn't lead to a wholesale collapse of conditions conducive to an ongoing narrative.

Aspects of the episode point to the writers' interesting and also very risky response to this problem, which is to begin extending throughout the show's world something like the extreme anomie that was earlier given more condensed form in season three's 'Kafkaesque' (3.9) and 'Fly' (3.10). (I say this presents a risk because it chances extinguishing or suffocating the flame of extreme drama that has drawn and kept viewers to the show.) One way that 'Box Cutter' forecasts this ambition is through its frequent scenes of Walt and Jesse sitting immobilised in the superlab under the armed guard of Mike and Victor. Walt's agitated desire to get things moving again emerges in his attempts to convince

Mike that he and Jesse should be allowed to resume cooking. Yet Walt is repeatedly stymied by Mike's increasingly sullen and frustrated commands that he should just *'shut – up'* and wait. Alongside Walt's growing anxiety these scenes contrast Jesse's relative remove from the situation; Aaron Paul plays most of the episode in a flat, empty stare, barely responsive to anything at all until Gus eventually makes his shocking intervention in the show's state of affairs, and Jesse's eyes become lit from within and draw Gus's iron gaze.

Gus's entrance to the superlab and his murder of Victor is the dramatic and stylistic centrepiece of the episode, and makes a considerable impression in regard to the tenor of the season's storytelling we might expect to unfold from this point. Crucial to this is its use of duration. This is largely internal to the scene in the way that Gus's unhurried execution of his ostensibly banal task of undressing carries a grave and merciless sense of purpose, while at the same time conveying an unmoved passivity, which renders his intentions obscure and so terribly ratchets our desire for – and dread of – an outcome. Yet the basis for this is provided by a handling of duration that is *external* to the scene, and it is one that suggests a platform for the plot to come, in which the battle between Walt and Gus will pivot around whether or not Walt is replaceable, and which one of them can best earn Jesse's commitment. We have already been waiting half an hour – two-thirds of the episode's running time – for Gus's arrival, to the point that Victor has impatiently commenced the long-delayed cook. Walt jealously studies Victor's progress with withering scepticism, wishing at every turn for Victor to make a mistake and so unwittingly prove that Walt's special abilities cannot be taught and that he therefore cannot be replaced.

Gus slamming the superlab door decisively redirects this dramatic line. All attention within the fiction is drawn to Gus up above on the catwalk, and the scene's stylistic designs come to cohere around him also. The harmonious relationship is first formed as if in recognition of a shifting centre of gravity, in the way that Gus's initial stride to the mezzanine rail draws the camera towards him as he silently surveys the figures assembled below. Victor offers a boyish smile in proud hope of fatherly encouragement, and then Gus begins his clanging walk along the length of the mezzanine, step-by-step down the spiral stair, and throughout the lab to a dressing station, where – as an increasingly desperate Walt pleads to be allowed back to work – he removes and hangs up his jacket, shirt, and tie (in an echo of Walt's carefully hung shirt in the pilot episode) before donning the orange rubber overalls and spray jacket designated for purposes of cleaning up the lab before resuming its cycle. The camera glides in Gus's unhesitant train, silently exploring a range of fluid options and perspectives unmoored from any fixed grounding in the lab itself, guided instead by each of Gus's clicking footfalls so that as he stands before Walt and Jesse we assume something like the God's eye view he took up upon entry. Against this freedom of movement is set Walt's stuck immobility. He is here framed mainly in tight static close-ups that, if they move at all, only pivot in small panning movements around his lynchpin seat. This sense of restriction is amplified by Cranston's jittery, agitated performance, which peaks at Victor's claim to have learned Walt's cook by rote repetition: Walt rises in indignation but Mike pushes him back down in his place.

Yet, despite the camera's elegant waltz with Gus's walk through the lab, the relationship between his preparations for Victor's murder and his recovery from it is handled to suggest no movement of any real consequence at all. This is in the way there is almost perfect symmetry between Gus's entrance to and exit from the lab. Gus's response to his gruesome and bloody slitting of Victor's throat is to perform in reverse his tasks prior to the murder – he piece-by-piece removes his splattered rubber slicks and, after a shower to rinse the blood from his face and eyeglasses, returns to his suited form. Untouched and without a word he again climbs the stairs and strides the catwalk, his footfalls a metronome measuring constant tempo – an unquickened pulse. Before exiting, Gus pauses in the same position from which he first surveyed the scene. The arrangement of the figures below is unchanged but for Victor's body collapsed in a spreading pool of blood, which by the episode's end will be dissolved in another anonymous barrel carried away by a truck under Gus's mast. 'Well?' Gus says. 'Get back to work.' Gus's command, around which our manner of involvement in the fiction has turned, fixes things as they were.

The choice to hold-up the story until Gus's arrival meets the handling of his presence in the superlab to signal his dominance of the series' world at this beginning point of the season. That a world ruled by Gus is one of ultimate inertia is suggested by Jesse's interpretation of Victor's highly theatrical murder. 'At least we're all on the same page,' he later says to Walt over breakfast in a diner. 'The one that says: "If I can't kill you, you'll sure as shit wish you were dead".' Jesse and Walt are each dressed in ill fitting, hastily purchased outfits in place of their own, now contaminated clothes. So in addition to the breakfast diner setting, the costuming raises the ending of *Pulp Fiction*, at which Vincent and Jules (Samuel L. Jackson) – also dressed like 'a couple of dorks' – get breakfast together after disposing of a body. The evocation of those characters resonates with the idea of being trapped in a closed circle. At the end of *Pulp Fiction*, Vincent and Jules are allowed to walk away into the rising light of the Los Angeles morning, having survived a number of catastrophic, potentially fatal encounters. Yet we know that Vincent, at least, walks towards his imminent doom. Further to this, Jesse's words look forward to a future condition in which there will be no hope of meaningfully pursuing anything worth living for – as he says, 'you'll sure as shit wish you were dead'.

Such a prognosis, in the wake of what we have seen in 'Kafkaesque' and 'Fly', has some of the colourings of nihilism as Pippin describes its regular 'figures and tropes' in Nietzsche's writing:

> images of death, decay, illness, the absence of tension, a 'sleep' of the spirit (as in his beautiful claim that what is needed now is 'an ability to dream without having to sleep'), and perhaps the most intuitive metonymy of failed desire: boredom. These images suggest that the problem of nihilism does not consist in a failure of knowledge or a failure of strength or courage or will but *a failure of desire*, the flickering out of some erotic flame.[7]

Just such failure casts a dark and suffocating shadow elsewhere in 'Box Cutter' and across a number of the following episodes. Towards the end of season three ('Half Measures', 3.12), Hank – trapped and seemingly helpless in his hospital bed – loses a bet with Marie that he is incapable of arousal, and the season's final image of the couple shows Marie triumphantly wheeling Hank from the hospital and towards their home. Despite the horror of Victor's murder by Gus, 'Box Cutter' plunges to its most awful depths in its earlier scenes revealing how Hank's physical and psychological paralysis persists and has deformed the state of his marriage with Marie. It is a pall that will only begin to gradually lift from the end of episode three ('Open House', 4.3), as Hank becomes slowly involved in the investigation of Gale's murder, and comes to suspect – prodded partly by Walt and partly by the remnants of Gale's apartment – that the Heisenberg case is still alive and presents something worth pursuing.

Alongside Hank's storyline of physical paralysis runs a parallel plot of *dramatic* stasis around Walt's continually frustrated attempts to arrange an ultimate confrontation that might allow him to kill Gus. The stifling of drama is signalled in episode two ('Thirty-Eight Snub', 4.2). The episode begins with Walt buying the titular pistol from a gun dealer (played by the wonderful Jim Beaver, here gifted rich dialogue that reminds us of his work with David Milch on *Deadwood*). With the Chekhovian weapon suitably in place, we are then introduced to the new regime governing life in the superlab, and relations between Walt and Gus. Walt and Jesse are now supervised by the menacing Tyrus (Ray Campbell), whose oversight lets little to no room for the kind of autonomy and exercise of will that would allow the characters the space in which to shape and transform their situation. Further, Mike offers this dispiriting information to Walt, who is keen to speak with Gus in person: 'Walter, you're never going see him again.'

Walt's desire to confront Gus, and his continuing inability to arrange such a confrontation, is then handled in ways that self-consciously raise and then disappoint or deflate anticipation of the grand dramatic posturing that *Breaking Bad* has so far regularly traded in and led us to expect. 'Thirty-Eight Snub' ends with Walt arming himself and driving to Gus's home, and his stalking approach towards the house is handled as a call-back to his confrontation with Mike and Gus early in season three's 'Full Measure'. Both scenes carry carefully calibrated airs of menace. Walt's deliberate stride seems to lead the camera that follows just behind his shoulder, picking out the 'Heisenberg' silhouette cut by his trademark pork pie hat, everything coloured by the threatening tone of Dave Porter's instrumental piece 'The Long Walk Alone (Heisenberg's Theme)'. Yet in 'Thirty-Eight Snub', Walt's attempt at heroism sees him reduced to the status of an errant boy, chastised by a grown-up to put away his cheap costume. This is when Walt's careful air of danger is punctured by the tinny, high-pitched ring of his cell-phone, and by Gus's voice, tinged only by a tiresome sense of irritation: 'Go home, Walter.' And in 'Shotgun' (4.5), when Walt storms into Los Pollos Hermanos demanding to see Gus, a cashier insists Gus is not present, and makes Walt sit and wait in a plastic seat with all the other customers, watching the clock. Eventually forcing his way to Gus's office, Walt finds the room empty. It is such a cloaking in disappointing or disappointed hopes of drama that will find Walt exhausted and resigned across much of the midseason. In episode seven ('Problem Dog', 4.7), after pointlessly destroying his recklessly purchased Dodge Challenger, Walt lies slumped on Saul's couch – the lawyer calls him 'Rebel Without a Cause' – and offers this lament: 'Fring will see me dead, and there's nothing I can do about it. All that's left to do is to wait.'

Just as Walt is restricted in his capacity to create a drama in which he might be able to assert himself, Jesse's storyline across the first five episodes is one of being trapped in or by the past. Jesse is haunted by memories of Gale's murder, and, in an intensified repeat of how his romance with Jane disintegrated in season three, he dedicates himself and his home to an endless drug-fuelled party that devolves into an increasingly extreme and nightmarish den of self-annihilation, in which Jesse seems to take little part himself, instead passively watching from the couch as others mindlessly destroy themselves and his home around him. Jesse's aimlessness is further figured in a motif built around driving, either endlessly in circles as in the scenes of him go-karting or playing video games, or possibly towards his doom as in his drive into the desert with Mike in 'Shotgun'. Jesse seems nonplussed about the obviously threatening context of their trip, yet when they arrive at their destination, he clenches his keys between his knuckles and prepares to fight to the death, even if he has no sense of what to live for.

This return to story material in a shape that is apparently so familiar from season three might suggest that, at this point in its now rather extended run, *Breaking Bad* began to lapse into a sort of creative narrative exhaustion. The editors of a special issue of *Cineaste* dedicated to serial television describe such a state in terms of 'dramatic wheelspinning', 'difficulties sustaining [. . .] inventiveness or sense of narrative purpose', and claim that this is 'clearly a function of the demands of long-form storytelling'.[8] The quoted words evoke an inherently negative taint of cloudy intentions and artistic failure. Yet, across the early episodes of *Breaking Bad*'s fourth season, in what might look like 'dramatic wheelspinning', the series' makers can be seen to self-consciously manifest in creative designs the difficulties of advancing the show's 'inventiveness' and 'sense of narrative purpose'.

A scene in episode four ('Bullet Points', 4.4) helps demonstrate that what at first appears to reflect a lack of ideas and dramatic vitality *outside* the fiction (a struggling, dead-end writers' room), may instead be purposefully pointing towards enervating attitudes or ambitions within it. With the money laundering car wash purchase in mind, Skyler hopes to 'come clean' to Hank and Marie over dinner by spinning them a story in which Walt's secret is presented as being in fact his irrepressible gambling addiction, one that, through an ingenious card-counting system, netted the family close to one million dollars.

Even in summary Skyler's story is unwieldy, and the scene in which she and Walt rehearse it is striking for its flat, expository sense of characters explaining the plot to one another. However, choices in how the action is presented to us suggest that this tone is not (entirely) a witless failure of the scene but is rather, to some extent, a self-conscious feature of it, and that there is more than garden-variety dramatic weakness that needs to be accounted for. This is in the way that the camera placement frames Walt and Skyler's extended dialogue in a deliberately theatrical manner to an extent that is seen little elsewhere in the series. Walt and Skyler sit opposite one another in their living room, clutching the pages of script Skyler has written, which they will perform for Hank and Marie as their cover story. (In an echo of 'Box Cutter' Walt is, once again, stuck still in a chair.) Long stretches of the couple struggling with the incredulity of the utterly forced and fake material are covered by a single, static, frontal master shot, the camera placed so that we see the width and depth of the room laid out flat before us. The position and perspective of the camera squarely frames the action within the room's interior ceiling arch, now transformed into a proscenium. The deliberateness of this choice is highlighted when Skyler, as if in an attempt to inject some conviction into the words that are failing to get a grip on her husband, stands and begins to walk around the room with her pages in hand, at one point aimlessly wandering out of the shot, with no attempt made to reframe her through editing or camera movement. From this view, Walt and Skyler are actors who can only fake their commitment to the story they are attempting to share.

The living room has been treated as a theatre on other occasions in *Breaking Bad*, but to markedly different effect, such as in the pilot episode, when Hank makes Walt's birthday party a stage for his lively and enlivening storytelling. But now, that mood of friendly improvisation is lost to the cold, hard imprint of rote repetition, symbolised in the story of card counting, a game of chance rendered lifelessly mechanical without intuition and risk. Towards the scene's end, however, there is a spike of genuine dramatic friction and convincing feeling when Skyler confronts Walt with the punishing nature of her own position in their story (a piece of dialogue that further reflects on contemporary responses to the show that celebrated the vicious masculinity embodied by Walt): 'At least you won at gambling. I'm just the bitch mom who wouldn't cut you any slack.' Walt is then moved to offer what sounds like a deeply felt apology to Skyler, and Cranston carries in his voice a convincing weight of hurt, touched with fragility and shame: 'I'm sorry. I'm sorry that I put you through all of this.' But in a cruel tone he then asks: 'How does that sound?' What seemed like true sentiment turns over a false hand. And as Skyler is left deflated, so are we, while Walt reaches across to revise his acting partner's pages.

The handling of Hank and Marie's storyline provides the most literal and direct manifestation of paralysis across the season's early episodes. The scenes anchored around Hank and Marie most richly demonstrate how the early parts of season four thematise the sense of restriction that can be seen to press upon *Breaking Bad* in the wake of its first three seasons. As noted above, Hank and Marie's story in season three ends on a triumphant note of renewal, and so it is a shock to see in season four that not only has Hank made such little progress but also that their marriage has so savagely disintegrated around him. We should feel a terrible loss in the viciousness and cruelty of Hank's attitude towards Marie and in the awful entrapment that her continued love and care for him comes to represent, shaded as it is by the dark hue of Hank's merciless resentments. I say that such scenes between this couple are an occasion for not just recrimination against Hank or sympathy for Marie, but also for mourning, because they represent the failure of those honourable and good aspects of Hank's character that he achieves in season three's 'One Minute' (3.7). In that episode, we are shown most clearly what is elsewhere available about Hank and Marie in a more ambient way: that in their fearless bickering and insults they are a couple not at odds but rather prepared to see and speak to each other with true clarity, without shame or embarrassment, and so any light that shines through Hank's examination of himself in 'One Minute' equally reflects and illuminates the quality of his life with Marie.

So we feel something like a wounding mystery, as Marie surely does, in the intensity of Hank's acrimony towards her in 'Box Cutter' and 'Thirty-Eight Snub'. It is in that second episode that we see how callous and intractable Hank's attitude is. Hank is visited by his physiotherapist, a very large and muscular man with a kind of military bearing – in this sense not unlike Hank himself – and immediately after their session ends the two enthusiastically share a strong bout of spirited self-congratulations and high-fives, from which Hank pointedly excludes Marie, leaving her hand hanging disappointed in the air. After the therapist leaves, Marie returns to Hank's room and we sense that, with some trepidation, she hopes to share in the afterglow of his restored mood. She instead finds Hank lying motionless as he grimly stares ahead at the wall. He does not turn to look at her. 'Get out,' is all he says.

In a cultural moment that valorises injury it would have been easily available for Hank's paralysis to be handled as a lightning rod of sympathy for the character, and an occasion on which to uncomplicatedly celebrate the healing capacity of Marie's caring therapeutic attitude. Instead, Gilligan and his writers take the opposite tack, presenting acts of kindness and generosity as the fuel of resentment. How should we understand such acts being received this way? What has Hank lost that he cannot turn his head to meet the eyes of his wife? It is not a physical paralysis that keeps him from her – as Marie has painfully witnessed, he is not so deathly still towards others who are less close. There is something about Hank's relation to Marie that in his condition he cannot bear, and the depiction of his paralysed existence is suggestive about what has gone missing. Crucially, one thing he is shown to still possess is appetite and obsession. Yet these at every point lack purposeful direction or meaning. At worst they are mere habit or diversion, and at best they form sterile stand-ins for more vital pursuits that are no longer felt to be possible. In episode three ('Open House'), Hank watches crude pornography but just stares at the screen, haggard and unstimulated. Although the litter of tissue paper that we have seen scattered about testifies to the remnants of whatever capacity for arousal got him out of the hospital in 'Half Measures', it seems to suggest only a basic, autonomic, animal responsiveness, rather than a more animating 'inner' desire. That Hank is driven by habit is seen later in the episode when he insists to Marie he is not hungry and yet is shown, moments later, robotically scooping spoonfuls of processed rice pudding to his mouth.

Hank's newfound obsession is his collection of minerals and it is this strange interest that is most suggestive about his inability to participate in anything like a life with Marie. The choice of these minerals as a pursuit for Hank to take up is astute in many respects; crucially, in the way his gathering of their crystalline forms stands-in for his abandoned hunt for Heisenberg and the tantalising blue meth. They are also – harvested from the earth's crust – emblems of the crushing force of geologic time, relics of a process of sedimentation that transcends any human experience of history. This is a kind of cosmic imagery towards which *Breaking Bad* points in the very first shots of the pilot episode, which highlight layers of sedimented rock face, the Earth's movement suggested by the passage of the sun across its surface. Yet at the same time, any suggestion that the minerals provide occasion for aesthetic appreciation of the transcendent in nature is undercut by the presentation of Hank's involvement with them. He lazily purchases the specimens through miserly bids on e-Bay, where they are reduced alongside any other commodity product, and he refuses to entertain Marie's frequent and well-meant attempts to share his interest, failing to realise any opportunity to educate her beyond his frustrated reminders that what she calls his 'rocks' have a higher status than that – they are '*minerals*'.

Further, Hank's desire to neatly sort and catalogue the minerals is placed in tension with what we are shown of how he treats his own surrounds. The detritus of his day-to-day life – newspapers, food waste, clothing, medical supplies, the minerals and their delivery boxes – is allowed to pile up as if the evidence or debris of his past cannot be adequately disposed of or neatly dealt with, instead contributing to a sense of aimless standstill accumulation. It is amidst this mess that in 'Open House' Hank receives a visit from an old friend, Albuquerque Police detective Tom Roberts (Nigel Gibbs), who wants Hank's help interpreting the case file on the shooting murder of Gale Boetticher. The exact way that Hank is initially sceptical is suggestive. He asks if the offer is 'some sort of charity thing', and offers his friend this assessment of his situation: 'I'm living from bowel movement to bowel movement – I'm not even useful to myself.' Important here is that we can understand the case files of Gale's murder as an accumulation of past relics waiting to be read as a narrative pointing towards an issue of great public importance, a matter of justice to be delivered at a future point. So in the context already described, what Hank betrays in his refusal of the case files is his lost sense of being able to find contact with, or to participate in, a meaningful history ('bowel movement to bowel movement'), one that requires for vitality and significance the imagination of a possible future worth inhabiting with others. And so the viciousness of Hank's bitter refusals of Marie's care make sense as a terrible defence against the way her attention brings home to him his disability, and in this way threatens his impossible wish to live as if he were outside the history in which he is trapped.

Such a wish can also be attributed to Marie. An unexpected storyline in 'Open House' concerns Marie's compulsive visits to various homes that are on display for sale. We see it is a fact about these homes that they are not new constructions – each displays the signs of its previous occupier who is now moving on. The visits provide Marie with occasions on which to tell a series of fictitious accounts of her life, each of which is highly fanciful yet still mirrors or echoes her real situation. She says that she has a husband deeply occupied in a demanding profession, and that his superiors have somehow let him down; she is divorced; she has suffered medical misfortunes. What is most pointed is Marie's persistent imagination of children as part of these fictitious lives, as if the redress of this absence in her real life would provide the impetus and justification for continuing on and attempting to build something anew.

That Marie's fantasies are less like openings into a liveable world and more like dead-end cul-de-sacs is suggested in the way that they yield only the trinkets she steals from these strangers' homes. Whatever significance the small objects hold in the lives of their true owners, in Marie's home with Hank they can only be private emblems of secrecy, the actual fact of their possession by her unable to be shared with anyone else under the pressure of guilt and the threat of shame. We are never shown Marie directly handle or even look at the stolen objects once she has them – it is as if her sole ownership of secrecy is all that she craves from a world now entirely collapsed into the black hole of Hank's wounding.

So in this context it is telling that in episode five ('Shotgun') our strongest picture of Hank's recovery – one that isn't theatrically prepared for others outside of his marriage to Marie – shows him surrounded by boxes of the case files on Gale's murder, looking over photographs of the various mundane objects found in the apartment: a kettle with a bullet hole, a hookah, a coffee table scattered with books. Hank is 'up and about' in his wheelchair. That his mobility is freely chosen and self-driven is suggested by the writers' choice to have Marie enter the scene by arriving home with the shopping, surprised by the situation in which she finds her husband – sitting up at the breakfast table, clean-shaven and in a butter yellow t-shirt that harmonises with the morning light streaming through the open windows. The episode ends with Hank making a discovery that he shares with Marie in a seemingly unthinking gesture that carries no sense of a special apology and so signals a return to the ordinary. Among the material that points to Gale's vegan and 'fair trade' lifestyle is a paper napkin from Los Pollos Hermanos on which a serial number has been carefully transcribed.

Two episodes later, in 'Problem Dog', we get another scene of renewal when Jesse, now under the tutelage of Mike and Gus, clears his house of its accumulated rubbish and filth and begins to repaint the walls a clean, pure white. Yet we see that it is not entirely a break with the past when Walt visits and pricks Jesse's memory of Gus's involvement in the murder of Andrea's brother. Paint roller in hand, Jesse agrees to help Walt murder Gus, and later in the episode the pair set about concealing a vial of ricin inside one of Jesse's cigarettes, the deadly object signalled by its being placed the wrong way around. The act of removing the cigarette's tobacco by gently twisting the tube's length, and then delicately balancing it on the end of its filter so the vial can be just dropped in to neatly sit as part of the parcel, is presented to us in a number of extreme close-ups that display an arresting degree of attention – shared also by the intensity of the characters' concentration – to the interplay of fingers and object so that we register a consuming purposiveness and tension now carried in this otherwise ordinary and indistinguishable item, earlier destined to be burned or trashed as with all others like it. Elsewhere in the episode, Hank is inspired by his discovery of the napkin to visit Los Pollos Hermanos, where he has the presence of mind to ask Gus Fring to personally refill his drink. In the parking lot, while Walt Jr is busy putting Hank's walker in the trunk, Hank gracefully slides the disposable paper cup into an evidence bag.

The discovery of the napkin, the plotting and planting of the poison-packed cigarette, and the meeting between Hank and Gus from which the DEA agent carries a loaded paper cup – these events all raise the pressure of season four's drama across its midsection, gearing anticipation of transformative confrontation and revelation to come. In this way, these moments are crucial in keying us to a sense of revived spirit and animated project on the part of characters earlier shackled by a sense of the past as a restriction they were each unable to shake loose. Crucially, though, the season's handling of objects suggests that rediscovering an animating and propelling inner desire is not achieved by the characters' 'freeing' refusals to take receipt of the debris left in the past's wake. For Hank, a renewal of spirit relies instead on being moved to strive, somehow, towards some way of discovering and transmitting the past's still-living and meaningful relation to an imagined future that is felt to be worth pursuing. That this aspiration is fragile is suggested in the way that Hank's discovery that points him towards Gus does not come from what we might most expect. The snaking '*Citizen Kane*' shot at the end of 'Box Cutter' pointed out Gale's lab notes as a lightning bolt booklet that might hold a 'Rosebud' key, but unlike Welles's earlier relic, one that would most definitely be uncovered by the search that is taking place around it. On its own, however, it leads only to Hank's dispiriting conclusion that with Heisenberg's apparent death he has missed his chance to do what he most desires: 'to be the one to slap the handcuffs on him'. It is a drunken Walt who, jealous at his genius being overlooked, convinces Hank that Gale's lab notes reveal him to be only the student of a more masterful teacher. And so Hank instead finds the meaning that will drive his revitalised pursuit by putting together two seemingly throwaway pieces of fast food trash, just as Jesse's future project inheres around a cigarette, one function and effect of which is to burn and poison.

Persistence and fragility

Both Jesse's and Hank's storylines lead towards *Breaking Bad*'s increased interest in Gus, who from 'Problem Dog' onwards comes to take up more screen time, allowing us to see more directly his pivotal role in the turning of events. The narrative tipping point arrives in the following episode, 'Hermanos' (4.8), which opens by returning to season three's eighth episode, 'I See You' (3.8), specifically to Walt's hospital lobby conversation with Gus following Hank's ambush. But then, in 'Hermanos', we are shown what was elided in the earlier episode: Gus visiting Hector Salamanca's retirement home, where he coldly taunts the stricken old man with the news of his nephews' respective deaths at the hands of Hank. The segment ends in a foreboding enigma: 'This is what comes of blood for blood, Hector – *sangre por sangre*,' Gus says, as we cut to a shot of shimmering green water that slowly stains with flowing blood. Watching season four for the first time upon its initial week-by-week release, it was this sequence's evocation of deep and untapped mystery that compelled my sense of *Breaking Bad*'s renewed dramatic vitality and promise, and it continues to point out the shift towards Gus as the move that most powerfully frees season four from its sense of being caught in a narrative straitjacket of the show's own making.

Yet later in 'Hermanos', the scene in which Gus is formally interviewed about Gale's murder articulates the problem that Gus presents as a potential source of new story material, while also suggesting the rich solution to this problem that Gilligan and his collaborators discover and come to mine. The difficulty partly comes across in the way the narrational shift towards Gus is handled – in an echo of his presence in 'Box Cutter' – to present him as a figure of unimpeachable omniscience and power. A sequence depicting Walt's submission to routine in the super-lab (which cuts against his statements to a fellow cancer patient that *he* is in control) ends on a high shot of the lab, as if from the closed-circuit camera, which then connects to a shot of Gus's oversight of the lab's surveillance system – Gus has Walt boxed into a sealed laptop world that can be snapped shut at Gus's controlling whim. Throughout the interview, Gus likewise displays his perfect manipulation of himself and his surroundings, answering with curious and seemingly improvised aplomb each question put to him, sensing and guiding currents of feeling as they flow through the men that are present, pulling without undue force those helpful ties of friendliness he has looped around his unwitting adversaries. Esposito cleanly parcels his character's command of self and setting into one neat gesture: taking his seat at the head of the table, in a swift sweep of each hand Gus clears the table top of any (invisible) dust before arranging his flattened hands, one atop the other, in a pointed arrow turned towards his interrogators.

That Gus's seemingly perfect control may at once compel and, over time, come to obstruct or repel viewer involvement with him is suggested in the way we are shown the exquisitely postured businessman wait in a corridor of the police station prior to his interview. As he stares at an identikit 'wanted' poster of the now non-existent Victor, we are drawn to the inscrutable mystery of Gus's (and of course Giancarlo Esposito's) face. The camera's slow glide towards Gus recognises the gravity felt in the ambient sense of withheld 'innerness' that always surrounds him, yet Esposito's performance is resolute in its refusal to suggest any shape of Gus's inner realm. This is most emphasised in the pressing close-up of Gus as he stands in the elevator following the interview, his eyes rendered as black sockets. The only hint of an inner tension is the metrical tapping of one finger to another, yet even this carries a sense of being mechanically determined, as if the stop-start interruption of an electrical contact, or the misfiring of a synapse. Such as it might exist, Gus's inner life remains a blank to us, a dark mirror of his apparently immovable capacity to be satisfied merely sitting and waiting on the hard wood of a bench seat in a state of utter stillness and statuesque containment.

David Milch's words on the character-based architecture of serial television drama suggest that bringing such a character into a more central role presents a potential storytelling difficulty. 'Ideally,' he advises, 'you place dozens of unique characters at odds with each other, set against a backdrop [with] which they are also at odds. The possibilities for exploration of a psyche could and should be endless.' But, Milch goes on to note, 'there is a limit to the amount of depth one can draw out of any character'.[9] Gus's ossified perfection of manner and purity of control represents a man brought to such a state. He becomes here a device through which to figure a threat that haunts *Breaking Bad*: that any one of its crucial characters, or dramatic dynamics, might reach such a point of stable cohesion that they come to what is effectively the end of their own history. If at this point in 'Hermanos' we were to imagine Gus's future it might resemble just such an endless stretch of exact repetition, a lack of potential dynamism that is figured in the next episode ('Bug') in the perfect replication of drives to and from work revealed by the tracking of his car. This aspect of Gus as a character is further acknowledged in the choice, or need, to discover new interest in him not by focussing on what his future might hold but instead by delving into his past. Towards the end of Gus's interview by the police, Hank asks whether Gustavo Fring is his real name, because he has been unable to find any record of it in Gus's native Chile. Gus smilingly deflects the problem as representing the chaos typical of the Pinochet regime. 'Keep digging,' he encourages Hank. 'I'm sure you'll find me.'

That (partial) excavation then takes place in the lengthy flashback that occupies the final act of 'Hermanos'. Along with his partner and chemist Maximino Arciniega (James Martinez), a young and nervous Gus – displaying none of the expressive restraint that characterises his later persona – visits the poolside seat of Mexican cartel overlord Don Eladio, played with a joyful menace by Steven Bauer, known for his grinning role as Manny in Brian De Palma's *Scarface* (1983). The captivating and ultimately shocking sequence, one of finely modulated conversation and negotiation – which should remind us of the centrality of compelling performative presence, gesture, and voice to our continued enjoyment of television drama – depicts, in Hector Salamanca's murder of Max, the historical origins and psychological terrain of the drama of recognition being played out between Gus and Hector in season four's present. (There is also a sense of the layering of historical sediment in the way that Gus and Max's gambit with Don Eladio replays, in a compressed form, Walt and Jesse's later upbuilding of their enterprise, and their subsequent struggles to sustain bonds of loyalty and love against the eroding force of the drug trade's merciless instrumentalism.) Gus's long-pursued quest to avenge Max's poolside killing by Hector culminates in 'Salud', when he returns to Mexico to appease the growing threat of the cartel's power. His plan is to trade Jesse to the cartel, who will only accept the deal if the meth Jesse cooks can meet the high threshold of purity set by Walt's product. Yet in the extraordinary sequence that closes the episode, one that returns us to the poolside setting of Max's murder, Gus's trade mission is revealed to have been a screen for his long awaited retribution, which comes in the form of a boxed gift of poisoned tequila.

Important to an appreciation of the climactic assassination sequence is the way in which the trip to Mexico is framed in terms of a shift in father–son loyalties. This context is set by two related events in 'Bug': Jesse's secret dinner at Gus's home, during which Gus (in the face of Jesse's fierce suspicion and opposition) recruits Jesse for the Mexico mission, but in such a way that the recruitment echoes his season three plan to replace Walt with Gale; and Walt and Jesse's fistfight that ensues when Walt uncovers Jesse's lie about the dinner and Jesse discovers Walt's paranoid GPS tracking of his car. Walt's resignation of his role as Jesse's surrogate father and teacher figure is to wish on him an especially cruel curse: 'You want advice? Alright, I'll give you advice – go to Mexico! Go and screw up like I know you will, and wind up in a *barrel* somewhere!' A contrast is introduced at the beginning of 'Salud' in the way that we hear Gus speak to Jesse as along with Mike they take off in a light aeroplane bound for Mexico. The plane's three passengers all wear headsets so as to communicate above the engine noise. Gus notices Jesse's anxiety, and, speaking into his mouthpiece, simply says: 'You can do this.' The texture of Gus's voice channelled through the electronic headset carries the force of a special link. Against the surrounding thrum it is clear and close and intimate.

The assassination sequence and its aftermath layers the breaking, re-forging, and ultimate overcoming or shattering of familial links under the pressure of the past that haunts Eladio's pool. Our sense of such links as being at issue here is heightened by the sequence being preceded by a number of scenes in which Walt ruminates on the disintegration of his relationship with Jesse, and is forced to confront his actual son's attitudes towards him, described in the introduction to this chapter. (The idea of Walt being a surrogate father is made most explicit when, under the influence of painkillers, he unknowingly calls Walt Jr 'Jesse'.) So it is fitting that an edge of patrilineal rift runs through two central moments of the assassination sequence at Don Eladio's hacienda.

Despite the occasion ostensibly marking the celebration of an already agreed deal, the meeting between Gus and Eladio is presented as a pressured reunion. Eladio walks down from the luxurious house that is set behind the pool deck but then he stops some distance from Gus so that his northern competitor must assume the status of a supplicant and be forced to make the conciliatory moves that will close the gap between them. The manner of the eventual bear hug between the two men, which seals Gus's apparent submission, takes advantage of the considerable disparity in size between the two actors. Bauer is a tall and heavily built man, and here his natural heft is inflated in his occupation of space – Eladio's posture as he stands and waits expectantly for Gus's deferential approach towers in our low-angled view. His immovability is on display in the slightly outstretched hands that in their only partial opening towards Gus make a demand rather than extend a welcome, and in the way his right shoulder is cocked back, pushing out and so accentuating his torso's bulk. The casting and presentation of Bauer opposite Esposito allows our established sense of Gus's physicality and manner to undergo a considerable and significant shift. At various points in this book I have described how elsewhere in *Breaking Bad* Gus carries a strongly collected presence, even in those moments when, as a respected businessman, he projects an affable sense of ease in place of machined menace. Yet by Eladio's pool in 'Salud', Gus approaches the nervous acquiescence of his youthful self that was on display in the flashback in 'Hermanos'. Confronted by Eladio's demanding and expectant gaze, Gus's eyes flick down, betraying a flash of humbling shame at his submissiveness before the irresistible power of the authority figure to whose side he is returning as if after a petulant attempt to set out on his own. There is a sense of a grown man being reduced to a childlike weakness in these moments, especially in the hug itself, in which Gus submits to the enveloping force of Eladio's arms that hit with a hard *slap*, and then pull in close a barely responsive Gus, who lies passive as he lets himself be manipulated by a larger and older man. That there is a filial aspect to this, rather than just a matter of bare power as such, is voiced shortly afterwards as a seemingly dejected Gus sits and stares into the water while a decadent party unfolds around his stillness. A buoyant Eladio sits with Gus and tells him to cheer up. 'I had to spank you,' the overlord says. 'But what choice did I have?'

The rebuilding of the implicitly parental relationship of Eladio to Gus, forged anew by the domineering bear hug, is immediately followed by a moment that at once dissolves the father–son bonds that have gradually begun to develop between Gus and Jesse while imposing another, pre-arranged set between Jesse and Eladio. Gus's introduction of Don Eladio to Jesse is ostensibly a mere business meeting but small touches of style convey another facet of its meaning: that Jesse is being surrendered for adoption by a richer, more powerful foster father. This sense of transfer from one parent to the other emerges in the context of a wide, high shot looking down upon the pool deck from up behind Eladio's 'side' of the setting, which is occupied by the large group of henchmen gathered behind Eladio, as if the cobbled-together 'family' Jesse will be passed over to join. From this distance we hear Gus quietly speak to Jesse in English: 'This is your new employer. You will address him as "Don Eladio". It's a term of respect.' Esposito's delivery balances the softness of a hushed tone with a firm touch of non-negotiable demand, shaping the attitude of the line as that of a parent providing simplified explanation and order as a way of reassuring an anxious child. Furthering this sense is Don Eladio's greeting – 'Hello, young man' – which is framed so that we are again reminded of Eladio's size, giving him a patriarchal bearing in comparison to Jesse's much smaller frame, which is squeezed in tight at the right corner of the image. (Eladio is given much more command of space in the more expansive left hand side of the shot.) And Jesse's silence throughout, unable to understand or reply to any of the Spanish being spoken about him, seals his status as a helpless child being passed around in an adult world that is not his to comprehend.

This dramatic context of surrogate familial ties being fragmented and re-formed inflects and complicates the significance of how Gus's retribution is shown to take place. One risk of the sequence in which the mass poisoning starts to take effect and then becomes apparent to all the characters – Eladio's dropped cigar, a smashed glass, a number of men tumbling over dead – is that the filmmaking on display is so potent and arresting that it might appear to us as if Gus's vengeance consists merely in the naked and fatal execution of his irresistibly violent will, one that simply metes out death as an answer to death, blood for blood – '*sangre por sangre*'. We are partly led towards such an understanding in the way that the presentation of the poison plot's unfolding is keyed to Gus's clockwork vision. The poisonings take place in Gus's absence, after he excuses himself to use the bathroom, where we are shown – in another echo of his conduct in 'Box Cutter' – the austere, methodical discipline by which he forces himself to vomit the poison he has had to consume in order to win Eladio's trust. There is a monastic quality to his careful preparation of a folded towel on which to kneel before the toilet, and he is in every way exact as he takes his time to properly recover from his exertions, carefully rinsing his hands and spotting dry his face. It is with precisely placed footwork that he cleanly navigates the dead body of the man posted to guard the bathroom door. These aspects of Gus's manner are shared by the measured and calm Steadicam shot that follows his walk towards the inevitable scene of carnage that awaits only his final oversight (Figure 4.1). In this brief moment overlooking the poolside tableau of death, we share with Gus a picture of the world being brought into magical and merciless alignment with his intent. The idea of Gus's will being in almost total unity with the world around him is

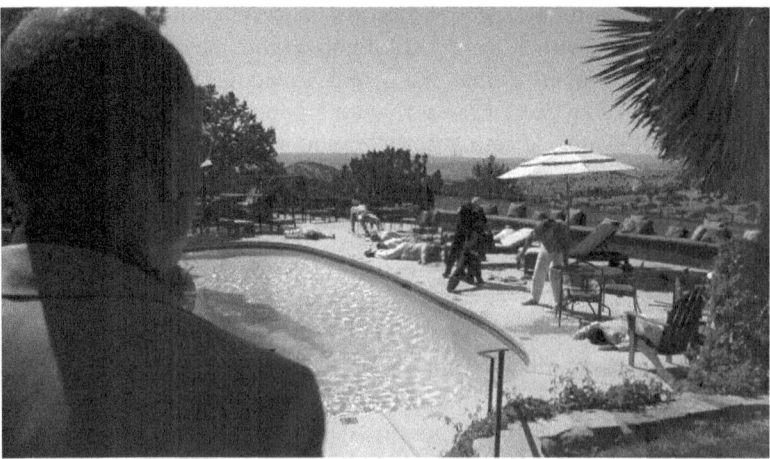

Figure 4.1 'Salud': Gus's oversight of his willed scene of carnage

figured even more suggestively when his eyes seem to actually direct or propel, rather than just follow or trace, Eladio's fall into the water.

Yet Gus's intent goes beyond the simple matter of delivering the death of Don Eladio, the man who ratified Hector's murder of Max. That delivery becomes only the crucial part of a much more extreme wish for the ultimate destruction of Eladio's entire family line. This is conveyed in the way that in the following episode, 'Crawl Space' (4.11), Gus glories in pronouncing the names of each and every relative of Hector's that Gus has seen killed, and in his announcement of what the culmination of that vision means: 'Now,' he tells Hector, 'the Salamanca name dies with you.' (That the continuation or erasure of a name is of fundamental importance to Gus's sense of Hector and Eladio's crime – and of his avenging it – is given earlier, oblique suggestion when he explains to the police that he knew Gale Boetticher as a recipient of the Max Arciniega Chemistry Scholarship, established by Gus at the University of New Mexico.)[10] So Mike's grim task of fishing Eladio's body to the edge of the pool and retrieving his necklace now makes sense as more than just the need to gather a receipt of the patriarch's death. Gus ceremonially unveils the necklace as he sits before Hector, and lets it dangle before the old man's eyes as testament to the destruction that has been wrought. There is more to this gesture than the surface matter of Gus's victory being recognised by his nemesis. Gus slips the silver medallion into the chest pocket of Hector's pyjamas, so that the crippled elder may receive his inheritance, and, in the cold weight resting against his dying heart, carry the knowledge that his family's one remaining heirloom has no future.

In light of these details, we might say that what interests Gilligan most about Gus's past and its relation to his present situation is not the matter of revenge as such. Rather, the purpose of presenting Gus's story as a drama of revenge – in just the way described above – seems to be to find an appropriate avenue of approach to the issue of permanence and impermanence, or the question of how things last, in matters of human achievement that unfold within a history. A vendetta provides an appropriate dramatic vehicle in this respect because it relies on the persistent force of past events and the capacity of their memory to sustain feelings of animosity, resentment, and malice towards others that, although eventually poisonous, may also instil a vitalising energy that can propel the design and execution of grand projects across time.

Gus's slaughter of the Salamanca family represents the fulfilment of such a project, yet it is suitably presented in ways that persistence is shadowed by impermanence. I have already pointed to the treatment of the silver medallion necklace as an emblem of an inheritance that is without a future into which it can be meaningfully passed on. Further to this is what we are shown of the immediate aftermath of the killing of Eladio and his men. With the last of his strength, Gus, in a desperate attempt to clear a path for his escape, makes a stand and screams in Spanish this message for whoever remains: 'Don Eladio is dead! His capos are dead! You have no one left to fight for! Fill your pockets . . . and leave in peace! Or fight me . . . and die!' As Mike and Jesse drag Gus outside we are shown the women and waiters from the party hurriedly scrambling away from the house with armfuls of cash, then making off in a variety of sports cars and luxury sedans left by their dead owners. The episode's final shot – of Jesse fishtailing a limousine towards the gates – leaves us with a brief image of what remains of Eladio's stronghold: only a few abandoned banknotes in the foreground, scattered in the dust that is kicked up in the car's wake.

Throughout *Breaking Bad*, money is central as an index against which Walt is shown to both measure his achievements in life and calibrate what his life will mean to others once he is dead. In the first episode of season two ('Seven Thirty-Seven', 2.1), Walt calculates what he must get done in the short remainder of his life in terms of how much money Skyler will need to raise their two children and see each of them through college. And in an early third season episode ('I.F.T.', 3.3), Walt, attempting to forge a reunion with Skyler, presents her with a duffel bag stuffed with the half a million dollars in cash collected from his initial deal with Gus Fring at the end of season two (and which he attempted but could not bring himself to burn in contrition at the beginning of season three). Walt's speech to Skyler frames the money as the basis for everything, both ordinary and momentous, that will come to pass in the family's life following his death. 'That', he says, 'is college tuition for Walter Jr. And Holly, eighteen years down the road. That is health insurance for you and the kids, for Junior's physical therapy, his . . . SAT tutor. That's money for groceries, and gas. For birthdays, and graduation parties.' That Walt wants the money to be seen by his family as a lasting testament to his personal achievement – persisting as a reminder woven into the very material fabric of their everyday lives – is made clear when he insists on this point of distinction: 'This money – I didn't steal it. It doesn't belong to anyone else. I *earned* it.' And yet the vulnerability of this potential legacy is evoked in Walt's final (self-pitying, exculpatory) plea. 'All that I've done,' he says to Skyler, 'all the sacrifices that I have made for this family . . . *All* of that will be for nothing if you don't accept what I've earned.'

So it is fitting that the fragility of money as the basis for a legacy becomes pivotal to the episode that follows 'Salud', 'Crawl Space', which in its closing sequences sets up the atmosphere of inevitable and ultimate confrontation that colours the remainder of season four as it heads towards what, at the time of production, was thought to quite possibly be the series' final episode.[11] That claustrophobic sense of inevitability comes across in 'Crawl Space' through the way a number of plot strands, which have until this point seemed to be running in parallel, begin to converge around Walt's money.

One strand of season four has followed Skyler's plan to purchase a car wash in which to launder Walt's criminal earnings, but not just any car wash – Bogdan's car wash, at which Walt was shown to so bitterly resent working in the pilot episode. In the episode two scene in which Skyler first tries to negotiate a deal with Bogdan ('Thirty-Eight Snub'), her attempt to project a persona of rational, calculating business acumen is swiftly undone by her inability to imagine that the car wash could represent to Bogdan anything more than the money for which it can be exchanged. 'I have worked thirty years building this business from nothing,' he tells her, 'with my own hands, and my own sweat and blood.' In an astutely written line, Skyler says that she can 'appreciate' Bogdan's position, and asks for a figure. 'Ten million dollars,' says Bogdan, leaning back in his squeaking and battered looking office chair. When Bogdan is forced to sell due to Skyler's ruse of a fraudulent threat of government fines and shutdown for 'contaminated groundwater', Walt takes ownership of the premises 'as is' ('Cornered', 4.6), and insists on keeping the first dollar Bogdan ever earned, which is framed and hanging on the wall. Walt delights in smashing the frame and feeding this monument to Bogdan's enterprise into a vending machine, dissolving into a commodity the bill's unique importance to its former owner. Yet Walt earns too much money, and too quickly, for it to be laundered through the car wash, and so in 'Hermanos' Skyler stores the bundles of cash in vacuum-sealed laundry bags. In an expression of the money's corrosive potential, the weight of the bags snaps the wardrobe rack on which they are hung, and so Skyler deposits them in the space underneath the house, where we see them placed and lit to resemble piled body bags.

These stacks of cash become relevant to the return, in episode nine ('Bug'), of a seemingly forgotten season three storyline: Skyler's participation in the tax evasion scheme improvised by Ted Beneke (Christopher Cousins), for whose family-owned business she worked as a book-keeper across seasons two and three (and with whom she had an affair following Hank's refusal to grant her a divorce or leave the house). Ted – now effectively bankrupt, his business in ruins – is under investigation by the IRS, which prompts Skyler to secretly pay his more than $600,000 in back taxes in order to end the investigation and any threat it poses to her and Walt. And so to make a clean break from that part of her past, Skyler (without Walt's knowledge) has Saul funnel the hidden money to Ted, by way of the lawyer's invention of a comically ludicrous inheritance left by Ted's 'Great Aunt Bergot' of Luxembourg ('Salud').

Skyler's plot soon comes to bear upon Walt's disintegrating relationship with Jesse. In 'Crawl Space', following the events in Mexico, Jesse's loyalty to Gus is further cemented to the extent that he agrees to run the superlab alone, effectively rendering Walt superfluous to Gus's requirements, although Jesse maintains that he will not cook for Gus if Walt is harmed. Nevertheless, Gus has Walt kidnapped, hooded, and dragged out to the desert, where Gus makes clear that he will kill Hank, and that if Walt attempts to intervene he will murder Walt's entire family. In an echo of his torment of Hector, Gus details for Walt his lethal vision, and its cold malice captures a sense of things tending towards an ultimate destruction that Walt is powerless to halt. We feel this in part through the way that Esposito plays Gus's cruel listing of each future victim one-by-one, the repetitions of phrasing and tone carrying the ruthlessness of the methodical executions he will force Walt to witness: 'I will kill your wife,' Gus says. 'I will kill your son. I will kill your infant daughter.'

In the face of such indiscriminate and irresistable murderousness being ranged against his entire family, Walt surrenders his cherished pretence of being able to singlehandedly control and protect them from the forces he has set in motion. He desperately begs Saul for the number of a man who, earlier in the season, was said to be able to magically pluck Walt and his family from their lives and grant them new ones elsewhere, as if perfectly freed of all that once haunted them. (Walt also asks Saul to call the DEA and warn them of the danger to Hank, and although this is presented as a 'just in time' afterthought, Walt's passionate insistence is also testament to a genuine care.) The cost of Walt's family being lifted from the situation he has put them in will be at least $500,000 in cash.

The closing sequence of 'Crawl Space' sees all of these converging narrative threads meet at once. Walt, madly scrambling underneath the house, discovers the money is irretrievably gone, and, in his subsequent and inexplicable mania, Skyler senses but cannot grasp any understanding of the awful consequences her actions have brought about, while at the same time Marie phones the house in panicked terror at the unexpected return of the threat against Hank's life. As the sequence begins to take shape with Walt's desperate grab for the cash under the floorboards, we are keyed to a sense of inevitable disaster by our knowledge – which here runs ahead of Walt's – that he will find the bags empty. Yet the feeling of spiralling chaos is then pitched even higher as Walt, after ripping the bags open with his teeth, realises his cash, almost all of it, is gone. With the music building to its crescendo, Skyler arrives and, terrified by the intensity of her husband's fear, peers down into the supply closet manhole, as Walt, lying on his back on the soil below, a few meagre bundles of banknotes clasped in each hand, asks in dry panic: 'Where is it? Where is the rest?' Skyler cannot answer, and he continues more insistently once again, 'The *money*, Skyler, where is the *rest*?', and then finally explodes and screams – '*Where is the money?!*' – as the music cuts out to only dead quiet. Porter's score limps back onto the soundtrack but no longer carries the force of a panicked pulse of blood beating in one's temples, instead only the slow, regular thrum of a lingering electronic heartbeat. Skyler tells Walt that she gave the money to Ted Beneke and he collapses into what sound like sobs but which then give way to unrestrained cackling as the phone starts to ring. So while we sense the neatly plotted coming-together of the season's various narrative strands, the sequence's expressive effect is of spreading madness and disorder and collapse, the central figure for which is its closing shot of Walt lying on the dirt floor of the crawl space, framed by the narrow confines of the supply closet and its manhole, laughing at fortune as he lies as if buried in a crude tomb along with a useless fraction of the cash he hoped to leave behind as a monument. The grain of the floorboards especially gives the image a striking resemblance to a timber-framed portrait, as if a metaphorical rendering of death through the stasis of a framed picture. Yet cutting against this feeling is our knowledge that two episodes remain, and so that a great deal of the unravelling chaos is left to be played out. And it is around this tension – between neat closure and continued future disintegration – that the season's ending is balanced.

The sense that impending closure looms in the form of an ultimate, vaguely apocalyptic showdown is pointed up by the episodes' titles: 'End Times' (4.12) and 'Face Off'. This is further given clear and, in its reiteration of the thematic keywords 'choice' and 'consequences', somewhat crude expression in Walt's speech to Skyler at the beginning of 'End Times'. Walt refuses to enter protective DEA custody at Hank's home with the rest of the family, and in explaining this to Skyler, appears ready to take responsibility for his deeds and to face the fact that he will probably die in his effort against Gus:

> I have lived under the threat of death for a year now. And because of that, I have made choices. [. . .] I alone should suffer the consequences of those choices. No-one else. And those consequences – they're coming. No more prolonging the inevitable.

The arrangement of the ultimate showdown between Walt and Gus, who are competing not only for survival and dominance in their ruthless trade but also for Jesse's loyalty, is then played out around the suspected poisoning of Jesse's own surrogate son, Brock. That Walt does little to earn but instead must violently force his intimacy with Jesse is seen in his pivotal winning of the younger man's trust when Jesse confronts Walt at his home. In a measure of Walt's unsuitability as a figure required to keep safe the commitments needed to bond a family, the White's living room is now a dark and paranoid space, barricaded against an enveloping sense of suspicion and threat that might erupt into fatal violence from any direction and at any moment.

And that fatal violence appears to visit now, in the guise of Walt's former partner, who aims at Walt his own snub-nose pistol earlier intended for his planned close-up killing of Gus. (That it is *this* possible shooting that might deliver the pistol's Checkovian payoff seems to recognise our desires for the closure of a neat plot, while rendering a caution against such desires by offering their satisfaction in a deadly form of unintended consequence.) Against Jesse's accusations that he is responsible for Brock's poisoning – by lifting and using the ricin cigarette – Walt pulls the psychological lever of Jesse's now-dormant wishes for vengeance against Gus's season three murder of Andrea's brother, a crime against which Walt at the time displayed no natural opposition. 'Who do you know who's okay with using children?' he asks. 'Jesse, who do you know who's allowed children to be murdered?' That Walt's trust of Jesse is premised on violence is suggested when he seizes control of the situation by forcing Jesse's hand, pressing the pistol barrel between his own eyes and daring Jesse to shoot. (Does Walt's gamble rest on an intuitive sense that his own cold lethality is missing in Jesse?) Walt's trust is repaid in Jesse's inability to pull the trigger. Now convinced of Gus's guilt, Jesse makes to leave with the plan of killing him, but finds the door locked – he is stuck in Walt's living room trap. The momentary delay allows Walt to offer his help with the assassination, a gesture of apparent solidarity that usefully ties Jesse's project to his own.

Walt's capacity to exploit Jesse's grief is plumbed even further in the way that Jesse's love towards Andrea and Brock becomes crucial to Walt's plot against Gus. Despite now being estranged from Andrea's family by their hazy suspicions of his responsibility for Brock's condition, Jesse maintains a devoted vigil in a public corridor of the hospital. Jesse's continued presence there disrupts the superlab's schedule and motivates Gus's visit to speak with him in the hospital's chapel. In the following sequence we see how this allows Walt to plant a pipe bomb under Gus's car. Here again Walt treats the love and devotion of others as merely planks to be yoked to the building of his deadly plans, complicating any simple sense that the season's closing drama squarely pits his heroic underdog against the merciless instrumentalism of Gus.

The chapel scene further blurs easy distinctions between the two opponents. An air of menacingly restrained violence surrounds Gus as he meets Jesse, and it is deepened by Gus's seemingly remorseless indifference to Brock's plight, seen in his unmoved response to the news of the young boy's poisoning. (On first viewing, this of course serves as a suspicious marker of Gus's plausible guilt.) Yet these overt tones are balanced against the patient calm with which Gus graciously accepts the cost of the lost batch, while allowing Jesse a generous reprieve: rather than being violently forced back to work, he may return when he is ready, 'next week'. The residual menace is felt when Jesse flinches as Gus raises his hands to Jesse's shoulders. But the apparent intimidation also extends Gus's condolence, a gesture of sympathetic accommodation that gently collects Jesse under Gus's wing and into his debt.

In the suspenseful closing sequence of 'End Times', Walt's attempt to cleanly kill Gus with the car bomb is frustrated by Gus's almost animal responsiveness to the world around him. Walking towards his car, Gus is stopped by something in the distance he cannot see, but nevertheless senses as a threat. After a stilled moment of consideration he turns and walks away. In 'Face Off', Gus's sensitivity to danger and risk will only be overcome by the weakness of his need for recognition from Hector Salamanca. And it is through Jesse's understanding of this need, gleaned by witnessing Gus torment Hector in 'Crawl Space', that leads he and Walt to arrange the meeting at DEA headquarters between Hector and Hank. After Gus has Jesse kidnapped (we will see that it is to make him cook in the superlab under armed guard), Gus is informed of Hector's visit to the DEA. Convinced that his nemesis is now an informant, Gus insists on travelling to the retirement home to kill Hector himself: '*I do this.*'

Gus's approach to the retirement home is presented in a sequence that lingers, eventually in slow-motion, on close-ups of his stilled, enigmatic face, the tone of the shots coloured by an elegiac score that soars loud in the sound mix, powerfully freighting these moments with a sense of monumental importance and arrival.[12] Such finality is felt by Gus himself. Looking over his helpless victim, he offers this assessment: 'A crippled little *rata* [rat] – what a reputation to leave behind. Is that how you want to be remembered?' And, as Gus prepares the syringe with which he will end their decades of interpersonal history, he says: 'Last chance to look at me, Hector.' It is a chance that in his last moments on earth Hector takes, and his unexpected stare has the power to still Gus's hand. The meeting of their eyes suddenly interrupts the tone of deliberate and full culmination, as Gus is captured by a strange confusion in finally receiving what should have been the satisfaction of his desire (Figure 4.2). His perfect mastery of self is undone in those last precious moments when he sees the bomb attached to Hector's ringing bell, and in a reflex of terror and rage gives an almost animal roar. Seconds after the explosion that kills him, Gus – seemingly untouched – walks into the corridor. In the manner of a creature's nerves firing after death, he habitually straightens his tie, as if to preserve the comportment he cemented in life. Yet on Gus's other side facing away from the camera, a nurse shrieks in horror as she rounds the corner and confronts the grotesque that he presents in death.

After Walt rescues Jesse and with his help destroys the superlab, the pair reunite on the rooftop of the hospital carpark as the late afternoon

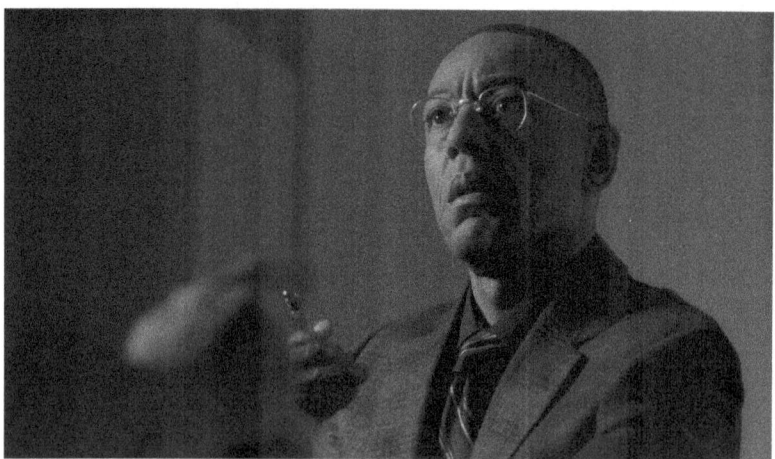

Figure 4.2 'Face Off': Gus undone before Hector's gaze

sun prepares to set over the city. Although the outcome of the negotiations between Sony Pictures Television and AMC meant that this and surrounding scenes would not come to be *Breaking Bad*'s final gestures, they nevertheless continue to impart a strong mood of ending in their way of showing us Walt and Jesse's efforts to arrive at a point of closure. Jesse tells Walt that, fortunately, Brock will recover from his poisoning, and that the young boy's illness was caused innocently enough by his accidentally ingesting berries of the common plant lily of the valley. Each man helps reassure the other that, nevertheless, Gus 'had to go'. Needing to get back to Andrea, Jesse extends his hand in a gesture of farewell. The mutuality that is expressed in this image is not forged here alone but is signalled in the preceding sequence as they together set the superlab to burn, able to work together wordlessly and with bright energy in their shared commitment to undo what they have helped build. Leaving the laundry for the last time, their harmony is captured in the mirrored way they each toss to the side the yellow cloths used to wipe clean their fingerprints at the superlab's entrance, together throwing in the towel while leaving no trace.

Yet in ways that are fitting with season four's messy entanglements of the past with the present, we are reminded that it is a self-deception to see one's life as a finished extract, able to be cleanly lifted above an otherwise ongoing history. When Walt clasps his young partner's hand, the act of reconciliation cannot be coloured by anything but darkly mixed feelings, coming in the shadow of how we have seen that perverse loyalty won. Difficult currents of feeling have been kept in play around the hand that Walt has had in repeatedly shattering and reinforcing their commitment to one another, and this mix of feelings continues to swirl through the next moments in which Walt is left alone on the rooftop. In Jesse's absence he lets out a sharp shudder of seemingly long-held breath and holds his cupped hands against his eyes and forehead; as he controls his breathing we see his eyes are beginning to redden with held-back tears. The hint of a satisfied smile appears to creep into those eyes but Bryan Cranston's typical expressive restraint means we cannot pin down the mix of sentiments that flood Walt in these brief moments. Yet we do feel precisely that a composed act is now gratefully surrendered. This understanding bleeds back across the preceding moments, which are now tainted by Walt's capacity for calculated falsity, leaving the pair's renewed friendship lined by lingering toxicity. That the awful extent of Walt's manipulations remain to be discovered by Jesse is pointed up in the season's final shot, which resembles the echo of *Citizen Kane* at the end of 'Box Cutter'. The first time we watch season four, its reveal of the lily of the valley in Walt's backyard works first and foremost as a stunning confirmation of his capacity for evil, yet the force of the pot plant's reveal persists on repeated viewing as more than a final turn of the screw: it takes its place as another of the season's relics from the past that awaits meaningful discovery, or erasure through destruction.

Walt then remembers to call Skyler. He assures her that the threat to their family is 'over', and in a further declaration of finality offers only this claim as explanation: 'I won.' Walt ends the call without saying goodbye to his wife, and, with a last, satisfied look at Gus's abandoned car, he drives away as the sun sets. Walt's victory, such as it is, consists only in part in his triumph over Gus. What lies at its heart is suggested in Gilligan's design of the season's plot so that in his moment of triumph Walt's family would be gathered together in Hank's living room watching a television news report. This arrangement resembles Hank's hijacking of Walt's birthday party so that the assembled guests could appreciate Hank's success that was broadcast on the nightly news. Now it is Walt's exploits that his family watch in awe. Yet we might sense in this the impermanence of Walt's achievements, a hope that the ascendancy of his secret and terrorising violence cannot hold for too much longer behind his cloak of privacy. As Skyler speaks with Walt we see her come to a radically changed understanding of what her husband is capable of, and so therefore a radically changed understanding of the kind of person he is: 'Was this you?' she asks. This is only the dawning of a clear view of Walt, and one that is far from being made public, but it at least moves in the direction of an unmasking. And, in the background, we can hear the news reports continue to unfold the still-breaking story of Gus Fring's death, and its dismantling of the face and name he left behind.

Conclusion: Facing Completion in Season Five

This book has aimed to make clear an appreciative understanding of the artistry that is manifest in *Breaking Bad*. I noted at the outset that the purpose of my attention and writing is guided by Christopher Ricks's summary of William Empson's aim as a critic. Here again are those steering words: 'The idea was not so much to show someone that a poem is good, as to go some way towards showing how it comes to be good, so very good'.[1] I can comfortably predict, on the basis of enough encounters with friends and colleagues and students whose views of *Breaking Bad* do not line up with mine, that not all readers will find full agreement with my appreciation for Vince Gilligan's show. Despite this, my conviction remains that the aspects of *Breaking Bad* that are described in the pages of this book are materially verifiable.

This means that the details of my interpretation may be tested against, to adapt V. F. Perkins's words, 'the reader's memory and renewed experience'[2] of the series. Perkins further suggests an important criterion for arriving at a judgement of any particular interpretation that has been offered, a criterion relevant to this book's interests in the opportunities that serial television drama affords for achieving expression and meaning through part–whole relations. Reflecting on his analysis of a fragment from Max Ophuls's *Caught* (1948), Perkins notes that an account of a film's elements 'can never constitute a description of the whole'.[3] So, in addition to testing a reading's plausibility in terms of the accuracy with which it describes the elements upon which the interpretation rests, 'there is a further judgment to be made, of the degree to which the whole is illuminated by the critic's account of the parts and of the logic of their configuration'.[4]

How to take *Breaking Bad* as a whole – the issue of how the show's completeness might bear on our sense of it – became an especially live question following the mid-2011 agreement between Vince Gilligan,

Sony Pictures Television, and AMC to end the series with a fifth, final season of two eight-episode parts. In the introduction to this book, I raised the problem that the 'flux' of serial television storytelling poses for coherence as a criterion. 'How do we judge a television work's unity,' ask Jacobs and Peacock, 'if it is open-ended, changing and building across episodes, still in flux? How can we make decisive discriminations of a particular moment if its relationship to the (incomplete) whole is as yet undecided or undeclared?'[5] Further to this, we may ask a related question: If a series' still-unfolding flux might somewhat relieve the pressures of accounting for the settled place of a part within the whole, how do our obligations shift once the entire series has been decisively and – as in the case of *Breaking Bad* – deliberately brought to a state of finished completion? That is to say, to what extent should the closure of the ending now bear the burden of illuminating the whole?

Writing as the second part of season five first went to air in 2013, Corey Creekmur noted *Breaking Bad*'s apparent invitation for viewers to anticipate or expect such illuminating closure:

> *Breaking Bad* has never shied away from indulging in the pulpy pleasures of cliffhangers and plot twists, nor has it (like a few notorious shows) frustrated viewers by perversely withholding satisfying answers to the enigmas it poses. Like most good crime fiction writers, the creators of *Breaking Bad* understand that the enjoyable anxiety of delay is tolerated insofar as it yields the regular *satisfaction of resolution*, of both big and small puzzles.[6]

Yet, for Sean O'Sullivan at least, the 'satisfaction of resolution' is antithetical to the art of serial television:

> 'Satisfaction' speaks, among other things, to the values of unity, harmony, and fully integrated design – values that champion precisely the forms of art that serial narrative works against. Unity and harmony represent rote norms that privilege the well-made play, the symmetrical picture, the clockwork story. Serial narrative, at its most compelling, taps into those norms as its raw construction materials in order to create its own modes and rhythms, its distinctive commitment to the multiple rather than the single, the broken rather than the whole, that which frustrates rather than that which completes.[7]

These tensions – between the potential fulfilment of completion and the frustrations of persisting partiality – become especially acute around the ending of a serial. O'Sullivan notes that it is at this point that 'cries for satisfaction are at their loudest and most insistent'. But, he goes on to ask, 'does the need for satisfaction not run counter to the fragment, the partial, to the incomplete that are the defining elements of serial narrative?'[8]

In light of this view of what serial fiction best offers – leaving aside for the moment the question of whether or not we would support it – does the ending of *Breaking Bad* represent a failure of serial storytelling nerve? In the lead-up to the final season and in the days and weeks following the finale itself, Gilligan regularly spoke of his desire to tie up his narrative in a clean finish, sometimes evoking the enigmatic ending of *The Sopranos* as a picture of what he would *not* do.[9] And the closing sequence of *Breaking Bad*'s final episode ('Felina', 5.16) speaks strongly to this ambition to achieve resolution and cohesive structural unity across the show as a complete whole. This is in the way that the show's ending is shaped so that it closes a circle, the line of which was first drawn by the opening sequence of the pilot episode, the sense of closure further heightened by a play of tensions between that which is suggested to be open and unresolved, and which then seems to become neatly tied-off.

Episode one of season five's first part ('Live Free or Die', 5.1) begins with a strange and inexplicable flashforward cold open in which we see a bearded and haggard Walt having breakfast at a Denny's restaurant, arranging the bacon on his plate to mark his fifty-second birthday, another iteration of what, in the pilot episode, was shown to be an annual series or tradition for Walt. The sequence ends with Walt receiving a car from the gun dealer (played by Jim Beaver) we met back in season four's 'Thirty-Eight Snub' (4.2); in the trunk of the car is an M60 machine gun and crates of ammunition. The mystery of this weapon's purpose persists across season five, providing no more than a hazy promise of some spectacularly violent and destructive future confrontation. (We are once more reminded of the gun's presence in the opening episode of the season's second part, 'Blood Money' [5.9], bringing up again its importance to the climactic events that the narrative is moving us towards.) As the final episode unfolds, we might begin to piece together a vague sense of a plausible scenario for the gun's use, as Walt is set for a standoff with the neo-Nazis who have kidnapped Jesse. Yet the M60's role as part of an incomplete 'puzzle' persists as we see Walt strangely rig the machine gun to the control mechanism that he has removed from his garage door. At the height of Walt's confrontation with the neo-Nazis, he activates his planted device – the trunk of the car springs open and the machine gun lets loose upon Jesse's captors, relentlessly pumping round after round from left-to-right in its merciless, mechanically determined arc.

So these disconnected parts of object and dramatic scenario are here brought together in such a way that the odd, almost Rube Goldberg device of the autonomous M60 can be seen to emblematise *Breaking Bad*'s frequent operation as a piece of improvised storytelling, a determined but makeshift clockwork contrived on-the-run. (And this unlikely mechanism is more plausible if we remember Walt's eager line to Skyler in season two's 'Down' [2.4], in which he attempts to find some impetus for conversation with her by announcing that he has spent the day fixing the garage door opener; that Walt's engineering of his deadly device can be connected with a seemingly throwaway part of a much earlier episode deepens the M60's place in the show's self-reflection on serial television and improvised cohesion.) Further to this sense of perfectly formed clockwork is the way that in pursuing this final project Walt risks his life in an effort to save Jesse's, and, in the series' final moments, dies at his own hand, bleeding to death from an M60 bullet wound to the gut, his criminal identity now fully exposed, surrendered, and his dead body left for the swarming police. All of this might be read as asking us to recognise, and perhaps take satisfaction in, something like the completion of what Walt fails to do in the opening sequence, in which we see him abandon any commitment to Jesse above himself, refuse a moment of final confession, and then be interrupted by outside chance (the safety catch) when he puts a pistol to his head and pulls the trigger. In a telling detail, Walt now shares Walter Neff's fatal stomach wound – both of which bleed beneath the men's jackets – as if to suggest that the initial distance between the two characters, which was marked in Walt's refusal to acknowledge his crimes and their 'deep down' motivation, has now been closed.[10]

Do these points of structural patterning and seemingly closed rhyming signal something like *Breaking Bad*'s fully cohesive 'unity' that any satisfactory interpretation of the series should reflect? Given this book's argument about the series' interest in tensions between the unified and the fragmentary, and the show's frequent reflections upon the kinds of self-deceptions and rejections of human actuality that a commitment to fixed personal unity and complete autonomy often involve, how could a last gesture so seemingly invested in wholeness and final cohesion not represent the show's betrayal of itself, some kind of ultimate failure to understand the meaning of what it has been doing this whole time? A way of responding to this question is suggested to me by Stanley

Cavell's consideration of how an interpretation could be brought to its own state of completeness. That is to say, how, in the face of multiple possible meanings, 'one may end a reading'. 'Completeness,' Cavell writes, 'is not a matter of providing *all* interpretations but a matter of seeing one of them *through*.'[11] Seeing through the reading of *Breaking Bad* prepared and put forward so far in this book – seeing it through to the end of *Breaking Bad* – renders the meaning of the show's final season and of its final gestures rather differently to the way I have described them above, as primarily expressive of a finally sealed cohesion, or wholeness (of the work, and of our understanding of the characters presented by it). Those qualities of the fifth season are of course important to our sense of it, and of *Breaking Bad* more generally, yet they are not manifest in anything like a pure or uncomplicated way. The final season, and its relation to the rest of *Breaking Bad*, should instead be interpreted in terms of the many ways in which its reflections on serial artistic practice (including *Breaking Bad*'s own tradition of that practice) puts any sense of unified completion, or desire for it, in considerable tension with those forces of time and history that mitigate against the wish for our lives to achieve some ultimate or perfect form and meaning. Absent the space for anything like a thorough excavation and working-over of the sixteen-episode season in all of its fine meshing of dramatic event and stylistic detail, let me more modestly draw the book to a close by offering a partial series of observations towards a particular view of the final season, and of some of the ways in which that view asks us to cast our eye and mind more widely across the show, and some aspects of its significance to us. (I hope at most to offer a few remarks that will provide some useful ground, and mark out some trails, upon which to pursue further appreciation of the final season, not only leaving room for but hopefully also inspiring future critical voices, by which so much of *Breaking Bad* still waits to be addressed; like Perkins reflecting on his study of *The Magnificent Ambersons* (Orson Welles, 1942), I have not found room for some of *Breaking Bad*'s 'most famous and stirring' moments, and have regretfully needed to 'omit favourite vignettes'.[12])

I begin by taking the lead of the season opener itself. I have already summarised the cold open of 'Live Free or Die', noting the repetition of the bacon ritual that partly serves as a temporal marker providing firm narrative orientation – we are two years since Walt received his cancer diagnosis the day after his fiftieth birthday. Yet Walt claims the restaurant's offer of a free birthday breakfast by presenting a New Hampshire driver's licence, one in the name of 'Mr Lambert'. So in addition to the mysteries of Walt's degraded appearance and of the heavy machine gun in his car, the juxtaposition of a newly assumed name with an established family ritual – performed in an elegiac manner in a context in which it is unintelligible to others – suggests at the outset of the final season a concern with the persistence of meaningful continuity placed in tension with its apparent breakdown. This tension is to be understood in relation to how the birthday ritual and the signs of Walt's returned illness (his gaunt face and neck, the prescription pills he swallows in the bathroom) raise again and make pressing the issue of Walt's mortality, his imminently terminal condition that has been the catalyst for the series' drama since the beginning, even if its force has at times diminished.[13]

The pressing sense of a terminal condition is further felt in the specific ways this flashforward cold open achieves its particular fatalistic air. Walt's driver's licence and his conversation with the restaurant's waitress let us know that he is returning to Albuquerque after some absence, that he has a climactic appointment here. And the M60 machine gun, which he doesn't know how to use (he asks the gun dealer if there is 'an instruction manual'), suggests that this appointment will be one of such violence and danger that we doubt his capacity to survive, giving a suicidal colouring to this glimpse of where the series might end up. Jim Beaver is aptly attuned to this mood in the way he plays the gun dealer's parting words to Walt. 'Well,' the character says, 'good luck, I guess.' More than the ambivalence of the written words, the actor finds a modulation of voice that speaks to a sense of fatality that evokes something like recognition of impotence in the face of events that are beyond influence or control. Beaver discusses the execution of his and Walt's underhand business with a strong, unyielding fullness carried deep in the throat. But then for his final words the actor moves to a tone that retains the distinctly gravelled texture of his voice, while lowering the volume to a whisper that strains at the top of the mouth. In the gun dealer's pause after he says 'Well . . .', we see and hear an otherwise eloquent man finding himself without ready words, and this brief moment of hesitation joins with Beaver's vocality to express a tension between some need to acknowledge the moment's weight, and an awkward uncertainty as to what could count as an adequate response to it.

A similar tension of feeling is evoked when, following his meeting with the gun dealer, Walt seems stopped by something – as if struck by an unarticulated thought – as he walks past his uneaten breakfast. After what seems a moment's consideration (but what is it that he is considering, exactly?) he leaves the waitress a $100 bill. We are shown this in a close-up that tracks the money as Walt quite deliberately takes it from his wallet and tucks it underneath his breakfast plate so that, in an echo of the inheritance theme discussed in the last chapter, it will be found after he has left. The choice to lavish such attention on the gesture freights it with importance, while our sense of its precise meaning for Walt remains obscure. And whatever significance Walt's choice to leave this money carries for him, he must surely be in some way reconciled to the fact that this meaning can only remain private, unable to be shared with the money's recipient, who is a stranger likely to understand it as no more than an instance of random and inexplicable generosity. (Or, perhaps more positively, she might imagine or believe that the money holds some deeper meaning, but will know nothing of that meaning itself – there is no firm meaning for her to grasp, rather only an air of 'meaningfulness'.) This moment's purpose in the design of the season opener emerges in relation to the recurrence of Walt's cancer and the suicidal lining of his return to Albuquerque, evoking the desire that a looming end be met in a way that might carry some kind of special meaningful weight, while colouring that desire with a deep uncertainty as to the very possibility of imbuing one's departing gesture with such significance.

Our sense of all of this is of course largely shaped by our knowledge that the show itself is coming to its own deliberate end, and so the narrative and stylistic choices that we are seeing unfold are available to be read in terms of what might seem to be their responsiveness to, or their acknowledgement of, that fact. This aspect of our involvement in season five is related to, but distinct from, the way in which an interpretation of season four needs to take some account of how that season's ending was to a great extent shaped so that it might have provided a possible conclusion for the whole series (while still holding in abeyance a range of avenues down which to pursue a hoped-for continuation). The fifth season was instead entirely conceived and produced towards the *certainty* of the series' ultimate ending, rather than that ending's possibility or likelihood. I believe we can fruitfully imagine that in facing this certain end, those involved in the creation of *Breaking Bad*'s fifth and final season would have found themselves in something resembling an artistic analogue to Walt's terminal condition from which the series' drama first emerged, a condition in which the sense that one is 'out of time' places upon one's remaining actions an intensified pressure to make things 'count'.

I want to suggest that this intensified pressure, this anxiety around the need to make things count – really matter in some kind of ultimate way – suffuses *Breaking Bad*'s final season. And this concern suffuses the season in forms that condense what has come to be one of the most persistent subjects of the series' drama from the very beginning: namely, the problem of purpose and meaning as aspirations in a historical period in which some crucial aspects of any secure basis for confidently pursuing or achieving such aspirations are felt to have given way; imagine moving to place one's foot on a rung of support below – out of sight but nevertheless strongly sensed – yet on placing one's weight there is found to be only air, a phantom or ghost of what used to be a solid structure upon which to stand and climb. In this book's introduction I identified this historical period as the era of seemingly ever-accelerating industrialised modernity. A characteristic of this period that helps cast light on *Breaking Bad* is its increasing complexity of social and commercial and technological organisation, such that an intensified degree of specialisation is required of individuals whose lives take shape within these structures. A plausible consequence of living in such a world is an attendant fragmentation of the self. 'Might not the division of individual lives into watertight compartments,' asks Tzvetan Todorov, 'be an understandable response to the progressive compartmentalization of the world at large?'[14] Such a condition can be thought to undermine any stable sense of personal coherence – a sense captured in the commonplace want to somehow be able to say 'who one really is', or 'what one's life really stands for' – while at the same time this fragmented condition conceivably amplifies one's desire to achieve such unity. And along with this psychological fragmentation of individual subjectivity, a technological instrumentalism has 'pervaded' the realm of intersubjective relations between people.[15] One potential consequence of these developments is a transformation of how individuals are able to bond to one another and to a community, those commitments threatening to become increasingly contingent upon their capacity to serve some instrumental purpose, to satisfy the material demands of the present moment. So absorbed in the present, lacking confident commitment to something that will outlast one's own existence, an individual's sense of being tightly bound into a historical continuity that links past and future becomes acutely vulnerable to erosion.

This potential breakdown of historical continuity – what Christopher Lasch has called 'the waning sense of historical time'[16] – is an implicit subject of Todorov's analysis of industrialised modernity against which I have seen fit to read *Breaking Bad*. Todorov undertakes his analysis within a study of the Nazi and Soviet concentration camps, the camps shown to manifest in an extreme form what are otherwise ordinary and inescapable aspects of modern life, but which might otherwise pass unnoticed amidst the conduct of the everyday. 'In the camps, however,' writes Todorov,

> where it is sometimes necessary to choose between holding on to one's bread and holding on to one's dignity, between starving physically and starving morally, everything is out in the open. [. . .] The deprivation of some is hastened and is there for all to see; but the betterment of others [through defiant acts of care and good] is also intensified.[17]

(*Breaking Bad*'s melodramatic character, the frequent extremity of its dramatic scenarios, needs to be understood in a similar way.)

And so it is in eyewitness accounts of the camps that we get, in awful clarity, pictures of instrumentalism and personal fragmentation combining to effect – in certain instances, though certainly not all – the complete breakdown of those fundamental bonds between people through which meaningful human continuity is achieved across generational time. It is in the camps that all human activity seems reduced to the mere calculation of momentary individual survival. 'Even the closest family ties were vulnerable in this fight [for survival],' Todorov writes.

> [Tadeusz] Borowski, for example, tells how a mother, to save her own life, pretends not to know her child. And Elie Wiesel, another Auschwitz survivor, describes in *Night* how a son snatches a piece of bread from the hands of his father, and he speaks of the relief he felt when his own father died, because it increased his own chances for survival.[18]

The situation in the camps was of the greatest extremity, an imposed starvation designed to reduce humanity to its most animal aspect. Yet these stories nevertheless speak with power to the loss of commitments between parents and children in a context that no longer seems to make available any real way of carrying into the future what has been built between people in the past. The eclipse of a person's sense of connection with past and future may leave them bereft of any meaning or purpose beyond attaining whatever necessities or satisfactions the immediate moment might provide. Todorov captures this futureless condition when he quotes the recollections of a man tasked with cleaning out the trains upon the arrival of prisoners at Auschwitz. The man explains why he and others remorselessly pilfered for private use or trade whatever things of value those doomed people had left behind (food, personal possessions): 'we had only one thought: why not take advantage of the last moments of life since everything else already belongs to the land of dreams?'[19]

'Everything else already belongs to the land of dreams.' By evoking a sense that whatever exists beyond the limits of one's life is not a possibly real destination – that the fact and imminence of one's mortality means that the world has in effect already ended – these words speak to a loss of confidence or belief in something to which a person can commit themselves in such a way that their actions might achieve some 'higher' meaning or purpose, beyond just the material satisfaction of their own life, some sense of what one's activities are all 'for', in the end, an end that lies beyond our own. Robert Pippin, considering the anxiety of meaning in Henry James's fiction, raises the question as to 'whether and if so how a certain community could be said to suffer a loss of meaning, in the way we sometimes speak of that happening to an individual'. And Pippin then gives us this vivid picture of what such a condition may be understood to consist in at the individual level:

> We usually mean thereby that some teleological structure has lost its authority for the individual and no longer seems, or is experienced as, worthy of allegiance. A hierarchy of ends, whereby this was important for that, and that for some higher goal, and so on, has broken down in some way, or some crucial element in it has failed (can no longer command allegiance) and caused all else to topple over. Accordingly, the desires animated by and animating such a structure have also simply failed. It is not easy to find the words to describe how such a thing could happen (that nothing could now seem 'worth wanting'), but it would be foolish to deny it happens.[20]

It is the art of *Breaking Bad* to turn the form of serial television drama in ways that address precisely such a condition, as being our condition, and as being necessarily caught up in the continuities and interruptions of historical time experienced at a personal and psychological level, at the level of characters living-out and reflecting upon their personal histories as these take shape through intimate, ongoing connections with other people, both the still-living and the now-dead. The densely serialised yet seasonally contained form of US television drama series that rose to such prominence and success in the early decades of the twenty first century provides a vital and rich means for the fictional exploration of historical time in such a way.[21] This is, in part, because the improvised realisation of character and identity as a provisional matter of practical meaning, and the retrospective dimension of such meaning itself – that the meaning of a particular choice is available only in retrospect, and that this meaning is itself open to retrospective revision, such that what one took a certain choice to mean at a particular point in time is not what it comes to mean now – these aspects of human identity and historical meaning are more than a potential subject for the drama of these series: they are available to be made a constituent part of the creative practice of their making, and of the imaginative experience of their viewing.[22] In *Breaking Bad*'s final season, all of this takes the form of a persistent internalisation of the series' impending completion, its own sense of an ending, and the intensified pressure upon meaning that this brings about. This pressure can be felt in the ways that some of the final season's most crucial and memorable sequences find their interest and force in matters of purposefulness, retrospection, perdurance, and death.

The storyline of season five's first part largely turns around Walt's quest for ownership over what is left in the wake of his killing of Gus Fring, and of the subsequent disintegration of everything that Fring had built. This effort itself depends upon Walt's capacity to first attract and then keep the allegiance of both Jesse and Mike, in spite of all that has passed between the three of them. Jesse's pitch to Mike in 'Madrigal' (5.2) is telling as to the absence of much purpose in Jesse's life, which the work might well fill: 'we figured, "why not?" [. . .] lot of money to be made . . .' But Mike is resistant, effectively retired (to his armchair, to drink beer and watch old movies), although by the episode's end he commits to Walt's scheme, after the DEA – led by Hank – seize the two million dollars that Mike has stored in an offshore account in the name of his granddaughter Kaylee.

The DEA's investigation of Fring's death and the exposure of his drug empire publicly validate Hank's suspicions and ratify his skill, intelligence, and tenacity as a detective. Yet his continuing desire to definitively fix and expose the ultimate identity of Heisenberg is not shared by his bureaucratic superiors, who are pleased by what they see as an effectively closed case – and on this basis Hank is promoted to Assistant Special Agent in Charge of the Albuquerque office. Accepting the post (and the prestige and pay that comes with it) Hank must abandon his incomplete quest, instead becoming immersed in the minutiae of allocating and balancing budgets, payrolls, fundraising. His remove from the immediacy of law enforcement is marked when he is given a dressing-down for personally serving Mike a search warrant, and, when the blue meth emerges once again, for continuing to spend money on Heisenberg-related surveillance of Mike.

Alongside these developments of Walt's re-emergent meth enterprise – now directly owned and 'controlled' by Walt, Jesse, and Mike – is the story of Skyler's growing capacity to believe and face Walt's murderousness and terrorism that she indirectly witnessed at the end of season four ('Face Off', 4.13). An ongoing dramatic issue since the beginning of season three has been the question of what Skyler is prepared to surrender in order to acknowledge, or to avoid, the fact of who Walt has become; whether she can accept that this fact in some sense destroys everything in her life 'as it was', or whether she must somehow pretend that, no matter what she or Walt has done, the life of their family can be preserved 'as it were'. For the first few episodes of the season Skyler is effectively paralysed, as in episode one's closing image ('Live Free or Die'), of Skyler in rigid flinch from Walt as he closes around her in a calculated embrace that shifts his sin on to her ('I forgive you', he whispers). Skyler breaks from her static and effectively mute condition in episode four ('Fifty-One', 5.4). The catalyst for this shift is a moment early in the episode when, at the family dinner table, Walt says to Walt Jr, 'and if you show me just a modicum of respect, maybe I'll teach *you* one day.' Skyler's mood of crushed despair sharpens to cold horror at these words – we might imagine that in hearing them she clearly sees a family and a future not worth having, one in which Walt is a tutor to his children. And so Skyler sets about splintering the family, first – fitting the theme of education – by suggesting that Walt Jr be sent away to a distant school, and later – interrupting Walt's deceitful birthday dinner reminiscence upon the cancer-forged bond of intimacy between he and Skyler – by walking into the freezing cold swimming pool as if in a spectacle of suicidal depression. That it is this act that succeeds in (temporarily) removing the children to the care of Hank and Marie suggests that the only form Skyler's acknowledgement could properly take would be one in which Skyler herself publicly assumed her part of responsibility for the ruin and severance of the family, the effective orphaning of Walt Jr and Holly, her suicidal gesture being intended to have Hank and Marie see not Walt but *Skyler* as the potential menace of the children's healthy upbringing. It is finally the seeing-through of an admission – both to herself and to Walt if not fully to Hank and Marie – that as a couple she and Walt are no longer fit to participate in the raising of the young, not fit to safeguard the future in this way.

Overcoming the past collapse of a family unit and rebuilding its future is further at stake in the brief storyline concerning Jesse's reunion with

Andrea and Brock. This part of the season effectively takes its shape in only a few short vignettes in episode three, 'Hazard Pay' (5.3), in which we catch glimpses of Jesse and Andrea's restored domestic life. Whatever reunion took place between the couple occurs in a scene that we do not see. This elision helps us encounter the sudden reintroduction of their resumed life together in a manner that is akin to Jesse's later description to Walt of his recovered situation: 'instant family', the word 'instant' here working with the elision to evoke a kind of timelessness, a neat excision from the past and its accumulations of memory, and the marks these leave upon and between people. When we later hear Jesse pledge to Walt his commitment to a future with Andrea and Brock, it is in a living room that advertises a picture of the domestic everyday such as we earlier see Jesse and Andrea inhabiting. But here it is presented as an assumed domesticity (as in the wearing of a guise), one commandeered by the toxic criminal trespass of Walt and Jesse's tented mobile meth lab (unfixed and traceless against the rootedness of a home in which to live), the chiaroscuro exposure further pitching the house around them into blank shapes of darkness, to the extent that we see only a black void behind Walt as he interrogates the depth of Jesse's preparedness to share himself with Andrea – to trust in her the things that he has done and so the person he knows himself to be. It is at first touching to see these two in what starts out as ordinary and genuinely friendly conversation, such as two people might have if they were unburdened by history. But the surrounding void suggests that for these two men the mise-en-scéne of family and the home can perhaps only be something like a veil or cover, a theatrical set, no more than living room pieces on an otherwise black stage.

Jesse's crisis seems to be whether he can trust Andrea with the fact that he is a murderer, whether he can trust a relationship of respect and love to survive such a revelation. But early in season four ('Thirty-Eight Snub'), Andrea confronts Jesse with the thick envelope of cash that she found stuffed in her letterbox the night that Jesse disappeared from her home and that her brother's murderers were themselves gunned down. That she brings this money to Jesse's door, and brings with it this story of the money's discovery, shows that she knows where it comes from, that it in some way comes from killing and that he is the likely killer. She pockets this knowledge when she pockets the money and builds from it her new life with Brock, into which Jesse later steps. In light of this, Jesse's dilemma is less to do with the question of revealing his past to Andrea as such (she must already know it, or enough of it), and more to do with the question of what one's respect and love could be worth if they must be couched in such a mutual self-deceit. Later in 'Hazard Pay', Jesse sits slouched on the sofa and watches Andrea and Brock play a video racing game. His mood is distant from theirs, perhaps because he might see in them a reflection of his own earlier attempts at distraction from nihilistic despair, finding in their mutual enjoyment of the game only a picture of his own cravings for sound and light and rush as routes of escape from a shadow of pointlessness. It is not a footing for the faith that he needs.

In the episode's disturbing final scene, following Mike's economics lesson that carves into allotments the thick bricks of cash earned from the first cook, Walt asks Jesse how he is feeling. Jesse tells Walt that it is over with Andrea, as if to continue the earlier living room closeness, and begins to explain why the relationship failed. Walt cuts him off. 'I meant *this*,' he says, 'how are you feeling about the *money*?' Walt lifts his duffel bag of cash, and in the heft of his clenched fist we register the weight it has for him. Jesse tries to encourage Walt to find satisfaction in getting 'a bigger piece of the pie', and in being 'owners, not employees'. But this only moves Walt to reflect on what seems to be for him the persistently troubling thought of what Gus meant by slitting Victor's throat in front of him. 'Maybe he flew too close to the sun?' Walt wonders, almost to himself. 'Got his throat cut.' The episode ends on Jesse watching Walt walk to his car, and in the young man's uncomprehending stare we see reflected our own unsatisfied desire for a clear grasp of significance. The garage door shutter rolls down a relentless machine as Jesse turns slightly, as if further towards introspection, and with a final crash of the gates we are plunged into the dark.

Early in this book's first chapter, I noted a small moment in the first act of the pilot episode in which Walt, after using his exercise machine in the half-decorated nursery, pauses to 'measure his progress'. This interest carries on across the seasons in persistent images of characters hanging on the outcome of drugs being weighed and their purity calibrated, exact sums calculated and projected, stacks of banknotes counted and parcelled out, often coming up short in Walt's view, not measuring what there is but rather what there could or should have been, such as in Mike's allocation of the groups' increasingly dwindling share of the gross at the end of 'Hazard Pay'. And in the final episode of the season's first part, 'Gliding Over All' (5.8), the collection or accumulation of money is made the focus of an expressive register around weight as an index of meaning and purpose, or of their absence.

The episode is distinctive within the series for its covering of a three-month span of time, much of that passage elided by the central

'Crystal Blue Persuasion' montage that expresses the repetitive rhythms of life that unfold within Walt's now fully secured and protected scheme cooking meth for the overseas market of the Czech Republic. And the episode comes to be coloured by a sense of the characters' exhaustion and resignation in the face of apparent futility and endlessness. The other major montage sequence in the episode depicts the execution of Walt's plan – assisted by the neo-Nazi crew of Todd's uncle – to wipe-out Mike's imprisoned 'guys' whose paid-for silence is threatened when in the previous episode ('Say My Name', 5.7) the DEA arrests the lawyer responsible for the payments, who then gives them a potential lead on Mike. In the wake of these gruesome killings we see Hank arrive home from work. He barely speaks to Marie (who kindly tries to lift his mood with offers of Chinese take-out), and then retires to the bar to share a drink with Walt, who is visiting Holly, still in the in-laws' care. After first sitting in silence, Hank quietly says, 'I've been thinking about this sum-mer job I used to have.' As a college student he would daily trek into the woods to mark trees for logging, gradually making his way through grid squares lined on a map, his words evoking an image of a measur-able and concrete task contained by clear limits, and the securities of repetition. 'Every day,' he says, 'I'd go back, hike in, pick up where I left off.' The aim of the work, says Hank, was just 'to make a few bucks, buy beer'. He complains of the sunburn, mosquitoes. But then he offers this: 'I've been thinking about that job more and more lately. Maybe I should have enjoyed it more. Tagging trees is a lot better than chasing monsters.' Here the duty to confront and strive to contain a spreading and shapeless evil is felt by Hank to be a burden that perhaps is not his to shoulder, that it might be better shed for the private enjoyment of a solitary task pursued deep in the woods, as if alone in the world, responsible only to one's own aesthetic pleasures. And even that pleas-ure is something that has gone irrecoverably missing for Hank, only desirable too late in hindsight, veiled at the time by the discomforting realities of work and the more prosaic payment of beer. And both these ends overlook another, quite different potential purpose to the summer job, one that goes unmentioned by both men but is available to our eyes. Visible throughout the house in which Walt and Hank sit and talk are numerous furniture pieces and architectural features (such as book-shelves, tables, chairs, doors, arches, and supporting columns) that are made from solid timber.

Towards the episode's end, Skyler shows Walt exactly what he has been working for: an immovable pallet-load of cash kept in a secret stor-age locker, a volume impossible to reasonably launder and so unable to be safely spent, but which must nonetheless be regularly tended against corrosion by silverfish and mould. Walt's alienation from the worth of this monument to his work is captured in Skyler's remark that she hasn't been able to count the money – even by weight – because the face value of the bundled notes is uncertain. Following this, a montage depicts Walt's visit to the oncologist in a way that suggests his cancer's recurrence. Washing his hands after using the bathroom, Walt is stopped by what he sees in the metal paper towel dispenser – the indentations left by his own fist when he pummelled the object after being told of his remission in season two's '4 Days Out' (2.9), good news that delivered Walt's sentence of having to live with his terrible history.

This moment needs to be understood in relation to various other features of the episode and of the season that prompt both the show's characters and its viewer to reach back and connect the series' 'present' with moments that lie deep in its past. Think for instance of the opening shot of 'Gliding Over All' in which Walt closely regards a briefly settled fly, and the later moment in which Walt tells Skyler he is out of the business in a scene staged to directly resemble that of his season one commitment to chemotherapy ('Gray Matter', 1.5); even more crucial is Hank's climactic discovery of the telling copy of Whitman's *Leaves of Grass*, and later in the season the fatal return to the site of Walt and Jesse's first cook in the desert, in 'To'hajiilee' (5.13) and 'Ozymandias' (5.14). In light of all this, Walt's and our confrontation with an object likely long-since forgotten, but that still bears this evidence of Walt's contact, points out an aspect of *Breaking Bad* that towards the show's end becomes an increasingly pressing interest of the series: its use of long-form serial television's access to the building and recovery of its characters' deep personal histories in order to craft what I want to call a dramatic narrativisation of the traces, or imprints, left by individuals upon the world – and upon those with whom they share it – and of those traces and imprints in turn left upon them.[23]

The show's return to these traces and imprints might be thought of as supporting an idea that unity forms one of the series' principal compositional concerns, an insistence upon connection across time, the persistence of coherent relations between human activity and the world that it builds. Yet, against such a view, the final season might be seen to present a picture of near-total human collapse, such traces becoming unintelligible or disappearing altogether. As if inviting this, the second part of the season was promoted through a roughly one-minute video of time-lapse photography of the landscapes and homes and businesses and city streets in which *Breaking Bad* is set, over which Bryan Cranston reads Percy Bysshe Shelley's 'Ozymandias'. The video is worth noting here for its depiction of a world as if denuded of human presence. Certain of the images (of the exterior of Fring's laundry, the streets of downtown Albuquerque) do indeed depict people going about their lives, yet the use of time-lapse photography, especially in those shots of the city at night, convey such human activity as only a blur, literally an ephemeral trace of light, a ghost of an event since passed, but lingering nevertheless. And outside of these shots we see a world abandoned to an empty nature that is presented in cosmic terms, as existing beyond the timescale of human life and history, measured only in the relentless sedimentation and shaping of the rock faces (against which we hear Walt's screams echo and fade early in 'Ozymandias'), rock that becomes sand to blow against the lengths of coiled barbed wire that we are shown stretch into the desert. The resonant and mysterious charge the images carry is addressed in the apt words of the poem, which raise the question of what human passions may be read as 'stamped on these lifeless things'.

Early in 'Ozymandias' – in what remains one of the series' most distressing moments – Todd's uncle Jack (Michael Bowen) shoots Hank dead upon the sands of To'hajilee. Gomez lies already killed nearby. A hole is then dug in recovering Walt's money that he desperately offered in exchange for Hank's life, and so the bodies of Hank and Gomez are dumped there and covered by the desert. In the wake of this and other unutterably cruel losses, the characters still alive at the end of *Breaking Bad* are left with a world so shattered, their bonds to one another and their views of the past so betrayed and tainted, that it does not seem excessive to say that the show leaves them in a condition that could be described as futureless, bereft of any guiding horizon, or history worth building on. This sounds despairing and pessimistic to a fault. The cruel snuffing-out of hope can be too easily taken as a mark of authorial courage, as if unflinching and clear-eyed in the face of what at times seem delusory beliefs in human possibilities for redemption and grace. Yet *Breaking Bad*'s ultimate commitment to seeing-through the ruination of the world that its characters inhabit does not leave us with anything so simple and mean as a picture of human capacity that has room only for the inevitability of failure.

One of the most moving scenes of the final episode is an unexpected flashback to a moment in Jesse's life that we had not previously witnessed. Cast in a haze of dusk light we see Jesse working intently and alone at carpentry. Slow-motion close-ups match the young man's dedicated attention to the grain of the wood and the fine application of his emerging craftsmanship. We see him lift to his face the wooden box he has built, lingering in the smell of timber and oils. Standing on his own, he cradles what he has made (Figure C.1). In 'Kafkaesque' (3.9), in what is perhaps Aaron Paul's finest moment in the series, Jesse is asked by his rehab counsellor (played by the excellent Jere Burns) what he would spend his life doing if money were no concern. 'I don't know,' Jesse says, 'I guess I would . . . make something?' He then tells the fellow members of his rehab group how, as a high school student, he was prompted to build the box seen in the flashback. Jesse remembers presenting to his teacher his first pitiful, uncommitted effort, and the teacher sincerely asking him, 'Is that the best you can do?' Jesse recalls how, moved by 'the way he said it', he started 'from scratch', and built one more box, and then another, in a process that is described as one of increasing intimacy and care for his creation:

> I built it out of Peruvian walnut, with inlaid zebrawood. It was fitted with pegs – no screws. I sanded it for days, 'til it was smooth as glass. Then I rubbed all the wood with tung oil, so it was rich and dark. It even smelled good. Y'know, you put your nose in it, and breathed in . . . It was perfect.

Later in season three, in the wake of the ruminations upon repetition in 'Fly' (3.10), another flashback shows Jesse and Jane visiting the Georgia

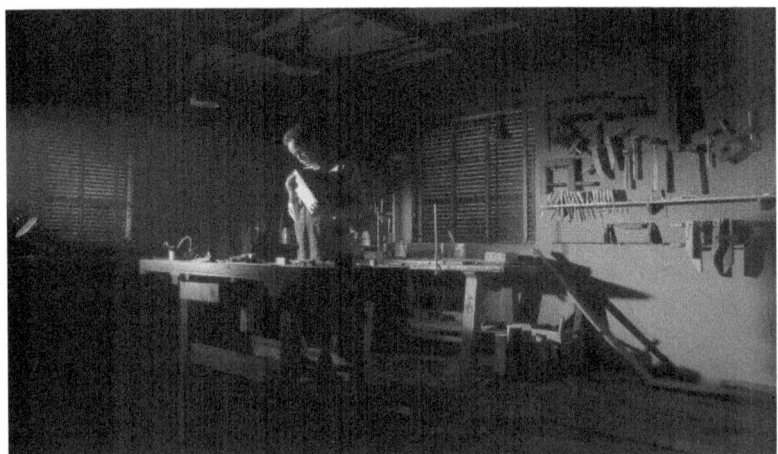

Figure C.1   'Felina': Jesse cradles his 'perfect' object

O'Keeffe museum in Santa Fe ('Abiquiú', 3.11). The couple argue good-heartedly about the motivation behind O'Keeffe's practice of painting apparently mundane subjects – such as the door of her house – over and over again. Jesse can only see a desire for perfection, a hunger to arrive at completeness of form: 'C'mon – that O'Keeffe lady kept trying over, and *over*, until that stupid door was *perfect*.' By contrast, Jane is alive to a different wish held out by the opportunity to repeatedly craft an image of the same subject. 'No,' she says, 'that door was her home, and she loved it. To me, that's about making that feeling last.' Jane stubs out her cigarette in the ashtray of Jesse's car. (Its filter is marked by her pink lipstick, which after her death will catch Jesse's attention in 'Fly'.) At the end of his monologue in 'Kafkaesque', Jesse's counsellor asks him what happened to the box. Jesse tells the group that he gave it to his mother. When the counsellor tries to find some encouragement in Jesse's story, reminding him that 'it's never too late', and offering 'adult extension classes at the local university', Jesse interrupts. 'Y'know, I didn't give the box to my mom,' he says. 'I traded it for an ounce of weed.' The scene ends in a silence broken only by the creaking of the listeners' weight shifting uncomfortably against the wooden folding chairs.

The significance of the box for Jesse's audience is felt to rest in what ultimately comes of it, as if its final place were the mark of its importance. Like them, we greet the picture of Jesse gifting his creation to another person as a saving gesture, one that makes the dedication shown in the box's crafting a symbolic expression and manifestation of the care and love shared between a son and his mother. The exposure of this image as a lie then becomes revelatory of the redemptive promise it carried, as we now experience a crushing of the heart in inverse proportion to its lifting only a moment earlier, as if a dashing of that promise. Yet it lingers as a ghost of what could have been. There are, though, more than phantoms of redemption and good to be found. Jesse's difficult and shameful expression of the truth of what he turned the box into represents the achievement of an honest self-relation before others. And the fact of the box's existence itself testifies to Jesse's capacity to be inspired by the voice of an elder, and to dedicate himself to creating from the world's materials ('Peruvian walnut, with inlaid zebrawood') an object of beauty and a potential emblem of his love for another person. That this potential goes unrealised in the box's commodification is a deep, irrevocable moral failure, and one that speaks to the unavailability of such an achievement – of love, of one's bond to another person – to completion, it being instead preciously vulnerable to the contingencies of loss and betrayal by the wavering of human faith or resolve over time. This speaks to the core of *Breaking Bad*'s art, one in which the persistent possibility of human connectedness is conveyed through irrecoverable moments of failure, of fragmentation and collapse. It is through forms that from a particular distance may impress upon the viewer a certain structural unity that *Breaking Bad* enacts a contrasting human drama within its fiction, of the compelling and vital forces through which individuals leave their mark over time, and of the permanence and fragility of those forces and imprints within a world that preserves them, while threatening them with insignificance, anonymity, or ultimate erasure.

Notes

Introduction

1. J. Jacobs (2001) 'Issues of Judgement and Value in Television Studies' *International Journal of Cultural Studies*, 4.4, 434. Jacobs discusses the 'cinematic' in relation to television drama in the context of analysing expressive achievement in medical dramas of the 1990s, yet the historical roots of this trend extend more deeply into the history of television production. For example, see J. P. Telotte (2010) 'In the Cinematic Zone of *The Twilight Zone*' *Science Fiction Film and Television*, 3.1, 1–17. There are also national contexts in which these overlaps take specific form, for example in European film and television production. See the discussions in: S. Peacock (2014) *Swedish Crime Fiction: Novel, Film, Television* (Manchester: Manchester University Press); and S. O'Sullivan (2009) 'The *Decalogue* and the Remaking of American Television' in S. Woodward (ed.) *After Kieslowski: The Legacy of Krzysztof Kieslowski* (Detroit: Wayne State University Press), pp. 202–25.
2. Tensions between unity and fragmentation, part and whole are important to early theoretical conceptualisations of television, broadly understood in terms of 'flow' between 'segments' of broadcast transmission. See: R. Williams (2003) *Television: Technology and Cultural Form*, Classics edn (London: Routledge), pp. 77–120 and J. Ellis (1992) *Visible Fictions: Cinema, Television, Video*, Revised edn (London: Routledge), pp. 115–26.
3. C. J. Clover (1993) '*Falling Down* and the Culture of Complaint' *The Threepenny Review*, 54, 32.
4. D. P. Pierson (2014) *Breaking Bad: Critical Essays on the Contexts, Politics, Style, and Reception of the Television Series* (Lanham: Lexington Books). See especially the section titled 'The Politics of *Breaking Bad*'.
5. See: A. Clayton (2011) 'Coming to Terms' in A. Clayton and A. Klevan (eds) *The Language and Style of Film Criticism* (London: Routledge), pp. 27–37.
6. This difficulty stems from the diminished clarity and force of moral language and concepts in contemporary secular societies. For an illuminating discussion of this context and how it gives rise to potentially enriching or violent desires for a renewed sense of the moral and ethical dimensions of human life, see S. Neiman (2008) *Moral Clarity: A Guide for Grown-up Idealists* (Orlando: Harcourt).
7. For an exemplary account of this trope's significance in these terms, see G. Perez (1998) *The Material Ghost: Films and their Medium* (Baltimore: Johns Hopkins University Press), pp. 237–8.
8. R. Pippin (2010) *Hollywood Westerns and American Myth: The Importance of John Ford and Howard Hawks for Political Philosophy* (New Haven: Yale University Press).
9. Perez *Material Ghost*, p. 237.
10. Perez *Material Ghost*, p. 237–8.

11. Wilson's inspiring study of cinematic point of view strikingly demonstrates how seemingly conventional Hollywood films may develop sophisticated alternative perspectives through which 'central aspects of their interest and significance bear only an *oblique* relationship to the forms of dramatic closure they employ'. G. M. Wilson (1988) *Narration in Light: Studies in Cinematic Point of View*, Johns Hopkins Paperback edn (Baltimore: Johns Hopkins University Press), p. 10; original emphasis.

12. M. Fried (2004) *Menzel's Realism: Art and Embodiment in Nineteenth-Century Berlin* (New Haven: Yale University Press), p. 13.

13. M. Fried (1967) 'Art and Objecthood' in his (1998) *Art and Objecthood: Essays and Reviews* (Chicago: University of Chicago Press), p. 167; original emphasis.

14. In an especially pertinent interrogation, Sianne Ngai questions Fried's emphasis on 'conviction' secured in instantaneous experiences of 'present-ness', noting how it excludes from judgements of value modes of 'ongoing temporality, so central to the serial, diachronic art of the novel'. S. Ngai (2012) *Our Aesthetic Categories: Zany, Cute, Interesting* (Cambridge: Harvard University Press), p. 163.

15. T. J. Clark (2006) *The Sight of Death: An Experiment in Art Writing* (New Haven: Yale University Press).

16. Jacobs eloquently evokes this critical problem through comparison of *Deadwood* (HBO, 2004–6) with *Moby Dick*. See J. Jacobs (2012) *Deadwood* (London: Palgrave Macmillan), p. 20.

17. C. Ricks (2010) *True Friendship: Geoffrey Hill, Anthony Hecht, and Robert Lowell Under the Sign of Eliot and Pound* (New Haven: Yale University Press), p. xi. I welcome Ricks's modification that allows for more than one useful handle. Cf. C. Ricks (2004) *Dylan's Visions of Sin*, First American edn (New York: HarperCollins), p. 1.

18. Fried *Menzel's Realism*, p. 13.

19. J. Jacobs (2015) 'Television Drama' in M. Alvarado, M. Buonanno, H. Gray and T. Miller (eds) *The SAGE Handbook of Television Studies* (Los Angeles: SAGE Publications), p. 316.

20. For discussion of these relationships, see the essays gathered in J. Jacobs and S. Peacock (2014) '"The Liveliest Medium": Television's Aesthetic Relation-ships with Other Arts' Special issue of *Critical Studies in Television*, 9.3.

21. Jacobs 'Television Drama', p. 317; original emphasis. For a more extended account of such a critical comportment, see: G. Toles (2001) *A House Made of Light: Essays on the Art of Film* (Detroit: Wayne State University Press), pp. 13–24.

22. A. Klevan (2000) *Disclosure of the Everyday: Undramatic Achievement in Narrative Film* (Trowbridge: Flicks Books), p. 2; original emphasis.

23. A. Clayton and A. Klevan (2010) 'Introduction: The Language and Style of Film Criticism' in A. Clayton and A. Klevan (eds) *The Language and Style of Film Criticism* (London: Routledge), p. 1.

24. S. Cavell (1981) *Pursuits of Happiness: The Hollywood Comedy of Remarriage* (Cambridge: Harvard University Press), pp. 36–7.

25. A. Martin (2010) 'Incursions' in A. Clayton and A. Klevan (eds) *The Language and Style of Film Criticism* (London: Routledge), p. 57.

26. V. F. Perkins (1990) 'Must We Say What They Mean? Film Criticism and Interpretation' *Movie*, 34.35, 4.

27. A. Klevan (2010) 'Description' in A. Clayton and A. Klevan (eds) *The Language and Style of Film Criticism* (London: Routledge), p. 71; original emphasis.

28. Cavell *Pursuits of Happiness*, p. 36; original emphasis.

29. Perkins 'Must We Say What They Mean?', 4.

30. J. Jacobs and S. Peacock (2013) 'Introduction' in J. Jacobs and S. Peacock (eds) *Television Aesthetics and Style* (London: Bloomsbury Academic), pp. 1–6.

31. J. Jacobs (2011) 'The Medium in Crisis: Caughie, Brunsdon and the Problem of US Television' *Screen*, 52.4, 510.

32. Klevan *Disclosure of the Everyday*, p. 2.

33. J. Jacobs and S. Peacock (2014) 'Editorial' *Critical Studies in Television*, 9.3, 1–2.

34. S. Cavell (1979) *The World Viewed: Reflections on the Ontology of Film* (Cambridge: Harvard University Press), p. 32.

35. *Breaking Bad*'s AMC stablemate *Mad Men* similarly produced its final season in two seven-episode parts. These decisions were taken during a period in which shorter seasons were becoming more common in US television, with shows such as *Luck* (HBO, 2011), *Game of Thrones*, and *True Detective* (HBO, 2014–), moving towards shorter seasons of ten episodes or less.

36. O'Sullivan 'Broken on Purpose', 68.

37. O'Sullivan 'Broken on Purpose'.

38. O'Sullivan 'Broken on Purpose', 74–5.

39. J. Gibbs and D. Pye (2005) 'Introduction' in J. Gibbs and D. Pye (eds) *Style and Meaning: Studies in the Detailed Analysis of Film* (Manchester: Manchester University Press), p. 10.

40. R. Durgnat (1971) *Films and Feelings*, First MIT Press paperback edn (Cambridge: MIT Press), p. 173; original emphasis.

41. Jacobs *Deadwood* and V. F. Perkins (2012) *La Règle du jeu* (London: Palgrave Macmillan).

42. Ricks *Dylan's Visions of Sin*, p. 7.

43. Ricks *True Friendship*, pp. 82–3.

44. O'Sullivan 'Broken on Purpose', 59.

45. S. Dias Branco (2010) 'Strung Pieces: On the Aesthetics of Television Fiction Series' Unpublished dissertation (University of Kent), pp. 79–80.

46. S. O'Sullivan 'Broken on Purpose', 59.

47. J. Gibbs (2013) *The Life of mise-en-scène: Visual Style and British Film Criticism, 1946–78* (Manchester: Manchester University Press), pp. 169–71.

48. Jacobs 'Issues of Judgement', 435.

49. Jacobs 'Issues of Judgement', 435.

50. Jacobs *Deadwood*, p. 158; my emphasis.

51. Jacobs and Peacock 'Introduction', p. 7.

52. S. O'Sullivan (2013) 'Story Land', Review of *Breaking Bad*, season five, episode fifteen, 'Granite State', *Kritik*, web, date accessed 11 November 2014.

53. The titles of the episodes break apart a line from *The Sweet Smell of Success* (Alexander Mackendrick, 1957). Across *Breaking Bad*, episode titles frequently allude to other movies, works of literature, and music, and also refer to the series' own internal history, which is especially notable across the titles in season two and season five. It is worth noting in regard to the present discussion how the titles of episodes two and three break up a quote that joins two parts of the series' story. Even at this level,

the series asks us to find unity in fragments, keeping complete cohesion in tension.

54. T. Todorov (1996) *Facing the Extreme: Moral Life in the Concentration Camps* (New York: Henry Holt).

55. Todorov *Facing the Extreme*, pp. 289–90. See also Z. Bauman (1989) *Modernity and the Holocaust* (Ithaca: Cornell University Press).

56. Again, see many of the essays gathered in Pierson (ed.) *Breaking Bad: Critical Essays*. As well, a great deal of journalistic discourse around the series can be seen to concentrate on these topics.

57. Jacobs *Deadwood*, p. 21.

58. My thinking about the importance of texture here is in part indebted to L. F. Donaldson (2014) *Texture in Film* (Basingstoke: Palgrave Macmillan).

59. G. Kateb (2011) *Human Dignity* (Cambridge: Belknap-Harvard University Press), pp. 5–6.

60. Todorov *Facing the Extreme*, pp. 59–70.

61. Todorov *Facing the Extreme*, p. 65. An important essay that accords with Todorov's account, while opening up an important distinction about the precise nature of the 'adequation' to which Todorov points, is Schiller's 'On Grace and Dignity'. Schiller sees dignity as consisting in the embodiment of reasoned mastery over, or resistance of, natural instinct or reflex, and provides the illustration of resistance to the expression of pain: 'But while his veins swell, his muscles become cramped and taut, his voice cracks, his chest is thrust out, and his lower body pressed in, his intentional movements are gentle, the facial features relaxed, and the eyes and brow serene. If a human were simply a creature of the senses, all his features would correspond with each other, since they would have a common source, and thus, in this case, they would all, equally, have to express suffering.' F. Schiller (2005) 'On Grace and Dignity' in J. V. Curran and C. Fricker (eds) *On Grace and Dignity in its Cultural Context: Essays and a New Translation* (Rochester: Camden House), pp. 159–60. The example is especially pertinent in that it points away from an emphasis on *total* unity of being (in which all aspects of oneself accord naturally with 'a common source'), but rather with a form of *tension* that expresses a comportment tending towards cohesion rather than division of intention and deed.

62. Todorov *Facing the Extreme*, p. 66.

63. R. Pippin (2000) *Henry James and Modern Moral Life*, First paperback edn (New York: Cambridge University Press), p. 29.

64. Pippin *Henry James*, p. 29.

65. For some examples, see H. Newcomb (1974) *TV: The Most Popular Art* (Garden City: Anchor Books), p. 255; G. Creeber (2004) *Serial Television: Big Drama on the Small Screen* (London: BFI), and O'Sullivan 'Broken on Purpose'.

66. Jacobs and Peacock 'Introduction', p. 12.

1   Humiliation and Shame in Season One

1. For this characterisation of first seasons, see S. O'Sullivan (2006) 'Old, New, Borrowed, Blue: *Deadwood* and Serial Fiction' in D. Lavery (ed.) *Reading Deadwood: A Western to Swear By* (London: I. B. Tauris), p. 118. See also

S. O'Sullivan (2009) 'Reconnoitering the Rim: Thoughts on *Deadwood* and Third Seasons' in P. Harrigan and N. Wardrip-Fruin (eds) *Third Person: Authoring and Exploring Vast Narratives* (Cambridge: MIT Press), p. 326.

2. Regarding narrative complexity, see J. Mittell (2013) 'The Qualities of Complexity: Vast Seriality Versus Dense Seriality in Contemporary Television' in J. Jacobs and S. Peacock (eds) *Television Aesthetics and Style* (London: Bloomsbury Academic), pp. 45–56. On the cold open, see: L. Coulthard (2010) 'The Hotness of Cold Opens: *Breaking Bad* and the Serial Narrative as Puzzle' *Flow TV*, 13.3, web, date accessed 6 December 2010. Cf. E. Logan (2013) 'Flashforwards in *Breaking Bad*: Openness, Closure, and Possibility' in J. Jacobs and S. Peacock (eds) *Television Aesthetics and Style* (London: Bloomsbury Academic), pp. 219–26.

3. For a detailed account of such issues and the relevance of flashbacks, see: R. Pippin (2012) *Fatalism in American Film Noir: Some Cinematic Philosophy* (Charlottesville: University of Virginia Press).

4. J. Jacobs (2012) *Deadwood* (London: Palgrave Macmillan), p. 53.

5. In interviews, Gilligan regularly discusses his stint on *The X-Files* as an apprenticeship that strongly influenced his work on *Breaking Bad*. For an example pertinent to the present discussion of cold opens, see J. Plunkett (2013) '*Breaking Bad* Creator Vince Gilligan: "How Long Can Anyone Stay at the Top?"' *Guardian*, 19 August, web, date accessed 27 November 2014.

6. G. Toles (2011) 'Occasions of Sin: The Forgotten Cigarette Lighter and Other Moral Accidents in Hitchcock' in T. Leitch and L. Poague (eds) *A Companion to Alfred Hitchcock* (Chichester: Wiley-Blackwell), pp. 529–52.

7. Toles 'Occasions of Sin', p. 534.

8. Toles 'Occasions of Sin', p. 533.

9. Thanks to Ted Nannicelli for inspiring me to push this issue further.

10. Cf. Gilberto Perez's comments on camera position and perspective in *The General* (Buster Keaton and Clyde Bruckman, 1926). G. Perez (1998) *The Material Ghost: Films and Their Medium* (Baltimore: Johns Hopkins University), pp. 111–12.

11. Pippin *Fatalism in American Film Noir*, p. 105.

12. P. Schrader (1988) *Transcendental Style in Film: Ozu, Bresson, Dreyer* (Berkeley: Da Capo Press), p. 42.

13. G. Kouvaros (2008) *Paul Schrader* (Urbana: University of Illinois Press), p. 27.

14. A. Martin (2013) 'Hands Across the Table' *The Cine-Files*, 4, 8.

15. A. Klevan (2000) *Disclosure of the Everyday: Undramatic Achievement in Narrative Film* (Trowbridge: Flicks Books), p. 32, n. 18.

16. For an illuminating reading of the film in terms of what the author calls 'melodramatic masculinities', see: D. Thomas (2000) *Beyond Genre: Melodrama, Comedy, and Romance in Hollywood Films* (Moffat: Cameron & Hollis), pp. 32–42.

17. See the reading of Callahan's comment about a .38 round bouncing off a windshield in E. Gallafent (1994) *Clint Eastwood: Actor and Director* (London: Studio Vista), p. 53.

18. Thomas *Beyond Genre*, p. 26.

19. T. Todorov (1996) *Facing the Extreme: Moral Life in the Concentration Camps* (New York: Henry Holt), p. 66.

20. These crucially important sequences are discussed in more detail in Chapter 3.

21. V. Gilligan (2011) 'Vince Gilligan Interview' *Archive of American Television*, web, date accessed 4 August 2012. The relevant section of the video is listed under 'Highlights' and is titled 'Vince Gilligan on the Moment He's Proudest of on *Breaking Bad*'.

2 Pursuing Success in Season Two

1. A simple formulation of the uncertainty principle is that the more accurately the position of a particle can be measured, the less accurately the momentum of that particle can be measured, and vice versa. For a more detailed overview of the concept and its history, see: Stanford University (2006) 'The Uncertainty Principle' *Stanford Encyclopedia of Philosophy*, 3 July 2006, web, date accessed 13 January 2015.
2. S. O'Sullivan (2009) 'Reconnoitering the Rim: Thoughts on *Deadwood* and Third Seasons' in P. Harrigan and N. Wardrip-Fruin (eds) *Third Person: Authoring and Exploring Vast Narratives* (Cambridge: MIT Press), p. 326.
3. See his discussion of David Milch's reflections on the second season of *Deadwood* in S. O'Sullivan (2006) 'Old, New, Borrowed, Blue: *Deadwood* and Serial Fiction' in D. Lavery (ed.) *Reading Deadwood: A Western to Swear By* (London: I. B. Tauris), pp. 115–29.
4. Murray Pomerance discusses this as 'performed performance'. See: M. Pomerance (2012) 'Performed Performance and *The Man Who Knew Too Much*' in A. Taylor (ed.) *Theorizing Film Acting* (Hoboken: Taylor and Francis), pp. 62–75.
5. J. Naremore (1988) *Acting in the Cinema* (Berkeley: University of California Press), p. 68.
6. S. Cavell (1996) *Contesting Tears: The Hollywood Melodrama of the Unknown Woman* (Chicago: University of Chicago Press), pp. 50–1.
7. H. Frankfurt (1999) *Necessity, Volition, and Love* (Cambridge: Cambridge University Press), p. 97; my emphasis.
8. E. Gallafent (1994) *Clint Eastwood: Actor and Director* (London: Studio Vista), p. 25.
9. The song is 'Crapa Pelada' by Quartetto Cetra.
10. A. Martin (2013) 'Hands Across the Table' *The Cine-Files*, 4, 3.
11. This reflects a discovery of the actor made by Vince Gilligan. As he says in interview: 'There's a lot of complexity to Dean Norris. It's a complexity that I didn't at first realise he possessed, way back when I hired him. And you say to yourself, "I've got to use this; there's more to this man, there has to be more to this character, therefore."' V. Gilligan (2014) 'Avenging Agent: Dean Norris as Hank Schrader' *Breaking Bad: The Complete Series* (Burbank: Sony Pictures Television), DVD. The chance to work upon the discoveries made of an actor as their performance and character takes shape over episodes and seasons is an opportunity peculiar to serial television drama, with important implications for understanding the art of the form; it is deserving of an independent study.
12. D. Thomas (2001) *Reading Hollywood: Spaces and Meanings in American Film* (London: Wallflower Press), p. 40.
13. The rich mining analogy for characterisation in serial television drama is William Rothman's. See: W. Rothman (2013) 'Justifying *Justified*' in J. Jacobs

and S. Peacock (eds) *Television Aesthetics and Style* (London: Bloomsbury Academic), pp. 175–84.

14. G. Toles (2011) 'Occasions of Sin: The Forgotten Cigarette Lighter and Other Moral Accidents in Hitchcock' in T. Leitch and L. Poague (eds) *A Companion to Alfred Hitchcock* (Chichester: Wiley-Blackwell), p. 538.

15. See my account in Chapter 1.

16. A. Martin (2009) 'The Social Mise en Scène of *How Green Was My Valley*' *Undercurrent*, 5, web, date accessed 8 December 2014.

17. J. Jacobs and S. Peacock 'Introduction' in J. Jacobs and S. Peacock (eds) *Television Aesthetics and Style* (London: Bloomsbury Academic), p. 12.

18. J. Jacobs (2012) *Deadwood* (London: Palgrave Macmillan), p. 94.

19. The song is 'Enchanted' by The Platters.

20. P. Adams (2008) *Fragmented Intimacy: Addiction in a Social World* (New York: Springer), p. 126.

3   Taking a Stand in Season Three

1. For a discussion of how returning to familiar scenarios may provide a rich dramatic resource, or risk a sense of exhaustion, see: J. Jacobs (2001) 'Issues of Judgement and Value in Television Studies' *International Journal of Cultural Studies*, 4.4, 434.

2. T. Todorov (1996) *Facing the Extreme: Moral Life in the Concentration Camps* (New York: Henry Holt), pp. 151–4.

3. Todorov *Facing the Extreme*, p. 153.

4. S. O'Sullivan (2009) 'Reconnoitering the Rim: Thoughts on *Deadwood* and Third Seasons' in P. Harrigan and N. Wardrip-Fruin (eds) *Third Person: Authoring and Exploring Vast Narratives* (Cambridge: MIT Press), p. 326.

5. O'Sullivan 'Reconnoitering the Rim', p. 327.

6. The use of the shower curtain brings to mind Cavell's reading of how the curtain in *It Happened One Night* (Frank Capra, 1934) 'dramatizes the problem of unknownness as one of splitting the other, as between outside and inside'. S. Cavell (1996) *Contesting Tears: The Hollywood Melodrama of the Unknown Woman* (Chicago: Chicago University Press), p. 90. Capra's film is a comedy, and so we are fairly assured by its genre and form that the man and woman will unite by story's end. *Breaking Bad*'s genre and serial form provide no such guarantees for our investment in the marriage between Hank and Marie.

7. S. Cavell (1981) *Pursuits of Happiness: The Hollywood Comedy of Remarriage* (Cambridge: Harvard University Press), p. 8. I am indebted throughout this section to Cavell's book and its understand of marriage in terms of conversation between a couple, and its potential failure.

8. Critics have noted that this not only mirrors the arc of Walt and Jesse's enterprise, but also the real-life historical development of the US-Mexican methamphetamine trade. For example, see P. R. Keefe (2012) 'The Uncannily Accurate Depiction of the Meth Trade in *Breaking Bad*' *The New Yorker* (Condé Naste), web, date accessed 4 September 2012. For a compelling account of this history, see N. Reding (2010) *Methland: The Death and Life of an American Small Town*, paperback edn (New York: Bloomsbury), esp. pp. 58–72, 150–66.

9. G. Toles (2001) *A House Made of Light* (Detroit: Wayne State University Press), p. 29.
10. The phrase is from R. Sennett (2008) *The Craftsman* (New Haven: Yale University Press), p. 243. I have been greatly helped in my thinking of these aspects of *Breaking Bad* by the discussion of routine in R. Sennett (1998) *The Corrosion of Character: The Personal Consequences of Work in the New Capitalism* (New York: W. W. Norton), pp. 33–45.
11. Quoted in N. Murray (2010) 'Vince Gilligan' *The AV Club*, web, date accessed 5 September 2012. Ted Nannicelli considers the episode's handling of its bottle episode status in terms of what he calls the 'Naturalist theatrical aesthetic' of such episodes. See: T. Nannicelli (2014) 'The Naturalist Theatrical Aesthetic of Bottle Episodes' *Critical Studies in Television*, 9.3, 54–64.
12. See the discussion of thymos in F. Fukuyama (2006) *The End of History and the Last Man*, First Free Press trade paperback edn (New York: Free Press) and R. Pippin (2010) *Hollywood Westerns and American Myth: The Importance of John Ford and Howard Hawks for Political Philosophy* (New Haven: Yale University Press), pp. 47–8; and the transcendence of material self-interest by the passions in S. Neiman (2008) *Moral Clarity: A Guide for Grown-up Idealists* (Orlando: Harcourt), pp. 99–100.
13. Fukuyama *The End of History*, p. 183.
14. This is something like the presentation of toy, or otherwise obvious and manufactured, symbols of 'the movie Western' that Robert Pippin sees as crucial to the irony of *Johnny Guitar*. See: R. Pippin (2014) 'Cinematic Irony: The Strange Case of Nicholas Ray's *Johnny Guitar' nonsite*, 13, web, date accessed 10 December 2014.
15. Todorov *Facing the Extreme*, p. 40.
16. G. Perez (1998) *The Material Ghost: Films and Their Medium* (Baltimore: Johns Hopkins University Press), p. 237.
17. Gilligan has made this claim in interviews. See: V. Gilligan (2011) '*Breaking Bad* Series Creator Vince Gilligan Answers Viewer Questions' *Breaking Bad Blog*, amctv.com, web, date accessed 16 June 2013.

4   Inheritance and Legacy in Season Four

1. J. Harvey (2002) *Movie Love in the Fifties*, First Da Capo Press edn (Cambridge: Da Capo Press), p. 158.
2. Tourneur's film is interpreted along these lines in R. Pippin (2012) *Fatalism in American Film Noir: Some Cinematic Philosophy* (Charlottesville: University of Virginia Press), pp. 27–49.
3. J. Jacobs (2012) *Deadwood* (London: Palgrave Macmillan), p. 142.
4. See Vince Gilligan's discussion of this period in D. Itzkoff (2011) 'Vince Gilligan of *Breaking Bad* Talks About Ending the Season, and the Series' *ArtsBeat, New York Times Culture Blog*, 9 October 2011, web, date accessed 13 November 2014.
5. This is the inverse of the situation in which those involved in *Deadwood*'s third season found themselves. The makers of *Deadwood* intended its third season to lead towards a range of future developments that they planned to depict across the proposed fourth and fifth seasons. But by the time season

three aired, any plans for future production had been shelved, and the third season became *Deadwood*'s end. For discussions of this, see: S. O'Sullivan (2009) 'Reconnoitering the Rim: Thoughts on *Deadwood* and Third Seasons' in P. Harrigan and N. Wardrip-Fruin (eds) *Third Person: Authoring and Exploring Vast Narratives* (Cambridge: MIT Press), pp. 323–32, and Jacobs *Deadwood*, pp. 172–5.

6. V. F. Perkins (2005) 'Where is the World? The Horizon of Events in Movie Fiction' in J. Gibbs and D. Pye (eds) *Style and Meaning: Studies in the Detailed Analysis of Film* (Manchester: Manchester University Press), p. 19.

7. R. Pippin (2010) *Nietzsche, Psychology, and First Philosophy*, Paperback edn 2011 (Chicago: University of Chicago Press), p. 54; original emphasis.

8. *Cineaste* Editors (2014) 'Editorial' *Cineaste*, 39.4, 1.

9. D. Milch (2014) 'Rethinking Television: A Critical Symposium' *Cineaste*, 39.4, 32.

10. There is another layering of legacy in the naming of this character and of the scholarship dedicated in his honour: Maximino Arciniega is the actor who played Krazy-8 in the pilot episode. He so quickly engendered himself with the crew that what was initially planned to be the character's death was revised so that he could return for two further episodes (in which the actor is superb in his scenes opposite Bryan Cranston).

11. As noted at the chapter's beginning, the uncertainty of the show's continuation shaped Vince Gilligan's intentions regarding the last episode of season four. As he said in an interview shortly after 'Face Off' first aired: 'We weren't sure that we would have a fifth season when we were plotting out the end of Season 4. So we wanted to make the end of Season 4 as satisfying and as complete as possible, not knowing what the future would hold.' Quoted in Itzkoff 'Vince Gilligan of *Breaking Bad* Talks'.

12. The music accompanying these scenes is an instrumental arrangement of 'Goodbye' by Apparat.

Conclusion: Facing Completion in Season Five

1. C. Ricks (2004) *Dylan's Visions of Sin*, First American edn (New York: HarperCollins), p. 7.

2. V. F. Perkins (1990) 'Must We Say What They Mean? Film Criticism and Interpretation' *Movie*, 34/35, 4.

3. Perkins 'Must We Say What They Mean?', 4.

4. Perkins 'Must We Say What They Mean?', 4.

5. J. Jacobs and S. Peacock (2013) 'Introduction' in J. Jacobs and S. Peacock (eds) *Television Aesthetics and Style* (London: Bloomsbury Academic), p. 7.

6. C. Creekmur (2013) 'Bad Breaks', Review of *Breaking Bad*, season five, episode nine, 'Blood Money', *Kritik*, web, date accessed: 26 March 2015; my emphasis.

7. S. O'Sullivan (2013) 'Serials and Satisfaction' *Romanticism and Victorianism on the Net* 63, web, DOI: 10.7202/1025614ar, date accessed 28 July 2014, para 2.

8. O'Sullivan 'Serials and Satisfaction', para 2.

9. For example, see: V. Gilligan (2013) 'Vince Gilligan Explains the *Breaking Bad* Finale' *Guardian*, web, 30 September 2013, date accessed 27 March 2015.

10. For the basis of this connection with Neff and *Double Indemnity*, see my reading of the opening sequence in Chapter 1.

11. S. Cavell (1981) *Pursuits of Happiness: The Hollywood Comedy of Remarriage* (Cambridge: Harvard University Press), p. 37.

12. V. F. Perkins (1999) *The Magnificent Ambersons* (London: BFI), p. 72.

13. See the section 'Enclosed in Repetition and Anonymity' in Chapter 3.

14. T. Todorov (1996) *Facing the Extreme: Moral Life in the Concentration Camps* (New York: Henry Holt), p. 150.

15. Todorov *Facing the Extreme*, p. 290.

16. C. Lasch (1991) *The Culture of Narcissism: American Life in an Age of Diminishing Expectations*, Norton paperback edn (New York: W. W. Norton).

17. Todorov *Facing the Extreme*, p. 42.

18. Todorov *Facing the Extreme*, p. 33.

19. Szyman Laks and R. Coudy qtd in Todorov *Facing the Extreme*, p. 33.

20. R. Pippin (2000) *Henry James and Modern Moral Life* (Cambridge: Cambridge University Press), p. 90.

21. On the distinctiveness of the period's seasonal television drama in comparison to other forms of more seemingly 'endless' television serial, such as soap opera, see: S. O'Sullivan (2010) 'Broken on Purpose: Poetry, Serial Television, and the Season' *StoryWorlds* 2, 59–77.

22. For a compressed account of identity as a matter of practical meaning, see: R. Pippin (2005) *The Persistence of Subjectivity: On the Kantian Aftermath* (Cambridge: Cambridge University Press), pp. 309–10. For Pippin, an individual's identity or self-image in this practical sense is not secured by their belief (or another's belief) in some 'inner essence'. It rather must also depend upon how an individual's actions are interpreted by others, interpretations (by both the individual themselves and by others) that are open to retrospective revision and re-making in light of future events, making one's self-image or identity in this sense always a provisional, unstable, and crucially social, historical matter.

23. I am indebted here to Michael Fried's chapter '"The Disenchantment of the World"; Walter Benjamin on Traces' in M. Fried (2004) *Menzel's Realism: Art and Embodiment in Nineteenth-Century Berlin* (New Haven: Yale University Press), pp. 231–46.

Bibliography

Adams, Peter (2008) *Fragmented Intimacy: Addiction in a Social World* (New York: Springer).

Bauman, Zygmunt (1989) *Modernity and the Holocaust* (Ithaca: Cornell University Press).

Cavell, Stanley (1979) *The World Viewed: Reflections on the Ontology of Film* (Cambridge: Harvard University Press).

Cavell, Stanley (1981) *Pursuits of Happiness: The Hollywood Comedy of Remarriage* (Cambridge: Harvard University Press).

Cavell, Stanley (1996) *Contesting Tears: The Hollywood Melodrama of the Unknown Woman* (Chicago: University of Chicago Press).

Cineaste Editors (2014) 'Editorial' *Cineaste*, 39.4, 1.

Clark, T. J. (2006) *The Sight of Death: An Experiment in Art Writing* (New Haven: Yale University Press).

Clayton, Alex (2011) 'Coming to Terms' in Alex Clayton and Andrew Klevan (eds) *The Language and Style of Film Criticism* (London: Routledge), pp. 27–37.

Clayton, Alex and Andrew Klevan (2010) 'Introduction: The Language and Style of Film Criticism' in Alex Clayton and Andrew Klevan (eds) *The Language and Style of Film Criticism* (London: Routledge), pp. 1–26.

Clover, Carol J. (1993) '*Falling Down* and the Culture of Complaint' *The Threepenny Review*, 54, 32–3.

Coulthard, Lisa (2010) 'The Hotness of Cold Opens: *Breaking Bad* and the Serial Narrative as Puzzle' *Flow TV*, 13.3, web, date accessed 6 December 2010.

Creeber, Glen (2004) *Serial Television: Big Drama on the Small Screen* (London: BFI).

Creekmur, Corey (2013) 'Bad Breaks', Review of *Breaking Bad*, season five, episode nine, 'Blood Money', *Kritik*, web, date accessed: 26 March 2015.

Dias Branco, Sérgio (2010) 'Strung Pieces: On the Aesthetics of Television Fiction Series' Unpublished dissertation (University of Kent).

Donaldson, Lucy Fife (2014) *Texture in Film* (Basingstoke: Palgrave Macmillan).

Durgnat Raymond (1971) *Films and Feelings*, First MIT Press paperback edn (Cambridge: MIT Press).

Ellis, John (1992) *Visible Fictions: Cinema, Television, Video*, Revised edn (London: Routledge).

Frankfurt, Harry (1999) *Necessity, Volition, and Love* (Cambridge: Cambridge University Press).

Fried, Michael (1998) *Art and Objecthood: Essays and Reviews* (Chicago: University of Chicago Press).

Fried, Michael (2004) *Menzel's Realism: Art and Embodiment in Nineteenth-Century Berlin* (New Haven: Yale University Press).

Fukuyama, Francis (2006) *The End of History and the Last Man*, First Free Press trade paperback edn (New York: Free Press).

Gallafent, Edward (1994) *Clint Eastwood: Actor and Director* (London: Studio Vista).

Gibbs, John (2013) *The Life of mise-en-scène: Visual Style and British Film Criticism, 1946–78* (Manchester: Manchester University Press).

Gibbs, John and Douglas Pye (2005) 'Introduction' in John Gibbs and Douglas Pye (eds) *Style and Meaning: Studies in the Detailed Analysis of Film* (Manchester: Manchester University Press), pp. 1–15.

Gilligan, Vince (2011a) *'Breaking Bad* Series Creator Vince Gilligan Answers Viewer Questions' *Breaking Bad Blog,* amctv.com, web, date accessed 16 June 2013.

Gilligan, Vince (2011b) 'Vince Gilligan Interview' *Archive of American Television,* web, date accessed 4 August 2012.

Gilligan, Vince (2013) 'Vince Gilligan Explains the *Breaking Bad* Finale' *Guardian,* web, 30 September 2013, date accessed 27 March 2015.

Gilligan, Vince (2014) 'Avenging Agent: Dean Norris as Hank Schrader' *Breaking Bad: The Complete Series* (Burbank: Sony Pictures Television), DVD.

Harvey, James (2002) *Movie Love in the Fifties,* First Da Capo Press edn (Cambridge: Da Capo Press).

Itzkoff, Dave (2011) 'Vince Gilligan of *Breaking Bad* Talks About Ending the Season, and the Series' *ArtsBeat, New York Times Culture Blog,* 9 October 2011, web, date accessed 13 November 2014.

Jacobs, Jason (2001) 'Issues of Judgement and Value in Television Studies' *International Journal of Cultural Studies,* 4.4, 427–47.

Jacobs, Jason (2011) 'The Medium in Crisis: Caughie, Brunsdon and the Problem of US Television' *Screen,* 52.4, 503–11.

Jacobs, Jason (2012) *Deadwood* (London: Palgrave Macmillan).

Jacobs, Jason (2015) 'Television Drama' in Manuel Alvarado, Milly Buonanno, Herman Gray, and Toby Miller (eds) *The SAGE Handbook of Television Studies* (Los Angeles: SAGE Publications), pp. 315–24.

Jacobs, Jason and Steven Peacock (2013) 'Introduction' in Jason Jacobs and Steven Peacock (eds) *Television Aesthetics and Style* (London: Bloomsbury Academic), pp. 1–20.

Jacobs, Jason and Steven Peacock (2014a) '"The Liveliest Medium": Television's Aesthetic Relationships With Other Arts' Special issue of *Critical Studies in Television,* 9.3.

Jacobs, Jason and Steven Peacock (2014b) 'Editorial' *Critical Studies in Television,* 9.3, 1–5.

Kateb, George (2011) *Human Dignity* (Cambridge: Belknap-Harvard University Press).

Keefe, Patrick Radden (2012) 'The Uncannily Accurate Depiction of the Meth Trade in *Breaking Bad' The New Yorker* (Condé Naste), web, date accessed 4 September 2012.

Klevan, Andrew (2000) *Disclosure of the Everyday: Undramatic Achievement in Narrative Film* (Trowbridge: Flicks Books).

Klevan, Andrew (2010) 'Description' in Alex Clayton and Andrew Klevan (eds) *The Language and Style of Film Criticism* (London: Routledge), pp. 70–86.

Kouvaros, George (2008) *Paul Schrader* (Urbana: University of Illinois Press).

Lasch, Christopher (1991) *The Culture of Narcissism: American Life in an Age of Diminishing Expectations,* Norton paperback edn (New York: W. W. Norton).

Logan, Elliott (2013) 'Flashforwards in *Breaking Bad*: Openness, Closure, and Possibility' in Jason Jacobs and Steven Peacock (eds) *Television Aesthetics and Style* (London: Bloomsbury Academic), pp. 219–26.

Martin, Adrian (2009) 'The Social Mise en Scène of *How Green Was My Valley' Undercurrent,* 5, web, date accessed 8 December 2014.

Martin, Adrian (2010) 'Incursions' in Alex Clayton and Andrew Klevan (eds) *The Language and Style of Film Criticism* (London: Routledge), pp. 54–69.

Martin, Adrian (2013) 'Hands Across the Table' *The Cine-Files*, 4, 1–11.

Milch, David (2014) 'Rethinking Television: A Critical Symposium' *Cineaste*, 39.4, 32–3.

Mittell, Jason (2013) 'The Qualities of Complexity: Vast Seriality Versus Dense Seriality in Contemporary Television' in Jason Jacobs and Steven Peacock (eds) *Television Aesthetics and Style* (London: Bloomsbury Academic), pp. 45–56.

Murray, Noel (2010) 'Vince Gilligan' *The AV Club*, web, date accessed 5 September 2012.

Nannicelli, Ted (2014) 'The Naturalist Theatrical Aesthetic of Bottle Episodes' *Critical Studies in Television*, 9.3, 54–64.

Naremore, James (1988) *Acting in the Cinema* (Berkeley: University of California Press).

Neiman, Susan (2008) *Moral Clarity: A Guide for Grown-up Idealists* (Orlando: Harcourt).

Newcomb, Horace (1974) *TV: The Most Popular Art* (Garden City: Anchor Books).

Ngai, Sianne (2012) *Our Aesthetic Categories: Zany, Cute, Interesting* (Cambridge: Harvard University Press).

O'Sullivan, Sean (2006) 'Old, New, Borrowed, Blue: *Deadwood* and Serial Fiction' in D. Lavery (ed.) *Reading Deadwood: A Western to Swear By* (London: I. B. Tauris), pp. 115–29.

O'Sullivan, Sean (2009a) 'Reconnoitering the Rim: Thoughts on *Deadwood* and Third Seasons' in P. Harrigan and N. Wardrip-Fruin (eds) *Third Person: Authoring and Exploring Vast Narratives* (Cambridge: MIT Press), pp. 323–32.

O'Sullivan, Sean (2009b) 'The *Decalogue* and the Remaking of American Television' in S. Woodward (ed.) *After Kieslowski: The Legacy of Krzysztof Kieslowski* (Detroit: Wayne State University Press), pp. 202–25.

O'Sullivan, Sean (2013a) 'Serials and Satisfaction' *Romanticism and Victorianism on the Net* 63, web, DOI: 10.7202/1025614ar, date accessed: 28 July 2014.

O'Sullivan, Sean (2013b) 'Story Land', Review of *Breaking Bad*, season five, episode fifteen, 'Granite State', *Kritik*, web, date accessed 11 November 2014.

Peacock, Steven (2014) *Swedish Crime Fiction: Novel, Film, Television* (Manchester: Manchester University Press).

Perez, Gilberto (1998) *The Material Ghost: Films and their Medium* (Baltimore: Johns Hopkins University Press).

Perkins, V. F. (1990) 'Must We Say What They Mean? Film Criticism and Interpretation' *Movie*, 34/35, 1–6.

Perkins, V. F. (1999) *The Magnificent Ambersons* (London: BFI).

Perkins, V. F. (2005) 'Where is the World? The Horizon of Events in Movie Fiction' in John Gibbs and Douglas Pye (eds) *Style and Meaning: Studies in the Detailed Analysis of Film* (Manchester: Manchester University Press), pp. 16–41.

Perkins, V. F. (2012) *La Règle du jeu* (London: Palgrave Macmillan).

Pierson, David P. (2014) *Breaking Bad: Critical Essays on the Contexts, Politics, Style, and Reception of the Television Series* (Lanham: Lexington Books).

Pippin, Robert (2000) *Henry James and Modern Moral Life*, First paperback edn (New York: Cambridge University Press).

Pippin, Robert (2005) *The Persistence of Subjectivity: On the Kantian Aftermath* (Cambridge: Cambridge University Press).

Pippin, Robert (2010a) *Hollywood Westerns and American Myth: The Importance of John Ford and Howard Hawks for Political Philosophy* (New Haven: Yale University Press).

Pippin, Robert (2010b) *Nietzsche, Psychology, and First Philosophy*, Paperback edn 2011 (Chicago: University of Chicago Press).

Pippin, Robert (2012) *Fatalism in American Film Noir: Some Cinematic Philosophy* (Charlottesville: University of Virginia Press).

Pippin, Robert (2014) 'Cinematic Irony: The Strange Case of Nicholas Ray's *Johnny Guitar*' nonsite, 13, web, date accessed 10 December 2014.

Plunkett, John (2013) '*Breaking Bad* Creator Vince Gilligan: "How Long Can Anyone Stay at the Top?"' *Guardian*, 19 August, web, date accessed 27 November 2014.

Pomerance, Murray (2012) 'Performed Performance and *The Man Who Knew Too Much*' in Aaron Taylor (ed.) *Theorizing Film Acting* (Hoboken: Taylor and Francis), pp. 62–75.

Reding, Nick (2010) *Methland: The Death and Life of an American Small Town*, paperback ed. (New York: Bloomsbury).

Ricks, Christopher (2004) *Dylan's Visions of Sin*, First American edn (New York: HarperCollins).

Ricks, Christopher (2010) *True Friendship: Geoffrey Hill, Anthony Hecht, and Robert Lowell Under the Sign of Eliot and Pound* (New Haven: Yale University Press).

Rothman, William (2013) 'Justifying *Justified*' in Jason Jacobs and Steven Peacock (eds) *Television Aesthetics and Style* (London: Bloomsbury Academic), pp. 175–84.

Schiller, Friedrich. (2005) 'On Grace and Dignity' in Jane V. Curran and Christophe Fricker (eds) *On Grace and Dignity in its Cultural Context: Essays and a New Translation* (Rochester: Camden House), pp. 123–70.

Schrader, Paul (1988) *Transcendental Style in Film: Ozu, Bresson, Dreyer* (Berkeley: Da Capo Press).

Sennett, Richard (1998) *The Corrosion of Character: The Personal Consequences of Work in the New Capitalism* (New York: W. W. Norton).

Sennett, Richard (2008) *The Craftsman* (New Haven: Yale University Press).

Stanford University (2006) 'The Uncertainty Principle' *Stanford Encyclopedia of Philosophy*, 3 July 2006, web, date accessed 13 January 2015.

Telotte, J. P. (2010) 'In the Cinematic Zone of *The Twilight Zone*' *Science Fiction Film and Television*, 3.1, 1–17.

Thomas, Deborah (2000) *Beyond Genre: Melodrama, Comedy, and Romance in Hollywood Films* (Moffat: Cameron & Hollis).

Thomas, Deborah (2001) *Reading Hollywood: Spaces and Meanings in American Film* (London: Wallflower Press).

Todorov, Tzvetan (1996) *Facing the Extreme: Moral Life in the Concentration Camps* (New York: Henry Holt).

Toles, George (2001) *A House Made of Light: Essays on the Art of Film* (Detroit: Wayne State University Press).

Toles, George (2011) 'Occasions of Sin: The Forgotten Cigarette Lighter and Other Moral Accidents in Hitchcock' in Thomas Leitch and Leland Poague (eds) *A Companion to Alfred Hitchcock* (Chichester: Wiley-Blackwell), pp. 529–52.

Williams, Raymond (2003) *Television: Technology and Cultural Form*, Classics edn (London: Routledge).

Wilson, George M. (1988) *Narration in Light: Studies in Cinematic Point of View*, Johns Hopkins Paperback edn (Baltimore: Johns Hopkins University Press).

Films and Television Series

2001: A Space Odyssey. Dir. Stanley Kubrick (1968).
Bigger Than Life. Dir. Nicholas Ray (1956).
Breaking Bad. Cr. Vince Gilligan (AMC, 2007–2013).
Caught. Dir. Max Ophuls (1948).
Citizen Kane. Dir. Orson Welles (1941).
Deadwood. Cr. David Milch (HBO, 2004–2006).
Dial M for Murder. Dir. Alfred Hitchcock (1954).
Dirty Harry. Dir. Don Siegel (1971).
Double Indemnity. Dir. Billy Wilder (1944).
Falling Down. Dir. Joel Schumacher (1993).
Forbrydelsen. Cr. Søren Sveistrup (DR1, 2007–2012).
Gaslight. Dir. George Cukor (1944).
Game of Thrones. Cr. David Benioff and D. B. Weiss (HBO, 2010–).
How Green Was My Valley. Dir. John Ford (1941).
Ikiru. Dir. Akira Kurosawa (1952).
In a Lonely Place. Dir. Nicholas Ray (1950).
It Happened One Night. Dir. Frank Capra (1934).
Johnny Guitar. Dir. Nicholas Ray (1954).
La Règle du jeu. Dir. Jean Renoir (1937).
Luck. Cr. David Milch (HBO, 2011)
Mad Men. Cr. Matthew Weiner (AMC, 2007–2015).
Once Upon a Time in the West. Dir. Sergio Leone (1968).
Out of the Past. Dir. Jacques Tourneur (1947).
Pulp Fiction. Dir. Quentin Tarantino (1994).
Scarface. Dir. Brian De Palma (1983).
Six Feet Under. Cr. Alan Ball (HBO, 2001–2005).
Strangers on a Train. Dir. Alfred Hitchcock (1951).
Sunset Boulevard. Dir. Billy Wilder (1950).
Taxi Driver. Dir. Martin Scorsese (1976).
The General. Dir. Buster Keaton and Clyde Bruckman (1926).
The Enforcer. Dir. James Fargo (1976).
The Godfather, Part II. Dir. Francis Ford Coppola (1974).
The Magnificent Ambersons. Dir. Orson Welles (1942).
The Shield. Cr. Shawn Ryan (FX, 2002–08).
The Sopranos. Cr. David Chase (HBO, 1999–2007).
The Sweet Smell of Success. Dir. Alexander Mackendrick (1957).
The X-Files. Cr. Chris Carter (Fox, 1993–2002).
Top of the Lake. Cr. Jane Campion, Gerard Lee (BBC Two, 2013).
True Detective. Cr. Nic Pizzolatto (HBO, 2014–).
Vertigo. Dir. Alfred Hitchcock (1958).

Index

Note: entries for *Breaking Bad* characters proceed from given names

2001: A Space Odyssey, 100

acknowledgement, 5–6, 60–4, 87–94,
 108, 120–2, 144, 152–4
acting, 4, 6–8, 22–3, 30–1, 34–6, 41–3,
 59–64, 66–73, 88–90, 91–4, 95,
 99–103, 107–8, 113–19, 125–31,
 137–40
 see also: voice
Adams, Peter, 81
AMC, contract negotiations with,
 110, 139
Andrea Cantillo, 101, 103–4, 123,
 136–7, 139, 152–4
 see also: Brock Cantillo
Arciniega, Maximino, 18, 169n10
autonomy, 82–4, 90–1, 96–100,
 102–5
avoidance, 60–4, 87–94, 120–2, 152–4

Badger, 50–2
Banks, Jonathan, 22
Bauer, Steven, 127, 128–9
Bauman, Zygmunt, 164n55
Bigger Than Life, 40–1
Bogdan, 41, 133
bottle episodes, 97, 168n11
Bowen, Michael, 157
Brandt, Betsy, 89–90
Breaking Bad, episodes of
 '4 Days Out' (2.9), 48, 77, 78, 97
 'Abiquiú' (3.11), 101, 159
 'ABQ' (2.13), 82–4
 'A No Rough-Stuff-Type-Deal' (1.7),
  56–7
 'And the Bag's in the River' (1.3),
  18, 20–4, 44, 113
 'Better Call Saul' (2.8), 69, 71–3, 77,
  78, 79, 92, 93
 'Bit by a Dead Bee' (2.3), 59, 73
 'Blood Money' (5.9), 143

'Box Cutter' (4.1), 112–16, 119, 124,
 139
'Breakage' (2.5), 63–4, 66–7, 71–5, 77
'Breaking Bad' (1.1), 2–8, 27–44,
 48–9
'Bug' (4.9), 65, 111, 126, 127, 133–4
'Bullet Points' (4.4), 118–19
'Buyout' (5.6), 19, 20–4
'Cancer Man' (1.4), 27, 45–7, 73
'Cat's in the Bag . . .' (1.2), 18, 44, 113
'Cornered' (4.6), 123
'Crawl Space' (4.11), 131, 134–5
'Crazy Handful of Nothin'' (1.6),
 56–7, 60, 63, 74–5, 85, 88
'Dead Freight' (5.5), 19
'Down' (2.4), 59–66, 73, 83, 144
'End Times' (4.12), 135–7
'Face Off' (4.13), 110, 135, 137–40,
 152, 169n11
'Felina' (5.16), 143, 157–60
'Fifty-One' (5.4), 152
'Fly' (3.10), 97–100, 107, 108, 113,
 116, 156, 158–9
'Full Measure' (3.13), 65, 105,
 106–8, 113, 117
'Gliding Over All' (5.8), 154–6
'Granite State' (5.15), 18
'Gray Matter' (1.5), 27, 50–5, 112,
 156
'Green Light' (3.4), 86, 87
'Grilled' (2.2), 59
'Half Measures' (3.12), 101–6, 108,
 116, 121
'Hazard Pay' (5.3), 48, 153–4
'Hermanos' (4.8), 124–7, 133
'I.F.T.' (3.3), 86, 132
'I See You' (3.8), 125
'Kafkaesque' (3.9), 48, 96–7, 98,
 113, 116, 158–60
'Live Free or Die' (5.1), 143, 145–7,
 152

'Madrigal' (5.2), 151
'Mandala' (2.11), 78–81, 101
'Más' (3.5), 85, 87–92, 95, 106
'Negro y Azul' (2.7), 69, 75–6, 77, 90
'No Más' (3.1), 85, 132
'One Minute' (3.7), 91–5, 120
'Open House' (4.3), 116, 121–3
'Over' (2.10), 60–1, 78–80, 83, 86
'Ozymandias' (5.14), 156–7
'Peekaboo' (2.6), 75, 79, 80, 101
'Phoenix' (2.12), 80, 81–2, 100
'Problem Dog' (4.7), 117, 123–4
'Salud' (3.10), 48, 111–12, 127–32
'Say My Name' (5.7), 155
'Seven Thirty-Seven' (2.1), 59, 83, 132
'Shotgun' (4.5), 117, 118, 123
'Sunset' (3.6), 48, 66, 91, 96
'Thirty-Eight Snub' (4.2), 116–17, 120–1, 133, 153–4
'To'hajilee' (5.13), 156
Brock Cantillo, 101, 136–7, 139, 152–4

Campbell, Ray, 117
Capra, Frank (*It Happened One Night*), 167n6
Caught, 141
Cavell, Stanley
  on artistic medium, 12
  on dignity in remarriage comedies, 91
  on *Gaslight*, 61
  on interpretation, 10–11, 145
  on *It Happened One Night*, 167n6
character (*see*: serial television drama)
Chiklis, Michael, 42
Cineaste, 118
cinematic television, 1–2, 76–7, 109, 161n1
cinematography
  camera movement, 57–8, 81, 82–3, 97–8, 99–100, 113–15, 130–1, 135
  camera placement, 7, 20–1, 29, 32–3, 36, 38, 41–3, 68, 71–2, 79–80, 82–3, 89, 94, 102–3, 108, 112, 118–19, 126, 128–9, 133, 135, 137–8, 147

focus, 37, 71, 104, 106
lighting, 37, 68, 76–80, 92, 97, 117, 123, 133, 153
slow-motion, 137–8
time-lapse, 48–9, 120, 156–7
see also: Steadicam
Citizen Kane, 113, 124, 139
Clark, T. J., 9
Clayton, Alex, 3
Clayton, Alex, and Andrew Klevan, 10
coherence (as a criterion of value), 16–18, 52–3, 82–4, 142 ff.
cold open, 28–9, 82, 165n2, 165n5
colour, 82–3, 106
Combo, 45–6, 51
  murder of, 79, 101, 105, 107
concentration camps
  and dignity, 24–5
  and industrialised society, 19–20
  and moral extremity, 148–9
cooking montages, 48–50
Coppola, Francis Ford (*Godfather* series), 63
corporations, in *Breaking Bad*, 94–7, 100–5, 108
Costabile, David, 65
Coulthard, Lisa, 165n2
Cousins, Christopher, 133–4
Cousins, The, 86, 91, 94
Clover, Carol J., 3
Creeber, Glen, 164n65
Creekmur, Corey, 142
Cranston, Bryan, 2, 6–7, 22–3, 30, 35–6, 41–2, 62–4, 71, 115, 119, 139, 156–7
criticism
  and description, 10–12
  expressive tradition of, 10
  and film style, 2, 3, 10, 14–15, 20–1, 38
  and interpretation, 10–12, 16–18, 141–2
  and medium, 10, 12, 16–18, 25–6
  and part-whole relationships, 16–18, 141–3
  and self-reflexivity, 15–16
  and sociohistorical context, 3, 19–20
  in television studies, 10, 11–12, 14

Deadwood, 15, 17, 20, 79, 109, 117
De Palma, Brian (*Scarface*), 127
de Lancie, John, 79
Dial M for Murder, 31
Dias Branco, Sérgio, 16
dignity
    as critical concept, 9–10, 25–6
    definitions of, 2, 23–5
    and dramatic stakes of *Breaking Bad*,
        2–8, 28–9, 55, 85, 111–12, 149, 160
    and embodiment, 23–5, 30–6
    and self-respect, 47
    and serial television drama, 8,
        16–26, 55, 73, 111–12, 160
    and time, 23–5
    and virtue, 91
    see also: acknowledgement;
        avoidance; humiliation; morality;
        resentment
Dirty Harry, 7, 42
disability, 4, 6, 39–40
Dixon, Kelley (film editor), 32
domesticity, 4–8, 36 ff.
Domingo Molina (*see*: 'Krazy-8')
Don Eladio, 111, 127–30
Donald Margolis, 82
Donaldson, Lucy Fife, 164n58
Double Indemnity, 34–5, 144
Douglas, Michael, 3
Durgnat, Raymond, 15

Eastwood, Clint, 6–7
editing, 32–3, 38, 48–50, 52, 74–5,
    96–7, 99, 104–5
education, 5–6, 45–53, 78, 80–1,
    148–50, 152–3
Eliot, T. S., 15
Elliott Schwartz, 53–5
Ellis, John, 161n2
Enforcer, The, 42, 165n17
Empson, William, 9–10, 141
entrepreneurship (*see*: work)
Esposito, Giancarlo, 64–6, 80, 95,
    102–3, 112, 114–15, 125–32, 134,
    137–8
everyday, the (*see*: ordinary, the)

Falling Down, 3
film noir, 29, 34, 70–1, 109 ff.

flashbacks, 18–19, 29, 34, 82–3, 126–8
    157–60, 165n3
flashforwards, 82–3, 143–4, 146,
    165n2
Forbrydelsen (*The Killing*), 1
Ford, John (*How Green Was My Valley*),
    76
Frankfurt, Harry, 61–2
Fried, Michael, 8–9, 162n14, 170n23
Fukuyama, Francis, 168n11–12

Gale Boetticher, 65–6, 95, 105–8, 112
    murder of, 105–8, 113, 116–17,
        122–4, 125, 127, 131
Gallafent, Edward, 64, 165n17
Game of Thrones, 1
General, The, 165n10
Gibbs, John, 16
Gibbs, John, and Douglas Pye, 14
Gibbs, Nigel, 122
Gilligan, Vince, 5, 19, 29, 32, 55, 97,
    143, 165n5, 166n11, 169n11
Godfather, The, Part II, 63
'Gomez', Steve, 42–3, 68, 87–8, 157
Greenberg, Clement, 12
Gretchen Schwartz, 53–5
Gunn, Anna, 2, 39–40, 62–4, 152
Gus Fring, 64–6, 80, 84, 85, 95 ff.,
    100–3, 114–17, 125 ff., 151

Hank Schrader, 42–4, 66–73, 74, 77,
    83–4, 87–94, 116, 119–24, 134–5,
    140, 151–2, 155, 156, 157
Hannibal (television series), 1
Harvey, James, 109
Hector Salamanca, 59, 125, 127, 131,
    137–8
Heisenberg (alter ego), 56–7, 59, 63,
    117, 124
Heisenberg, Werner, 56
Heydrich, Reinhardt, 86
history, and serial television form,
    14–15, 25–6, 58, 90, 109 ff., esp.
    150–1
Hitchcock, Alfred
    Dial M for Murder, 31
    Strangers on a Train, 70–1
    Vertigo, 39
How Green Was My Valley, 76

humiliation
  as exposure, 29–30
  and masculinity, 6–7
  and aspiration, 27–8, 36, 40–4,
    47–55, 69–70
  and the ordinary, 36–40
  and resentment, 5–6, 40–2, 53–5
  and self-division, 5, 33, 34–6
  and self-performance, 4, 31, 34–6,
    43–4
  and serial television drama, 27–8,
    69–70, 111–12
  and sociality, 42–4, 72–3

identity
  of *Breaking Bad*, 57–8
  instability of, 59–66, 67–70, 78,
    82–4, 88–91
  politics of, 3, 20
  and practical meaning, 151, 170n22
  surrender of, 79–81, 91–4
  see also: performance, of self
Ikiru, 57
interpretation (*see*: criticism)
improvisation, 16–18, 97–8, 118–19,
  144, 150–1
It Happened One Night, 167n6
Itzkoff, Dave, 168n4, 169n11

Uncle Jack, 157
Jacobs, Jason, 1, 10, 12, 15, 16–17, 20,
  29, 79, 109, 162n16, 162n19
Jacobs, Jason, and Steven Peacock, 12,
  17, 25–6, 77, 142, 163n30
James, Henry (morality in the fiction
  of), 25, 150
Jane Margolis, 73–84, 158–60
Jesse Pinkman, 22–3, 44–52, 73–84,
  95–9, 101–6, 108–9, 113–14, 115,
  117–18, 123–4, 127–9, 136–40,
  144, 151, 152–4, 157–60

Kateb, George, 24
Keefe, Patrick Radden, 167n8
Killing, The (*see*: *Forbrydelsen*)
Klevan, Andrew, 10–11, 12, 39
  see also: Clayton, Alex and Andrew
    Klevan
Kouvaros, George, 35

'Krazy-8', 18, 45, 169n10
Kubrick, Stanley (*2001: A Space
  Odyssey*), 100
Kurosawa, Akira (*Ikiru*), 57

La Régle du jeu (Perkins's study of), 15
Lasch, Christopher, 148
Leone, Sergio (*Once Upon a Time in the
  West*), 106
lighting (*see*: cinematography)
Logan, Elliott, 165n2
Luck, 163n35

MacMurray, Fred (as Walter Neff), 34
Mad Men, 1, 9, 163n35
Magnificent Ambersons, The (Perkins's
  study of), 145
Marie Schrader, 66, 87–94, 116,
  119–23, 152, 155, 167n6
Margolis, Mark, 59
marriage, 38–40, 59–66, 76–83, 87–94,
  118–23, 140, 152–4, 167n6
Martin, Adrian, 10–11, 38, 76
masculinity, 3, 5, 30, 35–6, 38–40,
  42–4, 66–73, 87–94, 117, 119,
  127–9, 132–3, 140
McDonald, Skip, 32
meaning,
  desire for in *Breaking Bad*, 98–9,
    145 ff.
  and practical identity, 151,
    170n22
  and modernity, 148–50
Measure for Measure, 105
medium
  as artistic medium, 12
  specificity, 10, 12
melodrama, 40–1, 43–4, 66, 88,
  103–8, 149
Mike Ehrmantraut, 22, 101, 102,
  105–8, 113–14, 117–18, 123, 127,
  131–2, 151–2, 154–5, 157
Milch, David, 117, 126
mise-en-scène
  as a tradition of film criticism, 14,
    16–17
  and television style, 38
Mittell, Jason, 165n2
Mitte, R. J., 2

modernity
  expression of in *Breaking Bad*, 20–3,
    95–100, 105–6, 147–51
  and fragmentation, 24–5
  and historical continuity, 149–50
  and industrialisation, 19–20, 147–9
  and morality, 4, 25
Moncada, Luis and Daniel, 84
montage (*see*: cooking montages;
    editing)
morality
  ambiguity, 51–5, 104–8
  and compartmentalisation, 84 ff.
  and dignity, 22, 24–5, 91 ff.
  and dramatic stakes, 4–7, 54–5, 98 ff.
  and lying, 61–4, 98
  in modern life, 4–5, 19–20, 94 ff.
  and narrational perspective, 29–36
  and serial characterisation, 73 ff.
  and sociality, 64–6
  and technological rationality, 23,
    148–50

Nannicelli, Ted, 168n11
narrative complexity, 35, 82–3
narrative structure (of *Breaking Bad*),
    13–14, 55, 57–8, 74, 81, 82–3,
    113, 118, 133–6, 140, 143–5
  see also: flashbacks; flashforwards
Naremore, James, 61
Neiman, Susan, 161n6, 168n12
neo-Nazis (gang in *Breaking Bad*),
    143–4, 155, 157
Newcomb, Horace, 164n65
Ngai, Sianne, 162n14
Nietzsche, Friedrich, 116
nihilism, 98–9, 116 ff.
Norris, Dean, 42–3, 66–73, 87–94,
    119–24, 166n11

Once Upon a Time in the West, 106
Ophuls, Max (*Caught*), 141
ordinary, the, 6, 36–47, 59–66, 77–9,
    123
O'Sullivan, Sean, 13–14, 16, 18, 27,
    58, 87, 142–3
Out of the Past, 109
'Ozymandias' (Shelley poem), 156–7

Paul, Aaron, 18, 22, 102–3, 111, 114,
    158

Peacock, Steven, 161n1
  see also: Jacobs, Jason, and Steven
    Peacock
Perez, Gilberto, 5, 161n7, 165n10
performance, of self, 6–7, 34–5, 42–7,
    56–7, 59–66, 67–70, 71–3, 75–6,
    77, 89–90
  see also: acting; identity
Perkins, V. F., 11, 12, 15, 141, 145
Pierson, David P., 3, 164n56
pilot episode (*see*: *Breaking Bad*,
    episodes of)
Pippin, Robert, 25, 34, 116, 150,
    168n12, 168n14, 170n22
Plemons, Jesse, 19
Pomerance, Murray, 166n4
Pulp Fiction, 73–4, 115–16
Pye, Douglas, 14

Quezada, Steven Michael, 42–3

Ray, Nicholas
  Bigger Than Life, 40–1
  In a Lonely Place, 109
  Johnny Guitar, 168n14
recognition, desire for, 6–8, 37 ff.
Reding, Nick, 167n8
resentment, 3, 27–8, 40–1, 54–5, 120,
    131
revenge, 6, 94, 101–8, 131–2
Ricks, Christopher, 9, 15–16, 141,
    162n17
Rios, Emily, 101
Ritter, Krysten, 73–4
Roberts, Tom, 122
Rothman, William, 166n13

satisfaction (as criterion of value), 142–3
Saul Goodman, 117, 134
Scarface (De Palma), 127
Schiller, Friederich, 164n61
Schrader, Paul, 35
Schumacher, Joel, 3
Scorsese, Martin (*Taxi Driver*), 35
seasons, of serial television, 13–14,
    17–18, 25
  artistic challenges of, 27–8, 56–8,
    86–7
  as expressive resource, 56–8, 83–4,
    86–7, 109 ff.
  and conclusions, 109 ff.

self-reflexivity
  in art, 15–16
  in *Breaking Bad*, 9, 60, 82–4, 96–8,
    144–5, 157–60
self-reliance (in *Breaking Bad*), 30–1,
    53–5
serial television
  and character, 14–15, 27 ff.
  and dignity, 16–26
  and history, 14–15, 25–6, 58, 90,
    109 ff., esp. 150–1
  and part-whole relations, 1–2,
    13–14, 16–18, 20–3, 58, 141 ff.
  and time, 25–6, 55 ff.
Sennett, Richard, 168n10
Shelley, Percey Bysshe, 157
shame (*see*: humiliation)
Shield, The, 42
Siegel, Don, 7
Six Feet Under, 1
Skinny Pete, 45, 51, 75
Skyler White, 2–3, 4, 38–40, 53–4,
    59–64, 66, 82, 86, 98, 100, 104–5,
    110, 118–19, 132–6, 140, 152,
    155–6
Sopranos, The, 1, 9, 13, 143
sound design, 71–2, 90–1, 95, 104–5,
    117, 127–8, 135
Stan, Marius, 41, 133
Steadicam, 130
Steve Gomez (*see*: Gomez)
Strangers on a Train, 70–1
Sunset Boulevard, 83
superlab, the, 84–6, 95–100, 112–17,
    125, 137, 138–9
Sweet Smell of Success, The, 163n53

Tarantino, Quentin (*Pulp Fiction*),
    73–4, 115–16
Taxi Driver, 35
teaching, or teacher (*see*: education)
Ted Beneke, 133–4, 135
Tellotte, J. P., 161n1
texture
  surface, 21–3, 63
  voice, 128, 146
Thomas, Deborah, 43–4, 67
thymos (*or* thymotic passion), 101 ff.
Todd Alquist, 19, 22

Todorov, Tzvetan
  on concentration camps and
    industrial society, 19–20, 148–9
  on dignity, 24–5, 47
  on morality, 86, 105
  on human fragmentation, 148–50
Toles, George, 12, 31, 70, 96, 162n21
Tomás Cantillo (murder of), 101–2,
    104–8, 123, 136–7, 153
Top of the Lake, 1
totalitarianism, 19–20
Tourneur, Jacques (*Out of the Past*),
    109
True Detective, 163n35
Tuco Salamanca, 56–7, 59, 67, 71,
    73–4, 85, 86, 93
Tyrus, 117

Victor, murder of, 114–16, 154
voice, 6–7, 39, 69, 80, 89–90, 93–4,
    102, 112, 128–9, 134, 146
  see also: texture

Walt Jr, 2–3, 6–8, 38–40, 60–1, 104,
    111–12, 128, 152
Walter White, 2–8, 18–23, 25–6,
    27–66, 70–1, 72, 81–3, 85–6, 94,
    95–108, 111–12, 116–17, 118–19,
    123, 125, 127–8, 132–40, 143–4,
    145–7, 151–7
Welles, Orson
  Citizen Kane, 113, 124, 139
  Magnificent Ambersons, The, 145
Western genre, 5, 28, 36–7, 104–8
Wilder, Billy
  Double Indemnity, 34–5, 144
  Sunset Boulevard, 83
Williams, Raymond, 161n2
Willingham, Lynne (film editor), 32
Wilson, George M., 6
work
  employment, 39–42, 94–8
  entrepreneurship, 45, 47–55, 73–5,
    96–7, 133
  purpose of, 36, 47–55, 64–6, 94–8,
    154 ff.
  and routine, 95–8

X-Files, The, 29

Printed and bound by CPI Group (UK) Ltd, Croydon, CR0 4YY